FLORIDA'S PAST

Richard —
Welcome to Florida
& the Diocese of Southwest
Florida — get sunburned!
☺☺☺ Love
Marcie + John
Lipscomb

FLORIDA'S

PAST

People and Events
That Shaped the State

Gene M. Burnett

Pineapple Press
Sarasota, Florida

To the body of believers everywhere
who made the days possible

Inquiries should be addressed to:
Pineapple Press, Inc.
P.O. Box 3889
Sarasota, Florida 34230
www.pineapplepress.com

LIBRARY OF CONGRESS CATALOGING-IN-PUBLICATION DATA

Burnett, Gene M., 1928–1991
Florida's past.

Originally published in Florida Trend,
1972–1986.
Bibliography: p.
Includes index.
1. Florida—History. 2. Florida—Biography.
1. Title.
F311.5.B87 1986 975.9 86–15048

First paperback edition
10 9 8 7 6 5 4

Printed in the United States of America

PREFACE

Gene M. Burnett genuinely loves Florida and its past. He has what some would call a "bird-dog nose" for a good story and gets all the nubs of truth that careful, determined research can produce before he writes about it. This volume contains some 63 sketches, most of which have been published in *Florida Trend* magazine over the past fourteen years. The book is a lode that will produce treasures unlimited for the Florida history lover to mine from its pages. Burnett is a skillful storyteller and writer. Each of the individual stories stands on its own base, but taken together they present a mosaic of the real Florida of earlier years.

Like all good historical writing, we learn from it, we are entertained and inspired by it.

—LeRoy Collins
Former Governor of Florida

ACKNOWLEDGMENTS

Over so lengthy a time period as that required for the gestation of this book, it is difficult to recall every form of assistance that lent aid to its birth. However, there are those to whom I am gratefully indebted for their singular contributions. I would like to express my deep appreciation to the founder of *Florida Trend,* Harris Mullen, who opened the door to the first efforts of this collection and whose publishing acumen went beyond a strictly business perspective, an attribute as much of aid to me as it was to his successful magazine. I am also very grateful to the present owners of *Trend,* the Times Publishing Company, and to *Florida Trend'*s former general manager, Andy Corty, for granting the author exclusive permission to copyright the articles, all of which appeared in *Florida Trend* since 1972, and to the magazine's current editor and publisher, Rick Edmonds. Each of these has lent aid and blessings to this project. I am thankful to editors, past and present, like Walker Roberts and Jeff Tucker, who wielded their blue pencils with a feather's touch and who were supportive down the line. I have a special gratitude to my editor, June Cussen at Pineapple Press, who, despite a harried schedule, kept a discerning and single eye as she guided the book through the sometimes knotty myriad of choices and detail that attend publishing. I have a very singular indebtedness to the honorable LeRoy Collins, a Florida history enthusiast himself, who graciously took time from his full and active days to peruse a core portion of this work and preface it with some kind and salutary remarks. Deep appreciation must also go to Cass Canfield, the distinguished senior arbiter at Harper & Row, New York, who, while regretting that marketing factors precluded them from handling the manuscript, nevertheless felt the book should be in print and urged me to keep searching for a publisher—advice which, thankfully, I followed. My sincere thanks go to the editors of the University of Miami Press, at Coral Gables, for permission to reproduce photographs from *Florida's Last Frontier,* by Charlton Tebeau, and *Pioneer Life in Southeast Florida,* by Charles Pierce, for my stories on Ed Watson and on early Lake Worth pioneers, respectively. For other photographs in this work I am indebted to the staff of the state archives at Strozier Library, Florida State University, and the staff of the Florida Archives at the Florida Department of Commerce. I must always be thankful to Joseph Hipp, Head of Special Collections at Tampa-Hillsborough County's Main Public Library, Tampa, and his able staff, and to J. B. Dobkins, Librarian of Special Collections, at the University of South Florida, Tampa, and the USF professor of history, Dr. Gary Mormino, whose knowledgeable aid has often eased my way in the search for elusive materials. Last but hardly least, a durable affection and gratitude goes to three "pests"—Ann, Laura, and Rachel—without whose persistent, loving pestering this book might not have been spurred to its fruition.

CONTENTS

Preface by LeRoy Collins   v

Introduction   ix

I. ACHIEVERS AND PIONEERS

1. Dad Gandy's "Crazy" Bridge   5
2. Dr. Wall Corrals Yellow Fever   9
3. Mary Bethune Builds a College   13
4. Mother Tuttle of Miami   17
5. "Dark Horse" Dave Wins Governorship   21
6. Zora Neale Hurston: Florida's Black Novelist   25
7. Dr. Gorrie Cools Florida Off   30
8. Young Whitaker Discovers Sarasota   34
9. DuPont Rescues Florida's Busted Banks   38
10. Florida—A Wellspring for Delius' Music   42
11. The Bohemian Birth of Coconut Grove   46
12. T. T. Fortune: Florida's Black Militant   50
13. Sidney Lanier: Poet Turned Promoter   54
14. Horticulturist Dr. Perrine's Senseless Death   58
15. Marjorie Rawlings Portrays Florida to the World   62
16. Educator Holt Remakes Rollins College   66
17. The Greeks Conquer the Sponge Industry   69
18. St. Petersburg's "Romanov Connection"   72

II. VILLAINS AND CHARACTERS

19. Banker Ed Romfh: Supreme Iconoclast   77
20. "Bone" Mizelle Was a Cowboy's Cowboy   81
21. The Notorious Ashley Gang   85
22. Miami's Horrendous "Guest," Al Capone   90
23. He Narrowly Missed Killing FDR   94
24. The Denouement of "Bloody" Ed Watson   98
25. Eccentric Prince Murat Dazzles Tallahassee   102
26. Florida's Dubious Dynasty: The Porkchop Gang   106
27. A Florida Boy Joins Lincoln's Assassins   109
28. When Palm Beach Courted Royalty   112

III. HEROES AND HEROINES

29. The "Little Alamo" at Cape Florida   117
30. Peggy O'Neale: "Scandalous" First Lady   121
31. Osceola: The Seminole Patriot   126

32. Jackie Cochran: Born to Fly 131
33. Sister Bedell Woos the Indians 136
34. Jonathan Walker: Freedom Symbol 141
35. He Replaced Another on the Gallows 144
36. Lake Okeechobee's "She-Doctor" 149
37. Lakeland's Female Lindbergh: Ruth Elder 152
38. Father Luis' Cross Conquers the Sword 155
39. Florida's Heroines for Suffrage 159

IV. WAR AND PEACE

40. Fast Cars, Rich Men at Ormond-Daytona 165
41. Pristine Lake Worth is Discovered 170
42. When Nazi U-boats Stalked Florida 175
43. The War Over a Rogue's Ear 179
44. Bartram Remembers Florida's Eden 183
45. Tampa's "Splendid Little War" 187
46. The "Dogs of War" Who Were Puppies 191
47. A Surgeon Assesses the Seminole War 194
48. Governor Milton: A Civil War Tragedy 197
49. The Healing Beauty of Bok's Tower 201
50. The Rise and Fall of Carl Fisher's Miami Beach 204
51. Florida's Great Train Race of 1901 207
52. Kissimmee's World-Famed Airplane Law 210
53. A Private's Eye-View of the Olustee Battle 213

V. CALAMITIES AND SOCIAL TURBULENCE

54. A Killer 'Cane Hits Okeechobee Land 219
55. To Burn in a Turpentine Hell 223
56. The Notorious Alston-Read Duel 227
57. The "Binder Boys" Burst the Great Boom Bubble 232
58. Tampa Terror and the Cigar Strike of 1910 235
59. The Infamous "Gulags" of Florida's Past 240
60. Armed Only with Integrity, Governor Carlton Faced Violence 244
61. The Flagler Divorce Law Furor 246
62. Near Riot at the Jacksonville Prizefight 250
63. Bad Faith and Avarice Felled a Banking Empire 253

Bibliography 257
Index 203

INTRODUCTION

While doing some free-lance writing in the summer of 1972, I wrote a historical article on George H. "Dad" Gandy and his Tampa Bay Bridge and sent it off to *Florida Trend* magazine. History has always been among my major interests but my writing of it tends to resist orthodox academic styles in favor of one more flexible and informal. *Trend,* on the other hand, was a staid and pillarish periodical devoted mainly to affairs of business and finance. Hence, I had little idea the story would be accepted. It was. I had even less notion that I would be writing a history piece for the magazine virtually every month for the next 14 years. I have. But a long time would elapse before the idea occurred of collecting and publishing the pieces in book form. Other parties suggested it; I was slow to come around to it. However, the topics I usually chose to write about were of broad, diverse and general human interest, and *Trend'*s readership was necessarily selective and limited, a minute fraction of the general reading public. Yet, not until the early 1980s did I make any serious effort to have the pieces published in book form. I am thankful that I did. I had unconsciously developed a special attachment to the work because it was written during years of often restrictive and trying circumstances. Conversely, the writing provided me with release and expression, an essential catharsis that made the efforts a labor of felicity if not of love.

The question recurs often among scholars and academicians: What is history? Just as often the query has provoked strenuous and ardent advocacy from various schools of thinking. U.S. historians from Bancroft to Beard have proffered interpretations ranging from theological to economic derivation. Noted British historians range similarly, from the distinguished Macaulay, who described his work as that of "half poet, half philosopher," to the "scientific" determinism of Toynbee. In our own state, among major Florida historians—Tebeau, the Hannas, Mahon, Patrick, or others—we likewise find rich variation. One might almost think it not too facetious to paraphrase Finley Peter Dunn's Mr. Dooley and conclude: "History is whut the historian sez it is." Almost but not quite.

One of our distinctive modern historians, Barbara Tuchman—who describes herself as simply a storyteller, a narrator who deals in true stories—affirms: "There is no such thing as a neutral or purely objective historian. Without an opinion a historian would be simply a ticking clock, and unreadable besides." But she stresses an essential qualifier: "The primary duty of the historian is to stay within the evidence." If he or she meets this requisite, then the reader is free to accept or reject whatever interpretation the chronicler gives such evidence. Another prime duty, she asserts, is to render the subject as interesting to the reader as it was to the writer. Thus one must "distill" the subject for the reader—assemble the information, make sense of it, select the essential, discard the irrelevant, and put it together into that form of dramatic narrative that is "the lifeblood of history." Such rules seem eminently reasonable, especially in a field of study where absolute certainty and precision can often prove elusive if not unattainable. At least hereby we may avoid that bane of the profession, what historian Allan Nevins called "Professor Dryasdust" and his "pedagogic gobbledegook," or his opposite extreme, the "Glib Popularizer." In short, one should strive to unite literary and scholarly qualities in a manner producing sound, readable history. If in this collection I have generally adhered to these broad but firm guidelines, I will be thankful; hopefully the reader will be too.

My own primary sense of history is that it belongs to human beings; they make history and are in turn affected by it whether they are noted, ordinary, or even obscure individuals. Therefore, letters, diaries, memoranda, notes, and even pictures are as much a part of history as are the great events themselves. Indeed, some obscure individual may actually be the catalyst for the larger event. To take a random example from this book, who would have dreamed that two powerful nations, England and Spain, would go to war in and over Florida in the 1740s simply because, years earlier, an obscure English trader had one of his ears lopped off for smuggling? Then, too, an ordinary individual can reach beyond the grave to throw new light on a historic event, as in the case of the discovery a century later of letters written by a young Union private who fought at the Battle of Olustee. Sometimes an individual's influence upon a given locality is subtler and less defined but no less tangible. The demonic presence of mobster Al Capone and friends in Dade County in the 1920s surely nurtured the seeds of gambling and corruption that would plague that area for another generation or more.

History can be exciting and intriguing as well as instructive. Thoughtful scrutiny of the activities of our forebears can often refresh and even change our minds and attitudes about the present. Basically, I believe that my own approach to history is that of a digger and a sifter, not unlike a miner who comes along after the main lode has been all but picked clean, panning the raw earth for hidden nuggets, or perhaps a nugget mistakenly cast aside as merely a rough stone. Herein the reader must himself assess to what degree this panning effort has been successful.

I have appended to this book only a partial bibliography, one or two sources for each story. These are given mainly for those who wish to read a further account of a particular topic. I believe that the nature of this presentation does not demand a massive and exhaustive list of sources. I can assure the reader that, were it so, the bibliography might entail a third as many pages as the book itself.

Gene M. Burnett

FLORIDA'S

PAST

For I will show you lessons from
our history, stories handed down
to us from former generations.
Psalms 78:2,3 (TLB)

Achievers and Pioneers

1.
Dad Gandy's "Crazy" Bridge

Everybody said a bridge across Old Tampa Bay was impossible until George Gandy's 20-year obsession proved them wrong.

When George Sheppard "Dad" Gandy's collossus—one of the longest toll span bridges in the world of that time—opened for traffic nearly half a century ago, it was the feat of its day.

The bridge surely was a financial and engineering marvel; it accelerated by years the residential and commercial development of the entire Tampa Bay area.

But the major wonder of the feat seemed to lay in its gestation, its birth, from the time that it was no more than a fixed glint in a pair of stern and flinty eyes, shortly after the turn of the century, to the day almost a generation later when the first piling hammered into water and bedrock.

In the early 1900s, however, it was not called Gandy's collossus but his folly. It was the apogee of Rube Goldbergism, technologically refined; it was simply a crazy notion that was greeted, at best, with patronizing guffaws from the more practical wags of the day.

In fairness to the scoffers, of course, it must be allowed that the scheme did present a far-out, high-risk aspect. Indeed, over the years, the project careened on the precipice of failure enough times to make the shrewdest stock market wizard hedge his bottom dollar for lunch money and a nice, sound U.S. savings bond. But it vaguely seemed to make a difference when the tall, imposing Philadelphian said simply, "I am going to build that bridge."

Gandy himself was the difference, the singlemindedness of a zealot mixed, sometimes precariously, with a razor will, unmitigated cheek, and more than a touch of the deGaullian *grande gesture*.

Born in Tuckahoe, New Jersey, October 20, 1851, Dad Gandy began life inauspiciously enough. A grammar school dropout, his first job was an office boy with Henry Disston & Sons, of Philadelphia. Within 11 years, the dropout had parlayed the Horatio Algeran virtues of the day into a top position in the Disston firm. This springboard was to launch him into a career as developer, builder, and transportation expert.

The latter vocation drew his singular interest and, by the end of the 19th century, he had major streets of Philadelphia's city and suburbs clattering with its first electric trolleys. It was his interest in an investment in a streetcar line that initially brought him to St. Petersburg, in 1903, at the invitation of the line's promoter, F. A. Davis, another Philadelphian.

At some point during this time, the visitor, then already in his 50s, gazed out over the broad expanse of Old Tampa Bay to the thin shore line on the far side and quietly whispered to himself: "Why not?" Thus began what Florida historian Charlton Tebeau has termed the old man's "obsession."

It was naturally, a pleasant fantasy, indulged by many a weary merchant or traveler who, as late as 1907, might spend up to three days making the Tampa-St. Pete trip by auto over nearly impassable, mud-clogged roads or, by boat, through hazardous and capricious winds and currents. But the staggering immensity of the concept confined it to just that category—fantasy and folly.

Gandy seemed to have had, however, a penchant for "folly." He once indulged a small folly on the side as if to prove it. In 1912, he purchased property at Central Avenue and Fifth Street in St. Pete and built a Plaza, with theatre and office buildings. For almost two years, he bore with patriarchal patience the derisive hoots of "Gandy's White Elephant." But the investment soon prospered many times over; the hoots became contrite squeaks.

Gandy's big dream was nursed in dormancy, however, until its initial spur came in 1910 when he began discussing with H. Walter Fuller, a nonskeptic who was also interested in such a bridge, the most feasible route the span might take. (They joined forces, but Gandy was later to buy out Fuller's interest for $500.) Nevertheless, plans dragged along in the lean year preceding World War I and it was not until 1915 that the exact bridge route was determined. By this time, Gandy had formed his Gandy Bridge Company and began to make the first formal surveys for the causeway dredgings.

The route itself was a propitious choice. They had discovered almost a straight line of broad, shallow flats ideal for dredging, this further enhanced by discovery of a long finger of natural rock bed lying several feet under the sand and forming a perfect foundation for the concrete bridge section.

The route as planned—and completed—called for three and a quarter miles of protruding causeway, at both ends, with two and a half miles of reenforced concrete bridge, 24 feet wide. It was looking good—on paper. The snags were to come.

By late 1917, Gandy had secured rights-of-way from both counties and, the following year, a tropic sun glinted off swinging machete blades as they hacked at palmetto clumps and mangroves to clear the survey lines. Meanwhile, Gandy was seeking state and federal rights for the span itself. But, after subduing one or two smaller competitors, he met formidable opposition from a Pinellas company, the Tampa, Atlantic & Gulf Railroad, which had already filed its own plans for a bridge along the same route. The old man also had been turned down earlier for a federal permit by Bernard Baruch's War Emergency Board.

Gandy fought back. He rushed all over both counties to get endorsements from powerful civic groups, banks, and businesses, while buttonholing legislators along the way. He turned out his own "form" endorsements and successfully sought signatures for them with which to deluge a hearing before the Board of Engineers of the U.S. War Department.

A high, tense moment in this hearing came when one board member obliquely suggested that the endorsements all appeared to bear the composing mark of one man. Gandy's reported retort:

"They bear the stamp of one man, you say?" he almost shouted, banging the table with clenched fist. "You bet they do. And I'm the man. And if that bridge is ever built, by myself or anyone else, it will be by some fellow who gets behind it like I have and never quits."

On February 11, 1918, the War Department approved his bridge.

However, Dad Gandy's other major obstacle—financing—had loomed with nagging constancy during the war years and after. The scarcity and high price of materials, post-war, had posed some problem, but nothing insurmountable. Also, in those years, the old man had courted, successfully, Northeastern U.S. interests (Stone & Webster of Boston via various Wall Street temples), and the money seemed ready. But—Northern money wanted Northern control and, on this point, Gandy balked. He finally cancelled all outside negotiations.

It was here that Gandy met his most imposing obstacle—himself—and the clash proved near-fatal to his dream. Nevertheless, with consistent adamancy, he refused to put one cent of his own money into the bridge; this even though he was a wealthy man. And, as if to compound the dilemma, he demanded controlling interest in the project, no matter who picked up the tab nor for how much.

These star-crossed elements of his nature induced a paralytic effect on the project that was to put it into limbo for over four years—and almost into oblivion. But history makes strange bedfellows and strange bedfellows make history. Rescue was in sight.

By 1921, the aberrant phenomenon called The Great Florida Land Boom was shifting into high gear. Land developers, promoters, speculators and tourists were flooding into the state by the thousands. Real estate prices soared astronomically, speculative fortunes came overnight, and the boom fever, its symptoms ranging from euphoric to manic, soon gripped the state.

It was a time, as well, of grandiose schemes—George M. Merrick's Coral Gables, Addison Mizner's mammoth Palm Beach estates, D. P. "Doc" Davis's Islands. It was not, therefore, an unlikely time for Gandy's grandiose project to draw attention, nor for an unlikely milieu in which to find a promoter like Eugene M. Elliott.

Gandy had decided earlier that he could build his bridge only by selling his friends and neighbors a piece of its future, and he hired Elliott (whose background remained a mystery), in September 1922 to sell stocks. The young promoter, with a crew of publicity men, immediately launched a blitz sales campaign throughout the bay area and beyond. Within an amazingly brief time, more than $2 million in preferred and common stock had been sold. By 1923, bridge construction was proceeding in earnest.

Historians suggest that Elliott was less enthusiastic about the bridge than in selling securities for it, and that his sales tactics, at times, bordered on the dubious. K. Ĥ. Grismer, for example, reports that Elliott would assure sales prospects, falsely, that the bridge was already "underwritten."

Grismer notes, further, that Elliott never imagined that Gandy was actually going to build. He relates a story of the time of how Elliott exclaimed one day of Gandy hitting "the million mark" in the sales campaign, and of Gandy's satisfied nod and reply that construction could soon begin. Elliott's jaw dropped. "What?" he gasped. "You're not really going to *build,* are you?" Finally convinced that Dad was sincere, Elliott was stunned. (Historian Page Jackson asserts that not every stock buyer received full return on his investment.)

But, apparently, the promoter decided later that the bridge was not a bad idea after all. In fact, he had scooped up some choice acreage along the bridge approaches and was last seen offering "Five Thousand Acres of Sunshine" to sun-enthused tourists, even though a good piece of the sunshine was still under water.

At all events, Gandy's 20-year dream was completed in record time and, on November 20, 1924, Governor Cary A. Hardee cut a rope of flowers to admit the first traffic.

Dad Gandy lived on (to a venerable 95), to savor his "obsession," and to realize that he had played poker with the Fates and, with not even a chip to ante, he had walked away a winner.

2.
Dr. Wall Corrals Yellow Fever

Dr. John Wall's observation that the tree-top mosquito was the carrier of yellow fever was ignored and ridiculed by those who felt filth was the cause.

A U.S. Army commission headed by Dr. Walter Reed in 1900 got most of the credit but, historically speaking, the first American to finger the lowly mosquito as the cause of the once dreaded disease, yellow fever, was a Tampa physician, Dr. John Perry Wall.

History has been less than kind in rendering credit to this versatile Floridian. Nevertheless, to the jeers and ridicule of both press and his medical colleagues, Dr. Wall accused the villainous insect 27 years prior to the Reed commission.

It did seem absurd. The word itself, yellow fever, once struck fear, panic, and terror into the hearts of men. For centuries that malady had caused epidemics the world over. It brought construction of the Panama Canal to a deadly halt and it was such a scourge of Florida coastal towns in the late 19th century that frightened inland communities once resorted to "shotgun quarantines" against their seaside neighbors. And to say that this pesky but innocuous-looking insect that barely weighs a milligram was the cause of it all—well, people said, we know the doctor is a wit of sorts but his humor is touching on the balmy now. "Skeeters," indeed!

Everyone knew, after all, that filth and dirt caused yellow fever. The medical sanitarians said so, and their theories held sway in the 19th century. Clean up those outhouses, pig pens, yards and streets—that will do it. Still others were certain that dank vapors from nearby marshes and swamps were the culprit. Get a tar barrel smoking on every corner.

But the good doctor was hardly jesting. He had contracted yellow fever himself and his young wife had barely nursed him back to recovery when she and their two-year-old daughter caught it. They both died. The grief-stricken doctor immersed himself in studies and research on everything relating to the disease. He conducted his own observations, too. And by 1873, he was convinced. He even zeroed in on the exact type of insect; the commonly known, far ranging "treetop" mosquito, later to be Latinized by its infamous genus—Aedes aegypti.

John P. Wall was born near Jasper, Florida, on September 17, 1836, to Perry G. and Nancy (Hunter) Wall. The elder Wall was a prosperous planter and his home outside Brooksville is still used today by the University of Florida as a biological experiment station. Young Wall took an M.D. degree from the Medical College of South Carolina in 1858, married 19-year-old Pressie Eubanks of Richmond, Virginia, served with the Confederacy in the Civil War. After the war, he came to Tampa to practice medicine.

Among the members of this early settler family of Tampa, the doctor's many-faceted character was perhaps the most distinctive. He was enthusiastically active in every part of the area's development—its industry, its port activities, its health needs and its politics. He was a brilliant writer and orator and he relished debates on any controversial issues of the day. He contributed articles to the local weekly newspaper and jousted with other state newspapers, wielding a satiric pen laced with trenchant wit—plus a saving humor. He once so infuriated Colonel Frank Harris of the *Ocala Banner* that the latter challenged him to a duel. The doctor accepted, but he shrewdly understood the curious truth that it was weakness, not strength, of character that prompted men to seek duels. As challengee, he could choose the place and weapons. For location, the doctor chose Mrs. Bunch's cowpens on Six-Mile Creek where cattle drovers rested before bringing their herds into Tampa. As weapons, he selected shovels, since the bovine beasts were mightily relieved at this rest stop. By the time the roar of laughter had died down over the state, the colonel had forgotten what it was exactly that he wanted to duel about.

The first yellow fever outbreak in Tampa in 1871 struck the doctor personally. He successfully treated for yellow fever a cabin boy on a ship in port and then came down with it himself. His wife, Pressie, nursed him to recovery but she and their two-year-old daughter succumbed to it. Their son, John P. Jr. was untouched.

The doctor's subsequent intensive study of the disease led him to conclude in 1873 that the common "treetop" mosquito was the carrier. He had already observed that both insect and disease prevailed only in summer months, both disappearing with the first frost. Adults whose work did not take them outside at night, when mosquitoes are most numerous, were rarely infected, as were children who were generally kept in at night. He was the first American to make these remarkably accurate observations and conclusions, but they were met with only scoff and ridicule from the medical profession and especially the lay press. Even when the noted specialist, Carlos Juan Findlay, pronounced the same conclusions after experiments in Havana in 1881, the theory was generally ignored at best.

Medical authorities of the sanitarian school, who held that dirt, filth and fecal matter were the causes of yellow fever, comprised the ascendant opinion on the subject until 1900 and no one questioned them—except Dr. Wall. He attacked the sanitarian theory by paper and lecture, before medical groups and public bodies both north and south. He labeled the theory "wild assumptions" and "a delusion." He reasoned: "It is now universally conceded that yellow fever is an exotic disease of infectious nature and has to be introduced to be an epidemic in this country. It would be about as logical to assume that the spread of measles was dependent on filth as that of yellow fever."

He noted studies of sanitation conditions in New Orleans where in 1877, "dirt and filth" caused only one death, whereas, the following year, it caused an epidemic of 4,000 deaths, and noted similar examples elsewhere. He added: "It is not to be inferred that filth is to be preferred to cleanliness . . . but we should protest against the use of these false teachings [by sanitarians] as both unscientific and harmful [since] they needlessly excite and alarm the public."

But the doctor's interests were not confined to his yellow fever theories. He was revealed to be far ahead of his time on a variety of issues. In a perceptive article written in 1966 by a Tampan, Dr. James M. Ingram, Dr. Wall was aptly labelled "a man for all seasons," and his activities seem to warrant the phrase. He was an early promoter of the then unaccepted ideas of Louis Pasteur, in bacteria, and Dr. Joseph Lister, in antiseptics. He anticipated— and wryly castigated—the modern pill and drug culture and did not hesitate to take his colleagues to task for relying heavily on drugs for therapy. Thusly: "Our stock of positive knowledge, as to the effect of drugs, is really much smaller than our professional vanity may be willing to confess. Is there any evidence that the average duration of life has been lengthened by our superior skill in the treatment of disease? On the other hand, is there not considerable ground for the belief that thousands of lives have been sacrificed by the exhibition of our [drug] remedies?" He was the earliest strong advocate of preventative medicine rather than cures, observing, "The truth is, the public faith in us as physicians far exceeds our ability—a fact whose recognition on our part . . . is likely to do more good for [the profession] than all of our boasted medical erudition."

Dr. Wall had one lamentable weakness—he was a hard and spirited drinker up to his mid-thirties. Then, after the death of his first wife, he met and wooed Matilda McKay, daughter of Tampa shipper Captain James McKay. The latter refused to consent to their marriage until Wall agreed to swear off the stuff. Love proved stronger than strong drink and the doctor remained thereafter a virtual teetotaller.

During these prolific years, the doctor also found time to serve a term as mayor of Tampa; as first president of the Tampa Board of Trade; and as president of the state medical association. During the 15 years that he also served as city health officer, his measures of protection and quarantine prevented any yellow fever outbreak in this period. Soon after he left these duties, however, an epidemic broke out in 1887, and people fled the city in panic, so hastily that they left lights burning in their homes and meals on the table. "Our city is desolate and distressfully quiet," plainted one citizen. All businesses were closed, hundreds fell ill and 79 persons died.

But yellow fever epidemics were almost an annual affair in Florida coastal towns in those years. Inland towns instituted the notorious "shotgun" quarantines and even prevented Governor-to-be Francis P. Fleming from campaigning in the interior of the state because his brother died in the severe Jacksonville epidemic of 1888. This enabled Dr. Wall, as a legislator, to "father" the state's first health board soon after.

In a speech to the medical association in Gainesville on April 18, 1895, the doctor still assailed his detractors: "The sanitarians offer no experimental evidence of the truth of their assertions [on yellow fever], but having come across a case of sickness, they at once set out to hunt up a cause for it, and perhaps, finding something offensive in the locality or environment, they at once exclaim 'Eureka!' and thus exalt humbug at the expense of science and truth." During this speech, a colleague noted that the speaker seemed under some stress and the doctor himself quipped to his audience that "high tones and toney meals do not seem to agree with me." A few minutes later he fell over dead of a heart attack.

Dr. Wall could not know that his theory would be vindicated five years later when Dr. Reed's U.S. Army commission team working among troops stationed in Havana, Cuba, in 1900, would isolate the insect and let it bite volunteers. The evidence was overwhelmingly conclusive, but not before one team doctor almost died from a voluntary bite, and another scientist—accidentally bitten—died within days.

At his death, his medical colleagues put together a huge wall plaque honoring the doctor's memory; the plaque still hangs today in Tampa General Hospital. Historic tribute for his "premature" conclusions on the cause of yellow fever may have eluded him, but Dr. Wall's vital interest in human welfare and his versatile and effective activities on behalf thereof, certainly might merit the later day colleague's assessment of him—scientist, naturalist, industrialist, journalist, politician, humorist, and crusader, "a man for all seasons."

3.
Mary Bethune Builds A College

With no money, she started a private school for blacks. It thrived. From there she gained national influence which she wielded to aid her race.

It seemed at least improbable—if not slightly mad—for the young black school teacher to attempt to found a school of her own with a total capital reserve of $1.50.

Especially when she picked as her school site an old trash dump, thickly choked with overgrowth and swampland, for which she promised to pay the owner $5 down—which she didn't have—and $5 a month, when she could get it.

But Mary McLeod Bethune, founder of Bethune-Cookman College at Daytona Beach, was innately convinced that God's ways seldom squared with man's ways, and that faith and prayer ("Nothing comes without it"), has often tipped the balance in favor of many a "fool."

And it did seem a primitive and quixotic endeavor, especially back in 1904 when even a simple education for blacks was tacitly frowned upon in the Deep South. It might give them "uppity ways," and no telling what that would lead to.

But this strong-willed "fool" was in earnest when she called her first pupils—five girls and her own son—into the first class in a tiny run-down, rented cabin. "We burned logs and used the charred splinters as pencils, and mashed elderberries for ink. I begged strangers for a broom, a lamp, a bit of cretonne to put around the packing case that served as my desk. I haunted the city dump and the trash piles behind hotels, retrieving discarded linen and kitchenware, cracked dishes, broken chairs, pieces of old lumber. Everything was secured and mended," she recalled.

Of course, this indomitable, industrious daughter of former slaves was too busy in those days to ponder her future. She certainly never dreamed that she would become one of America's foremost black educators and one of the most powerful spokesmen for the advancement of her race. Or that she would address national gatherings, receive honors, hobnob with royalty, advise presidents (and even scold one once—FDR—to his roaring delight).

13

Her single-minded desire, then, and ever after, branded into her soul when she was just an illiterate, knee-high cotton picker in rural South Carolina, was to raise the standards of her people and do so by bringing them what they needed most—education.

Mary McLeod was born July 19, 1875 in Mayesville, South Carolina, to Samuel and Patsy (McIntosh) McLeod, one of 17 children. The McLeods were former slaves who later sharecropped for their former owners and were finally able to buy a few acres of land from the owners for themselves. A childhood incident, at age 11, first ignited Mary's ambitions. One of the farm owner's daughters invited Mary to see her toys and playhouse. While viewing the scene, Mary spotted a book and in curiosity began to open it. At this, her white playmate turned on her sharply: "Put that book down! You can't read." A stunned Mary did so. But later, as she sweated through the long rows of cotton, she groaned silently, in gritty determined prayer to her personal God to let her learn how to read.

Mary was more than ever convinced that God could hear even an illiterate little black girl cotton-picker when, soon after, a Presbyterian mission teacher, one of many who fanned over the South in Reconstruction days, came to Sumter County. An excited Mary gladly walked the ten miles back and forth to school and, after two years, her big day came when she took down from the shelf the dusty, unread family Bible.

"That evening," she recalled, "Mama, Papa, and the family gathered around the fireplace of the tiny cabin, while in faltering words, I read from the great book. At that moment, I felt the joy of giving something to others."

Bright and diligent, the youngster soon after was picked for a scholarship to Scotia Seminary and, after graduation, was provided funds to attend Moody Bible Institute in Chicago. Upon graduation, she wanted mainly to be a foreign missionary to Africa, but the appointment never came. Instead, she went to Palatka, Florida, to teach school. In this period, she met and married Albertus Bethune, also a teacher, in 1897, and they had one son, Albert McLeod.

But Albert did not share his young wife's zeal, energy and determination to educate her race. After several uneasy, incompatible years, Albert decided to run off, and she never heard from him again.

An undaunted Mary moved to Daytona, opened her little cabin school, located the dump site acreage and offered the astonished owner $200 for it. He gratefully agreed to the $5 monthly payments on her "when possible" terms. Meanwhile, she worked night and day baking penny sweet potato pies which she sold to black construction gangs in the area, and raised the $5 down payment.

Organizing any private black school in those days was a formidable task but Mrs. Bethune, a born organizer endowed with a quiet dynamic force, relied heavily on that childhood faith that plucked her out of the cottonfields. Charging 50 cents a week tuition, she taught neighborhood children and boarded children of women who worked seasonally up north for winter tourist visitors.

She was keenly aware that the greatest need of her people in those days was not only skills in the basic "three-Rs," but practical training in domestic, farming, and technical skills, which they were so often denied. The school teetered precariously in its early struggles, but Mary Bethune worked tirelessly, begging, borrowing, and boldly buttonholing both visiting tourists and townspeople for school aid. At every crisis, she recounted, she prayed on faith for the need and she cannot recall a single time the need was not met. Appropriately, when her first large building went up two years later ("It was prayed up, sung up and talked up"), she named it Faith Hall.

Aside from its academic functions, Mrs. Bethune extended the school's activities to children in the primitive neighboring turpentine camps, along with adult evening classes, and she established the first black YMCA. The fast-growing institution was put on a firmer foundation when she persuaded the Mayor of Daytona and other local citizens to serve as school trustees. One valuable trustee, who served until his death in 1932, was James N. Gamble, son of the soap king of Procter and Gamble. Gamble also generously endowed the school at critical periods of financial need.

Reputation of the amazing accomplishments of both the school and Mrs. Bethune gradually became widespread, and in 1923 the Methodist Church Board of Education agreed to merge their Cookman School for Boys in Jacksonville with the Daytona school, making it coed. Five years later, the school was officially named Bethune-Cookman College.

The growth and success of Bethune-Cookman was phenomenal in the first half of this century. From six pupils in a crude cabin in 1904, the college would boast a faculty of 100, over 1,000 students enrolled, and a physical plant value of $1,000,000 at the time of the founder's death in May, 1955, at her Daytona Beach home. Mrs. Bethune would also serve variously over the years as president, president-emeritus, and trustee of the school.

The educator's renown and efforts in her field, as well as her battles against racial injustices on a national scale, gradually drew her into a variety of activities in the 1920s and the 1930s. At various times, she served as a national officer of the NAACP as well as the National Urban League and she wrote countless articles on racial affairs. She was the recipient of numerous honorary degrees as well as national honors, such as the Brotherhood Award of the National Conference of Christians and Jews. Ida Tarbell picked her as one of the 50 women who have contributed the most to the enrichment of American life, and she shared awards with Hugo Black, Will Alexander, and Frank Graham for outstanding service to the South.

In 1936, President Franklin D. Roosevelt named her director of Negro affairs in the National Youth Administration. She also served eight years in FDR's "black cabinet," as a special advisor on minority affairs. During World War II, she was named special assistant to the Secretary of War to select female candidates for officer training school in the Women's Army Corps (Wacs).

As N.Y.A. director, she saw hundreds of thousands of black children receive an education that they would have been denied otherwise. Once, as she quietly listened to the president outline the funding for the emergency education program, she noticed that Congress' funding for black children seemed grossly unequal. At this she rose, strode over to his desk and, shaking one large black finger at him, cried: "Mr. President, you've got to do better than that for me." Bursting into laughter, FDR warmly approved both her directness and her assessment of the program's funding disparity. He later sought, and received, a congressional correction of it.

She sparked national attention when she attacked discrimination by the war industry, noting that schools were refusing to train blacks for jobs because the industry was denying them jobs. A new policy was instituted to remedy this injustice.

President Harry Truman named her as a special emissary for the State Department at the organization of the United Nations in 1945, and she gained international recognition for quasi-official activities in both Africa and India.

Mrs. Bethune was never oblivious to the sting of prejudice in those years—the hotel she couldn't stay at, the restaurant she couldn't eat at, the back door she often had to enter. But the big woman had a warm, infectious humor and a kindly temperament, all sustained by her deeply-held Christian faith. She once noted: "I meet discrimination with great pity in my heart for those who inflict injustice or unhappiness." She felt that "the smallness of their souls, their failure to measure up to the Christ spirit," did them far more harm, in the long run, than it could for the moment to her. And this could only give her a sense of pity rather than resentment, she affirmed.

She had always believed, of course, that she could do as well as any white counterpart if given half the chance. Thus, it seemed the more remarkable that, with something less than half a chance, she took a run-down cabin and a dollar and a half and turned it into a million-dollar educational facility for hundreds of future black leaders, building along with it a distinguished record of national service that made her one of the outstanding women of her century.

4.
Mother Tuttle of Miami

Julia Tuttle had a vision. Out of the swamp, the palmettos, and mosquitoes of South Florida could rise a city.

The widow was still young and attractive with comfortable means, and she might have led a life of pleasant social ease, enjoying the relatively civilized and cultural amenities that a staid and established city like Cleveland had to offer.

Instead, she chose to journey to far off jungle wilderness where, amid dense exotic shrubs and woods and undergrowth, she envisioned the building of a brand new city.

Some, of course, scoffed at her "barmy" notions, like Henry Flagler who insisted that her Miami would never be more than a "fishing village." But the lady was persistent, determined and her soft and easy charm belied the intensity of her vision. There was a velvety toughness to this early shaker and mover; the birth of a sprawling metropolis could not have been served by an abler midwife.

Nevertheless, the "Mother of Miami," Mrs. Julia DeForrest Sturtevant Tuttle, was not always so sure of her destiny. In Cleveland, at 18, she married the scion Frederick L. Tuttle, of the big H. B. Tuttle & Son ironworks, and promptly delivered to him first a daughter, Frances Emmalie (Fannie), then a son, Henry E. (Harry). Later, when her husband took to bed with tuberculosis, she displayed a solid astuteness in managing the business' affairs.

During this period, her father, Ephraim Sturtevant, came to Biscayne Bay with another early settler, William Brickell. Both were captured by the idyllic unspoiled beauty of this bay country and both purchased land on either side of the Miami River, Brickell on the south bank, where it met the bay, and Sturtevant on the north. Julia, intrigued with her father's descriptions of this new frontier, brought her two small children along and came to see for herself, in 1873. Accompanied by a local settler, the versatile and erudite J. W. Ewan, a merchant, farmer, and legislator who would later be dubbed "the Duke of Dade," she toured the bay and river by sailboat. She not only lost her heart to the area, but saw the vision of a thriving city nestled along the wild mangrove-lined river. As she wrote to a friend later: "It may seem strange to you but it is the dream of my life to see this wilderness turned into a prosperous country and where this tangled vine, brush, trees, and rocks now are to see homes with modern improvements surrounded by beautiful grassy lawns, flowers, shrubs, and shade-trees."

Following the successive deaths of her father and then her husband, Julia decided that now was the time to follow her dream. In November, 1891, an enthusiastic woman came floating up to her inherited riverpoint homesite on a barge bearing her numerous household possessions, her daughter, now 23, and son, 21, a housekeeper, Maggie Carney, and two Jersey cows. They sheltered temporarily in the old Fort Dallas officers' quarters and, soon after, like some welcoming omen, a shipwreck yielded up to them bundles of rare, finely-worked Spanish tile which would form the floor of their new home.

An ever practical visionary, Julia gradually acquired more land to her river-bay section, mostly from Ewan who had moved a short way southward. She now had 640 choice acres. But the grandest visions of widows and men entail hard, practical requisites and the first requisite of a new city is people—merchants, craftsmen, doctors, bankers, butchers, bakers, and settlers generally. And these, in turn, need streets, waterworks, power plants, sewage, and drainage. Above all, people must be able to get to it, and Dade County then was virtually cut off by land from the rest of the country. Henry Flagler had pushed his railroad south as far as his Palm Beach resort by 1894 and he saw no reason to go any further.

The lady's soft voice intoned a persuasive manner as well. Historian Helen Muis once noted: "Julia Tuttle was a woman men liked. They admired her intelligence and were disarmed by her femininity. Julia could say no with a smile." "Duke of Dade" Ewan was strongly enamored of her for years; she gently declined his offer, yet kept his admiring friendship. Julia corresponded off and on with Flagler in the early nineties trying to persuade the tycoon to push his railroad to Biscayne Bay. He was polite but noncommittal. Meanwhile, she had imported both workers and building materials, first constructing a barnlike building to house the workers (which would later become her Miami Hotel), and then erecting buildings that could be used for business or residence, or both. Earlier, she had offered Flagler every other one of her 640 acres if he would railroad in and help lay out the town. She had persuaded William Brickell to make a similar donation on the river's south side. Elsewhere, a looming natural disaster was about to provide an untoward blessing.

In December 1895, Florida was struck with its severest freeze in history, heavily damaging its major industry, citrus. Then, during the next January, a second freeze hit even harder, as far south as Jupiter, virtually wiping out the growers and those dependent on the economy. Losses were estimated at $100 million.

Whatever Flagler earned from the lavish hotel playpens he built along the east coast for his wealthy peers, the greater portion of his hard coin derived from rail shipping. Figures reveal some idea of his losses: before the freeze, growers shipped by rail 5,550,367 crates of citrus; after the freeze, a mere 150,000 crates were shipped. A frantic Flagler rushed in with loads of free seeds to growers, plus tools, crates, and personal loans to help them start replanting. When his agent, James Ingraham, on a damage inspection tour, arrived in frost-free Miami, Mrs. Tuttle repeated her offer of free land. She then handed Ingraham a box to take back to Flagler—it contained on dampened cotton the fragrant sprig of an orange blossom cutting. No word or gesture could have been more effective. Within days, Flagler arrived in Miami for talks with Julia. He agreed to build his Royal Palm Hotel, clear streets, finance water and light plants, and make other improvements. Almost at once, he began the 66-mile laying of track southward. The march to build Miami had begun.

Speculators, tradesmen, merchants, and laborers poured into the village. Crude shacks went up. The sound of hammer and nails on pine lumber echoed over the bay. Flagler brought in visitors with free excursions from Jacksonville. Viewing the drab, unpainted buildings and tents and plank-board streets, while fighting an influx of mosquitoes and sandflies, many fled back to "civilization." But heartier souls shared Julia's infectious optimism and she set about at once to build quarters for them, charging a flat $25 monthly rent. J. E. Lummus soon opened shop, followed by Isidor Cohen in dry goods; John and E. J. Sewell, general store; Thomas Townley, drugstore; Dr. James and Mary Jackson, medical practice; J. W. Watson, hardware; E. C. Romfh, banking; and many others.

Yet Flagler's true perspective on the town was myopic at best. When Julia and the Brickells pleaded with him that the streets were too narrow, he retorted huffily: "The town will never be more than a fishing village for my hotel guests." The effects of that undersight are still visible today. His waste disposal planning, with short-fall pipes pouring tons of raw sewage into the beautiful Miami river, would create serious health problems within the decade. Flagler's ornate, palatial wonders for his millionaire friends aside, he demonstrated harmful ignorance in planning the community needs of lesser everyday mortals. Thus, when he became infatuated with the unique, free-spirited little settlement of Coconut Grove just south of Miami and sought to bless them with his brand of progress, Commodore Ralph M. Munroe, expressing the general sentiment of the people in the Grove, tersely informed the railroader: "Leave us alone."

But city planning problems were on nobody's mind that exciting day, April 15, 1896, when more than 300 area settlers, some of whom had never seen a train before, flocked in to watch the little wood-burning locomotive chug into town with a load of building supplies. The town's first newspaper, *Metropolis,* announced in apropos headline: "The coming metropolis of

South Florida," and the following July 28, the city of Miami was incorporated. Julia's dream was now a bustling, thriving fact—and she was jubilant.

The widow worked tirelessly thereafter, planning other town projects—school, church, hospital, government—whatever the need. But the city's—and Julia's—expectations took some hard lumps over the next two years. The country was in a financial depression. New tourists and settlers had not arrived, and efforts by Mrs. Tuttle to spur Flagler's assistance for the ailing town were in vain. Following a fire which destroyed 28 of the town's buildings, an exhausted Julia fell into ailing depression and secluded herself for a while in the confines of her bayfront home. Years later, Commodore Munroe recalled of the time: "Flagler continued to build ahead of actual demand. The result was bitter disappointment for Mrs. Tuttle, whose land remained vacant, weed-grown and in little demand until her death. In later years, of course, it became immensely valuable to her heirs."

And then one day, September 14, 1898, Julia complained of a violent headache. A friend who was staying with her at the time, Mrs. Fannie Comstock, gave her a headache powder and it seemed to bring relief. But within an hour, Julia was dead, at 50.

Activity in Miami came to a standstill and a town turned out to mourn her. Like some latter-day female Moses, she had brought her people to the threshold of a great city but did not get to enter it herself.

Nevertheless, she knew it was there. Speaking in the 1950s, an aging J. E. Lummus recalled the time he visited her and asked her point-blank: "Do you really think this place has a future? She replied: 'Mr. Lummus, if you live your natural lifetime you will see one hundred thousand people in this city.' " He did see them, many times over. It was a visionary's understatement.

Therefore, as citizens today cross the Julia Tuttle Causeway linking Miami with the Beach, it is just possible that some of them might feel a twinge of gratitude to the determined, soft-spoken woman who once long ago stood in a boat viewing the tropical splendor of the Miami River and exulted to a friend: "It may seem strange to you but it is the dream of my life to see this wilderness turned into a prosperous country." It was—and it did.

5.
"Dark Horse" Dave Wins Governorship

David Sholtz was the darkest of dark horses, but won nomination by the greatest majority ever won in Florida at that time.

The seers stood in puzzled awe in 1976's presidential election as they watched a little-known rise up to confound the major candidates, the party pros and machine bosses, the infallible prophets of TV and newspaper, and all the conventional odds involving religion, region, and financial resources, to win his party's nomination—and the election.

But about 45 years ago, a Florida gubernatorial candidate performed a similar "miracle" against odds at least as formidable if not greater, when David Sholtz moved quietly out of his dark horse stable to stun the state's powers and pundits and become Florida's 26th chief executive in 1932—and a New Deal protégé of President Franklin D. Roosevelt.

In a sense, Sholtz even "out-Cartered" Jimmy Carter because he had ethnic and regional image problems that would have hog-tied any mere tourist, much less a seeker of the state's highest office, in the hard-shell Cracker and Bible Belt land that was so much of Florida in the 1930s.

The son of immigrant parents, he was a Yankee (a Brooklyn-born one at that), and a lawyer who had lived in the state (Daytona Beach) only 15 years. He was an honors graduate of the symbol of Eastern Establishment "pointyheadedness"—Yale, class of 1915. He was also of Jewish ancestry. (This latter fact injected an ugly note of anti-Semitism in the race, but as it turned out, it may well have tipped the scale against the odds-on favorite who injected it.)

Staggering handicaps enough—but only openers. Sholtz was a relative unknown in his first try for major office. He had no support from the old-line political organizations or bosses and virtually no funds for media advertising. Above all, he was running against two powerful former governors of the 1920s, John W. Martin and Cary A. Hardee, who all pros agreed would easily be the run-offers. If these two sure bets were not enough, they were joined in the first primary by five formidable candidates—Stafford Caldwell, Charles M. Durrance, Arthur Gomez, Thomas S. Hart, and J. Tom Watson.

21

Sholtz was also strongly opposed in his own Volusia County with a clouty political machine bossed by Francis Whitehair.

Wiser wags and cynics smiled benignly if somewhat in disbelief at this genial, urbane, portly little upstart, as if to ask: What's a nice little Yankee Jewish boy like you doing among these native son giants who will cut you up like so much fish bait? No one took David Sholtz seriously, except the unnervingly optimistic David himself. Even up to final election eve, state gamblers' odds against him were 200 to one.

He was the darkest of dark horses. But he would win the nomination by the greatest majority ever garnered in the history of the state to that time.

David was born in Brooklyn, October 5, 1891, to Michael and Annie (Bloom) Sholtz, the father having immigrated from Germany at age 15. The elder Sholtz prospered in investments and real estate and moved to Daytona Beach in the early 1900s and became active in business affairs there. David, after Yale, came to Daytona to live and took a law degree from Stetson University in 1916.

Still practicing law, he offered himself for the legislature that same year and, with strong grass roots support, won against the opposition of the local "Courthouse Ring." But in World War I, he took a leave of absence and joined the Navy as an ensign, serving four years. In 1921, he resumed his Daytona practice and in 1925 married Alice Mae Agee. They had one son of their own and three adopted children.

Long active in local and state civic affairs, Sholtz was elected president of the Florida State Chamber of Commerce in 1927. While in this post, he not only developed a wide range of state interests but also nurtured a growing interest in government, along with some keen ideas on how it might best serve all citizens and not merely a few of the long-entrenched machines and special interests. And by now he had his eye on the only single post he knew that could help bring about such changes—the governorship.

However, by the time the elections of 1931 rolled around, the state needed more than a few changes. Already reeling from the heavy blow of the crash of the Florida Boom, the state was being drawn still deeper into the vortex of the great national Depression. The state was by now in an unconstitutional condition of debt and these woes were compounded further in that 150 Florida towns were in default on their obligations.

The legislature itself, struggling for urgently needed revenues, could engage in vehement and, yes, bloody debates over adoption of a then unheard of one-penny gas tax. The new rug on the floor of the Florida House was splotched with the blood of solons actually fighting over the tax and the session dragged into 100 days until a powerful west coast political boss, Peter O. Knight, who had opposed the tax, sent 38 telegrams, (one for each senator), reading "Pass gas tax bill and come on home." They did.

A mild Governor Doyle Carlton, fearful lest the state's business-tourist image be tarnished, wrote to President Herbert Hoover to reassure him that everything was just fine here, thank you, and the state needed no federal assistance, even though in the city of Tampa alone, one third of its people were unemployed and food riots were a daily threat.

Sholtz well knew the odds as the eight-man primary opened that spring, but not many knew the Sholtz personality. He had an infectious self-confidence but, moreover, he had an instinctive rapport with individuals of diverse background and he conveyed a feeling of sincerity to those he addressed. His law partner recalled him simply as "a kindly person with a sincere interest in helping people." It was at least a refreshing change from the winking, nudging, phoney croneyism, and pandering in the "good ole boy" tradition of the day.

As a public speaker, he seldom used notes and this emphasized the impression of sincerity and genuine concerns for individual needs. The urbane Yankee could in such manner convince the most skeptical Cracker that he, too, was against the rampant bossism of the day. Sholtz was an active Episcopalian by faith and when an audience in the panhandle Bible Belt asked what it meant to be an Episcopalian, the reply came that this was midway between a Baptist and a Methodist. The answer apparently satisfied both. Sholtz had no funds for radio, newspaper, or billboard advertising and often had to go door to door to get funds for mailing a few campaign letters. But he relied mainly on a flat-bed truck with two loud-speakers which he drove from town to town over the state under tireless schedule. And then came election day.

Martin indeed led the first primary with 66,940 votes. But no one could explain or understand dark horse Dave's second place win with 55,406, and Hardee trailing third—and out—at 50,427. The soothsayers went into apoplectic daze and a grim Goliath Martin took a more sober look at this menacing David. It would be a bitter run-off primary.

The ex-governor pulled no punches as his machine laid pressure on not only the losing candidates but every old-line boss in the state. But a desperate Martin went even further. Whatever demonic urge moved him, once he learned of Sholtz's Jewish ancestry (which Sholtz never denied) he began to inject a subtle tone of anti-Semitism into the campaign until finally he was elevating the evil smear into a major issue. He even wrote to Germany to get sworn depositions attesting to Sholtz's Jewishness. He would win—at any price.

Meanwhile, Sholtz completely ignored these attacks and refused to show any anger against Martin. Instead, he smiled, shook hands and listened to people. He talked of the Depression crisis, jobs for the hungry, opening schools and keeping them open nine months, free textbooks, and a reduced tax millage for small homeowners. He was serious, intensely sincere, and people listened. They were tired of the shopworn, Coolidge-type slogans of the old politicians as the Depression grew darker and heavier. And, again, Martin may have won the winking tacit approval of the party regulars with his rabid smears but he underestimated the solid sense of fair play of those very Cracker voters he sought to inflame. Election night once more stunned the political analysts: Sholtz, 173,540; Martin, 102,805, the largest majority ever given a candidate in Florida history. Sholtz easily swamped his Republican opponent, W. J. Howey, in November.

Sholtz could say truthfully, as he did at his inaugural, that he owed no political obligations anywhere and that in setting the state house in order it would surely arouse the anger of "selfish interests" and "political racketeers" and their "chicanery, conniving, and attacks." But he would "hew to the line and let the chips fall."

The 40-year-old upsetter was known as "the New Deal governor" for his strong support of F. D. R. and his policies. In fact, his closeness to Roosevelt redounded strongly to Florida's benefit as programs and critically needed federal aid began to pour into the state. Sholtz first pushed for an auto tag fee of $5 and diverted enough funds to pay teachers in cash instead of script. He beat the powerful publishers' lobby to make good a promise of free textbooks. He instituted needed reforms in prison camps and set up the highway patrol. He made jobs a priority and cut relief cases by 75% in three years and moved an inherited deficit of $2,124,000 to a surplus of $591,000 by 1934. Other enduring achievements made at his impetus were a park service and conservation commission, the state citrus commission, a workman's compensation act, a mechanics' lien law, a social welfare board, a state employment service, pensions for the aged and blind, and numerous other long-range improvements.

When he had finished his constitutionally-restricted one term in 1936, Florida had become one of the fastest states in the country in moving toward economic recovery.

But it all might have been otherwise if an affable New York Jewish lawyer had not looked over the odds—and the needs—and said to himself: "Why not?"

6.
Zora Neale Hurston: Florida's Black Novelist

She was born in poverty but raised herself to be among the nation's great black novelists. Then her world fell in.

Zora Neale Hurston: Florida's black literary heroine.

The light brown barefooted "waif" had traveled a piece of road from her rural Central Florida shanty and its trees and fields and chicken yards and outhouses and the pungent aromas of boiled collard greens and fried chicken.

Zora Neale Hurston, Florida author, folklorist, and anthropologist, never dreamed as she lay against her big "loving pine" tree in childhood reveries over Greek mythology that she would one day be regaling the leading literary lights of her day with stories of a more earthy, realist modern lore.

Her Baptist preacher father impressed upon her the grandeur, beauty, and poetry of the Bible for her imagery and her mother urged her to "follow your own heart and jump for the sun" and these dual influences combined to produce one of Florida's most remarkable literary figures. In fact, in the renaissance of black consciousness that first began to crack the shell of racial isolation in America in the 1920s and 30s—producing the Hughes, the Wrights, the Johnsons, the Cullens—perhaps no other person effectively translated and introduced the common black experience as did Miss Hurston.

She could feel at ease in the posh salons of New York City's intelligentsia, swapping vignettes with friends like Carl Van Vechten, Dwight Fiske, Sinclair Lewis, Alan Lomax, Cornelia Chapin or Max Eastman, and enjoyed warm friendships with figures as diverse as Fannie Hurst or the inimitable Ethel Waters. But she was likewise at home sauntering casually through the rough and primitive railroad and turpentine camps and juke joints of her native Florida, gathering the raw materials for her numerous books, articles, and short stories. Putting it all together, she gradually cut the clay away from a rich and long-hidden lode of mainstream Americana and, for the first time, made a huge segment of Ralph Ellison's "invisible" men vitally visible to a looking, unseeing world.

She stretched her canvas evenly and mixed her oils and colors with rich soil and warts and mortal fallibility. She declined the posture of either militance or bland "Tomism," top-heavy racial pride or condescending toadyism. To the occasional chagrin of her more sensitive brethren-in-letters, she etched the racial portrait "like it is," with the age-old human mix of good and evil but, far from depreciating its special richness, this only further enhanced its image and commonality with Everyman. This attitude was wryly marked once in her autobiography, "Dust Tracks On A Road," when she wrote,

"For me to pretend I am Old Black Joe and waste my time on his problems, would be just as ridiculous as for the government of Winston Churchill to bill the Duke of Normandy the first of every month, or for the Jews to hang around the pyramids, trying to picket Old Pharaoh. While I have a handkerchief over my eyes crying over the landing of the first slaves in 1619, I might miss something swell that is going on in 1942."

Her cool objectivity never lessened her deep sense of empathy with the real and imperative needs of "my people;" she could render these mute yearnings in lyrical and passionate cadences. But she learned early the subtle lure of the "bitter cup," and its poisonous effects, and she spurned the potion emphatically.

Zora Neal Hurston was born January 7, 1901, in the town of Eatonville, the first all-black community in America, just north of Orlando. It was a town strongly steeped in black folk tradition and history. To her, it was "a city of five lakes, three croquet courts, 300 brown skins, 300 good swimmers, plenty of guavas, two schools, and no jailhouse."

Her mother was the town seamstress and her father was at one time mayor of the town, a tenant farmer, a carpenter, and a sometime Baptist preacher who was as often "circulating" the state as he was at home. She was a zestful spirited youngster (sometimes too much so for her more passive kinfolk), and after her mother died when Zora was nine, the child was for a time "passed around like a bad penny" to stay with various relatives. This kept her from her major love then—the classroom—to such extent that she revolted at the age of 16 and ran off to take a job as a maid to a young stage actress.

She thrived in this novel and colorful theatrical world and was further rewarded when her white benefactress arranged for her to attend and graduate from the high school department of Morgan College in Baltimore. From here she enrolled in Howard University where she strongly benefited from the influence of the eminent black scholar, Dr. Lorenzo Dow Turner, head of Howard's English department. She attended Howard from 1921 to 1924, supporting her way as a manicurist, until lack of funds forced her to leave school.

But she had already won distinction as a short-story writer, having had several published in the national black literary magazine, *Opportunity*. The magazine's editor, Charles S. Johnson, urged her to come to New York and try her writing wings. She did, and after winning a short-story award, found herself the center of munificent attentions, first from the popular novelist, Fannie Hurst, who hired her as her personal secretary, and Annie Nathan Meyer, who secured for her a scholarship to Barnard. Miss Hurston had no "lurid tales" to tell of discrimination at the prestigious girls' school. With amused tongue-in-cheek she recalls: "The Social Register crowd at Barnard soon took me up, and I became Barnard's sacred black cow. If you had not had lunch with me, you had not shot from taw."

At Barnard, her special talents prompted the renowned anthropologist Dr. Franz Boas, to urge her to study anthropology and she took her B.A. in that field in 1928. She also won a Rosenwald Foundation fellowship for two years of graduate study at Columbia University and, at Dr. Boas' urging, went south—and home again—to study black folklore.

It was a tough assignment in that rural and shanty-town country that was black Florida in the 1920s and 1930s, in sharp contrast to our own day. As she herself commented: "Folklore is not as easy to collect as it sounds. The best source is where there are the least outside influences and these people, being usually under-privileged, are the shyest."

The black, in spite of his open laughter and seeming acquiescence, she found "particularly evasive," offering the questioner a smile and a few random thoughts that might satisfy his interrogator. "The Indian resists curiosity by a stony silence. The Negro offers a feather-bed resistance. That is, we let the probe enter, but it never comes out. It gets smothered under a lot of laughter and pleasantries."

But the months and years of work were rewarding. With the publication of a short story, "The Gilded Six-Bits" in the internationally known *Story* magazine, edited by noted anthologists Whit Burnett and Martha Foley, doors began to open. Miss Hurston then went home to Eatonville and wrote her first novel, *Jonah's Gourd Vine*. It was accepted by J. B. Lippincott publishers the day she was evicted from her tiny house when rent and grocery funds ran out.

The book, though somewhat crude and uneven by today's standards, was hailed by the *New York Times* as "the most vital and original" novel by a black about her race up to that time. Carl Sandburg, whose work Miss Hurston's resembles in poetic imagery, called it "bold and beautiful."

The lady had arrived. Commissions and requests for articles and stories began to pour in. During this period, while doing anthropological work in Haiti, she had another work "dammed up in me" and she let it gush out in seven weeks. *Their Eyes Were Watching God,* was an even better book, with the same black Florida setting, and it unfolded some of her finest character creations. It is considered today as her best novel. Meanwhile, she had also published one of her most valuable anthropological studies, *"Mules and Men,"* folklore collected from blacks in both Florida and Haiti.

She had also won a Guggenheim Fellowship which enabled her to study in the Bahamas. In these islands, she found the folklore and folksongs "more original, dynamic, and African" than some she had studied in America.

In the early thirties, she successfully organized and produced black song and dance groups featuring island and mainland folk and work songs and spirituals. The show made highly successful tours of the cities in the eastern U.S. In 1939, came her third novel, *Moses, Man of the Mountain,* a somewhat unusual work which retold the story of the emancipation of the Hebrews in modern colloquial terms. Her last novel, published in the early forties, was *Seraph on the Suwanee.* This tale was of poor white Crackers, rather than poor black, but just as authentic and skillful in language and characterization.

In the early 1940s, Miss Hurston was invited to Hollywood, as a writing consultant, by Paramount producer Arthur Hornblow. While there, she found time to rest, relax, and write her autobiography, *Dust Tracks.* It won rave reviews, as well as the Ainsfield award for the best book of the year on racial problems. But California was almost a foreign country to her and she returned to Florida where she lived on a houseboat, wrote magazine articles, and became a guest lecturer at Bethune-Cookman College in Volusia County.

But a tragic incident would enter her life while she was at a settled height of fame and career. In 1948, she was falsely accused and indicted on a morals charge which alleged that she had been a party in sexual relations with two mentally ill boys and an older man. The charge was lodged by the mother of the boys who had mistaken Miss Hurston for another woman. The charge, of course, was quickly withdrawn since Miss Hurston had been out of the country at the time of the alleged crime, but not before some Negro newspapers played it into a major scandal. Miss Hurston experienced first shock and disbelief and then the deepest despair. She wrote to her friend,

Carl Van Vechten: "I have resolved to die. My country has failed me utterly. My race has seen fit to destroy me without reason, and with the vilest tools conceived of by man so far." Noting that the affair occurred not in the South but "the so-called liberal North," she asked: "Where shall I look in the country for justice . . . . All that I have believed in has failed me."

And, aside from a few articles in the 1950s, she ceased all creative writing. She even went to work as a maid, until her employer discovered a story by her maid written in the *Saturday Evening Post*. Newspapers ran the story around the country of the successful black writer doing housework. Miss Hurston then went to Fort Pierce to live in relative obscurity and poverty until she died of a stroke on January 28, 1960. Shocked friends as well as local citizens saw to it that she was given a fitting tribute and burial.

Miss Hurston's intimate knowledge of Southern whites and blacks had long convinced her of the essential oneness of mankind. "I learned that skins were no measure of what was inside people . . . . I began to laugh at both white and black who claimed special blessings on the basis of race. Therefore, I saw no curse in being black, no extra favor in being white. I give you all my right hand of fellowship and love." The lady lived these words, and her writings, therefore, remain an enduring gift not only to American literature but to the race of man that it might truly constitute, "All God's Chillun."

7.
Dr. Gorrie Cools Florida Off

When Dr. John Gorrie invented air-conditioning he was trying to heal the sick. It was years before the invention caught on.

He wasn't really thinking of the sweaty brows or stuffy hot homes and offices of millions of people today when, back in the 1840s, he himself sweated in a modest workroom and tinkered diligently with the laws of physics and mechanics.

In those days, the father of modern air-conditioning and refrigeration, Dr. John Gorrie, was concerned only with the prevention of disease and the alleviation of human suffering. Particularly in the care of his fever-wracked patients in the thriving Gulf Coast cotton port of Apalachicola which, like most Southern seaports, suffered recurring epidemics of yellow fever and malaria throughout the 19th century.

If he could keep his patients cool and dry, the doctor theorized, he might cure their tormenting maladies.

So he ingeniously devised a way to cool their rooms and, in the process, discovered how to make a miraculous little machine that could produce "artificial" ice. He quickly foresaw its widespread use to preserve food indefinitely, after centuries of salting, pickling, sugaring, and drying.

And yet, amazingly, these wonderful inventions would lie in oblivion for almost 100 years before mankind in general would enjoy their blessings.

Dr. John Gorrie's origins were as romantically nebulous as his fertile mind was creative. His dark hair and dark eyes bespoke his Spanish descent and he always spoke Spanish fluently. He was born an illegitimate child, in 1802, in St. Nevis Island in the West Indies (where another distinguished American, Alexander Hamilton, was born, also illegitimately, a half-century earlier).

His mother, a handsome and educated young governess who presumably had tutored in a royal household in Spain, brought her year-old son to Charleston, South Carolina, in 1803, accompanied by an elderly Scotch officer, named Gorrie, who served in the Royal Spanish army. Gorrie never returned to Charleston, but the mother took his name for her own. She had been amply provided with funds from Spain which were deposited to her account annually. This enabled her to educate John in the best private schools of the area. Historians presume that John's father, unknown, was a member of the aforesaid royal household.

During political upheavals in Spain the funds stopped arriving, but by this time John was of age and able to secure work to support himself and his mother. After working several years with a U.S. Postmaster in Columbia, South Carolina, he studied at the College of Physicians and Surgeons in New York, from which he graduated in 1827. He practiced medicine for a while in Abbeville, South Carolina, before moving with his mother to Sneads, Florida, in 1831, on the Apalachicola River. Following his mother's death from an unknown illness in 1833, the doctor moved himself and his practice down river to Apalachicola, a bustling frontier town and then third largest cotton shipping port on the Gulf.

The young doctor's distinctive education, diffident charm, and deep social concerns prompted townspeople to thrust upon him many civic roles— postmaster, city council chairman, city treasurer, mayor, co-founder of the Trinity Episcopal Church, as well as an investor and officer in two banks, the Mansion House Hotel, and a land company. He also took a wife, Caroline Beman, the attractive widow of a Presbyterian missionary to Indians and they had a son, John Jr., and a daughter, Sarah.

But, to the gradual exclusion of other civic interests, the doctor's attention was increasingly absorbed with the town's recurring summer attacks of yellow fever and malaria. He was convinced that decaying vegetation in swamps, marshes, and wet places caused both fevers and he successfully persuaded citizens to fill in low waterfront areas, drain the higher wetlands, and construct their buildings of solid brick. Through a congressional act he secured funds for a marine hospital to treat the numerous seamen who brought the fevers to port and he also raised subscriptions to support a hospital for poor and indigent local fever victims. He was named resident physician for both hospitals.

Understandably, Gorrie associated the two fevers with hot and moist atmospheres in which victims inhaled the "volatile toxic end products of decaying vegetable and animal matter." Noting in 1842 that malaria could not exist in very dry or very cold climates, he deduced that cooling and drying the air surrounding a patient would eliminate his fever. (No one in the medical world of that time looked to the lowly mosquito as the fever carrier— except another noted Florida doctor, John Perry Wall, of Tampa, who would first suspect this insect some 40 years later.)

In his first experiment in 1844, Gorrie suspended a basin of ice from a hospital room ceiling and extended a pipe over the basin through the ceiling above to the chimney by which air entered the closed room. Another pipe installed at the floor level would discharge the room's air. The fresh air from the ceiling pipe—drawn into the vacuum that formed around the ice in the basin, which in turn absorbed the air's heat as it melted—diffused the cool air showerlike throughout the room.

Developing this physical principle further, Gorrie operated two compressor pumps by steam engine, one pump to condense the air, the other to expand it, while a storage chamber in between released the cooled, condensed air through pipes into the hospital rooms.

Then, one hot summer evening in 1845, an attendant accidentally left the steam engine of the air-conditioning compressors on overnight; next morning Dr.Gorrie found the air pipes clogged with ice. The excited physician began at once his blueprints for an ice machine.

In this same period, Gorrie was envisioning the future uses of refrigeration. In a scientific journal article, he wrote: "Animals or fruit, when divested of life, may be preserved entire with all their juices in a low temperature; this principle of producing and maintaining cold might be made instrumental in preserving organic matter an indefinite length of time, and thus become an accessory to the extension of commerce. We know of no want of mankind more urgent than a cheap means of producing artificial cold. The discovery would alter and extend the face of civilization; we trust that a measure that promises to be attended with such results will not suffer neglect or fall into oblivion."

The town was fortunate in drawing another eminent figure to its midst. A doctor more famed as a botanist, Dr. Alvan Wentworth Chapman, whose *Flora of the Southeastern United States,* is a definitive work on the subject, arrived in Apalachicola in 1846 and became a close personal friend and avid supporter of Gorrie. Gorrie had quietly begun filing for patent papers on his invention in 1849. Although many had heard of his efforts, no one had actually seen the machine until one day in June 1850 Gorrie called Chapman into his laboratory. Chapman recalled that Gorrie was "excited and nervous," traits he had never seen in the doctor before.

"Jokingly, I said, 'Well, have you found a way yet to freeze all your patients?' "

" 'Not exactly,' Gorrie smiled, 'but I've made ice.'

" 'The hell you have.'

" 'This has nothing to do with hell,' Gorrie responded, 'but with continued success I may be able to lower the temperature in that torrid climate too.' "

The first public exhibit of the ice machine came when a French cotton broker, M. Rosan, gave a banquet at the Mansion House for some wealthy Northern cotton brokers. Having already seen the machine, Rosan teamed with Gorrie to wager a basket of champagne with the brokers that, if the ice ship arrived too late in port for the banquet, Rosan would produce ice right there in the dining room. The incredulous brokers eagerly accepted the bet. By dinner time, the ship had not arrived, but Rosan suddenly drew back a curtain for the assembled guests who witnessed waiters hurrying into the dining room with champagne baskets and silver salves covered with ice. "Today it is an American who has worked the miracle," Rosan exclaimed, and the astonished guests were later taken to Gorrie's lab to see the machine in action.

Nevertheless, except for one wealthy New Orleans merchant who died before he could effectively assist Gorrie, the doctor was unsuccessful in finding any backers to put his machine into production. He had already exhausted his holdings and savings in developing the machine and having the Cincinnati Iron Works construct the first two small models (one of which is now in the Smithsonian Institute in Washington.) His patents were finally issued in Washington and London in the summer of 1851 but, for want of further improvements or production, they would expire 20 years later.

Perhaps the major stonewall to Gorrie's machine was the combined efforts of the powerful Northern monopoly of ice shippers who controlled this great and lucrative market, especially in Southern cities, where ice was a luxury only the affluent could afford. Cut in winter from northern lakes and 'rivers, packed in sawdust in thick-walled storage rooms and shipped southward, ice commanded prices of up to $1.50 a pound. Naturally, the industry foresaw certain extinction at the prospect of a machine that could produce, within minutes, fat ice blocks that would sell for only a few dollars a ton! Shrewdly, enlisting the aid of the press, the ice shippers organized a subtle campaign of ridicule. So effective was this manipulated laugh-in, that the doctor met only smiling skepticism wherever he sought funds for production. Typical was the New York editorialist who scoffed: "There is a crank down in Apalachicola, Florida, a Dr. John Gorrie, who claims he can make ice as good as God Almighty."

Deeply discouraged, his sensitive nature scarred by these orchestrated attacks, his health broken by illness, the doctor returned to Apalachicola, where he secluded himself at home until his death on June 22, 1855.

It was Chapman, who kept Gorrie's reputation and works publicized among contemporaries until his death in 1899, that prompted Floridians to recognize a great citizen. In 1911, Gorrie became one of the two distinguished citizens representing Florida in Statuary Hall in the Capitol at Washington. Later on, bridges, museums, squares, public schools, and other distinctive memorials appeared, not only in his hometown but throughout the state.

Gorrie is now ranked with the world's great inventors of the 19th century for discoveries that did in fact "alter and extend the face of civilization."

The wonder is that such a boon to mankind should, as Gorrie once feared, be neglected and fall into oblivion for nearly a century, due to the myopic ignorance and collective greed of the people who stood to gain the greatest benefits from his achievements.

8.
Young Whitaker Discovers Sarasota

Life was risky but not hard in 1843 when Bill Whitaker built his homestead in Sarasota. Being the only white resident of the county was lonely.

He bought up more than a mile of Sarasota's bayfront for $1.25 an acre, then rafted logs over Longboat Key's dense cedar forest and built a sturdy log cabin.

He went into the seafood business, selling salt-dried mullet at a penny a fish to roving Spanish traders; he soon prospered modestly.

Thus began the unique and solitary pioneer life of William H. (Bill) Whitaker, the father of Sarasota, and he would remain its first and only settler for almost a generation.

But settling down was the last thing on Bill's mind when, at age 14, in 1835, with his father's reluctant consent, he left his Savannah, Georgia home. Carrying only a few clothes, a few dollars and—his father's gift—a large key-wind Swiss gold watch "big as a biscuit," he signed as a deckhand on a schooner bound for Key West.

He sailed for about a year and then tried his hand as a fisherman at St. Marks. Here he met his half-brother, Hamlin Snell, a young Tallahassee attorney, who persuaded Bill to "get a little schooling" in that city. The boy consented but, still restless for adventure, he left his studies two years later and joined the army to fight in the Second Seminole War. When that long, bloody war ended in 1842, Bill had had his fill of "adventure" and, at age 21, was ready to find a home.

With the war's end, the government was offering 160-acre homesteads in South Florida to any man who would work it for five years. So with half-brother Snell in the latter's sloop, he sailed down the west coast to find a suitable homesite. They had found nothing by the time they reached Manatee Village where some other prominent Tallahasseans—Joseph and Hector Braden, Major Robert Gamble, Colonel William Wyatt and others—had staked homestead claims on the banks of the Manatee River, hoping to recoup their losses after the Tallahassee bank failures during the Panic of 1837. They visited awhile in Manatee and then continued sailing south. In December 1842, they entered Sarasota Bay.

As the sloop moved around the curtain of cedar forests on Longboat Key, Whitaker's pulse quickened at the sight of the high yellow bluffs on the mainland. They drew up into a small bayou north of the bluffs and eagerly went ashore. They found traces of an ancient Indian village, a crystal springs pool of fresh water on the bayou's east bank, and a transient Spanish fisherman "squatter" who informed them of the teeming abundance of fish and game in the area. The dense vegetation also indicated a richly fertile soil. As he stood on the bluffs and beheld a magnificent view of the entire bay, Whitaker knew he had found his home. The two men built a temporary shelter, rafted logs from Longboat Key, and by spring 1843, had built a sizeable, sturdy cedar log cabin. Snell then returned to Tallahassee law practice, leaving Whitaker alone in a primeval wilderness to work out his future.

With his government deed to 144.81 acres plus the later purchase of 48.63 acres at $1.25 per acre, extending his bayfront land over a mile, the lone pioneer of Sarasota County was firmly settled in.

In wintertime, immense schools of mullet churned through the bay so thickly that they resembled a shimmering silver carpet; Whitaker had no problem filling a cast net within minutes. Then came the hard job of cleaning, salting, then placing the fish on sun-lit racks to dry "hard as boards." Along with dried mullet roe, the fish were packed in handmade crates and sold for a penny a fish to the Cuban traders who plied the west coast. Ten dollars (1,000 mullet) would buy a lot of essentials in those days and, with the aid later of a temporary transient helper, Whitaker's savings steadily grew.

Whitaker had a small vegetable garden and also planted an orange grove which, over ten years, would become a full-bearing quality grove. If a lonely settler lacked other conveniences in this isolated frontier, he never had want of food. Nature's free supermarket was literally Cornucopian. The bay's clear water teamed with every kind of fish, plus the finest oysters, clams, scallops, and stone crabs; one could gather a dozen meals in half an hour. Or he could shoot a meal a few hundred yards from home—deer, possum, turkey, quail, duck, plus wild razorback hogs that roamed the woods in great packs. Whitaker learned how to herd these porkers into pens, then fatten them and sell them to Key West traders at an attractive profit. Their leanness also made the finest smoked hams and sausages, plus cooking lard, and grease to mix with leached ashes for soap. Squeezed fish heads provided oil for home-made lamps.

By 1847, Whitaker had saved enough money to ride up to Dade City and invest in some cattle—ten cows and calves. Over the years, he would build his '47-brand herd into a substantial cattle business.

But nature was not always such a source of benevolence to the young settler. On September 22, 1848, the acknowledged "grandaddy of all Florida hurricanes," struck the west coast with a fury it has never known since. Lighthouses, such as Egmont Key, toppled like matchsticks, homes were flattened, whole islands disappeared, and large ships were swept in and smashed to pieces on the mainland. Huddled inside his cabin facing the open bay, Whitaker felt the full center force of the blast. He recounted later: "I didn't believe I would live through the night. The logs in the wall groaned as though they were in agony. Every minute I thought they would tumble down upon me." But the sturdy cedar logs stood fast; only the roof was damaged. Next day, he looked out toward the beach strip on which he had left his nets. The nets were gone, so was the beach strip. A new pass was carved in the key, so Whitaker gave it that name, New Pass. But he would spend months at the long tedious task of making new nets. Other coastal settlers were not left totally bereft. Beach-strewn wreckage yielded up valuable furniture, farm and household implements, cloth and even scores of barrels of quality whiskey which may have offered some brief consolation to the heaviest losers.

But soon after this another storm hit Whitaker—an emotional one—and at age 30 he was about to end his long celibate years. She was a pretty, spirited, black-haired, blue-eyed 18-year-old, Mary Jane Wyatt, youngest child and only daughter of Colonel and Mrs. William Wyatt, of Manatee Village. She had been privately educated, but she knew frontier life intimately. On her father's ranch, she learned early how to ride, herd cattle and shoot a rifle. For two years, the love-struck suitor wore a good-sized trail in the 30-mile round-trek from Yellow Bluffs to Manatee. On June 10, 1851, they were married and the following April, 1852 the first child was born in Sarasota—Nancy Catherine Stewart Whitaker. Over the next 14 years, ten more sons and daughters would follow.

The young couple prospered as Spanish doubloons poured in from Key West traders for cattle, hogs, fish, and citrus. But during the Polk County–Seminole War in 1856, calamity struck Whitaker again. In his rage over the destruction of his famous banana grove by some reckless U.S. army engineers, Chief Bill Bowleg's tribesmen occasionally raided coastal settlers who, including Whitaker's family, had by now taken refuge at "Braden's Castle" at Manatee. One day, while Whitaker was on his way to seek help at a Peace Creek military camp 70 miles away, Indians raided his home, stole livestock, and burned his cabin to the ground. At war's end, Whitaker set about the long task of building a new two-story home, this time using mostly fine finished cedar lumber shipped from Cedar Key. The home would still be standing some 80 years later.

As his business activities expanded, Whitaker was pressed to find an assistant to help him, a difficult job since he was still the only settler in Sarasota County. But one day while out riding, he found one—in a palmetto thicket. The black man, Jeffrey Bolding, a runaway slave from North Carolina, lay half-conscious in the palmetto clump, his back laid open with raw, festering whip-welts. Slowly, Mary Jane nursed him back to health. Fugitive slave laws were harsh in the 1850s but Whitaker was determined not to return him to his cruel owner. Instead, he sent the owner $1,000 as take-it-or-leave-it compensation, suggesting strongly that he had better take it. The owner did. Though freed later in the Civil War, a grateful Bolding stayed on with Whitaker, becoming almost a family member and one of the settler's most industrious, all-round employees.

During the Civil War, Whitaker supplied the Confederates with beef and, when federal troops began confiscating food and livestock from coastal settlers, he operated a clandestine grist-mill deep in the Myakka region, with which to supply area families with vital corn meal and grits. Once, while he was away in Myakka, some renegade soldiers first ransacked his home and then turned to his wife and ordered her to get some matches with which to set the house afire. Without arguing, Mary Jane returned with a block of matches and calmly handed it to the head officer. But as she did, her voice soft and tense, she said: "Sir, I want to look into the eyes of a man who can stoop so low as to burn the home of a defenseless woman and her family." The words had a sobering effect. The surprised officer drew back, paused, then without a word led his men away. Thus their second new home was spared.

The war's end marked the end of an era—not only for the country but for the only homestead in Sarasota County over the past 25 years. U.S. homesteads were being offered once more and settlers began trickling into the Manatee and Sarasota area in ever-increasing numbers.

Whitaker's lonesome idyll had come to a close. Yet his prolific business activities would resume and his growing family prospered once more. Over generations, his descendants would scatter in droves over Florida's west coast, pursuing a variety of interests in professions, trades, and commerce.

But the lonely youth who began it all in a crude log cabin, selling fish for a penny apiece and building a thriving homestead in a remote and semi-tropic wilderness, was probably never aware that he had single-handedly laid the foundation of one of the most bustling and beautiful modern cities in the state.

9.
DuPont Rescues Florida's Busted Banks

Alfred I. duPont and other noted bankers minimized the damage in this state of the bank crisis which preceded the Great Depression.

When the champagne bubble of the Florida land-boom burst back in 1926, its inflated, high-rolling excesses shattered the state's financial structure, causing banks across the state to melt away.

By April 1929, on the eve of the stock market crash, some 80-plus banks—more than one fourth of all Florida banks—had failed. Customers lost millions, and "runs" on banks by panic-stricken depositors came to resemble a grotesque kind of marathon event in city after city. After the giddy, speculative binges of earlier years, it all seemed like some unreal, nightmarish hangover. But it was grimly real. And when the stock market crashed in October, 1929, the bank-bust pace just accelerated.

If ever a crumbling financial structure needed a propping hand—plus some hard lessons in sound banking practices—Florida's did in 1929. Fortunately, it found this remedial lift in the maverick figure of Alfred Irenee duPont, manufacturer, inventor and, despite his ostracism by haughty kinsfolk in the powerful Wilmington, Delaware, duPont family empire, still a major controller of duPont multimillion dollar holdings.

With an early interest in Florida development, duPont had already acquired about 900,000 acres in 11 counties of the Florida Panhandle, plus large properties around the state, and in 1927 had bought a controlling interest in the Florida National Bank of Jacksonville. Here he would make his initial move to stem the hysteric tideswell. In April, 1929, when jittery officials and stockholders sought to merge Florida National with neighboring Barnett National, duPont stepped in to block the merger. He knew it would not only give Barnett controlling interest in both banks but would incite suspicions about Florida National's own liquid stability. C. D. Dyal of Daytona Beach and E. C. Romfh of Miami hailed duPont's move as a tonic restoration of confidence.

But for months duPont had been reviewing the entire state banking scene, looking for advantageous sites where "sound banks" might be opened. However, duPont's notions of sound banking—such as keeping banks liquid with heavier cash reserves while reducing speculative chances for profits—grated like heresy on the ears of many Florida banking leaders. Only a few years before, any banker who did not indulge the frenzy of speculative loans and investments lacked at least vision and faith in the state's future, if he did not possess outright traitorous impulses. To them, duPont's public statements did, in fact, sound strange and unnerving, like the following: "Florida has lacked a conservative banking system. Banks are public trusteeships; their primary object should be the safe custodianship of the money entrusted to them, not the making of money for their shareholders. If all Florida banks had had this in mind there would have been no failures."

DuPont also instituted stringent loan policies, especially loans on real estate securities, which he rarely permitted. Nor would he let any officer or director borrow from his own institution. Of his banks' profits, 8% was set aside for reserves; 10% of what remained went into annual employee bonuses. Nevertheless, within two years of organizing seven banks in as many cities, duPont succeeded not merely in restoring morale and confidence in the midst of a skittish financial scene but, more importantly, demonstrated the operative principles for sound banking practice with thriving model examples.

A major source of antagonism toward Alfred duPont by his brothers and other duPont family relatives was the progressive social concerns shared by Alfred and his wife, Jessie Ball. Both poured substantial sums into philanthropies and charities, especially into aid for the elderly and for crippled children. In Wilmington he was nicknamed "Santa Claus" for his outlays of food, clothing, and coal to needy families. (The bulk of his estate would be left to such charities.) He shocked Herbert Hoover by advocating $5 billion in federal public-works spending to aid "millions of men with empty dinner kettles." DuPont also anticipated Franklin D. Roosevelt's New Deal (which he strongly but critically supported) by sending a fleet of trucks around the streets of Jacksonville to pick up unemployed blacks and whites and putting them to work on city beautification and other projects.

He had shrewdly predicted the market crash and, before departing for a European vacation in the summer of 1929, he gave Ed Ball, his brother-in-law and top business troubleshooter, power of attorney over his Almours Securities—worth $150 million—just in case. Ball did not share the political and social views of his sister and her eminent husband—his own such views would be later labeled conservative if not reactionary—but duPont wisely assessed Ball's business acumen. After duPont's death in 1935, Ball would parlay the estate's holdings into a vast economic Florida empire. Always a ubiquitous figure, Ball himself would become for years a powerful "gray eminence" in Florida politics. He would also provoke a swarm of detractors who would label this power "pernicious."

Despite his successes, two of duPont's banks would experience some tense and hairy moments of their own as the panic deepened. The first was a run on his Jacksonville bank. When the mighty Citizens Bank of Tampa failed in July, 1929, dragging 15 other banks down with it, the aftershock convulsed the state. It also triggered slow window-runs on three Jacksonville banks, including duPont's. The runs slackened for two days and then zeroed in on Florida National as frightened crowds jammed its lobby. Ball acted at once, taking $20 million in Almours Securities and expressing the paper to Northern institutions for stand-by loans of up to $15 million. He then rushed to the Jacksonville *Journal* with a statement to assure depositors. For fear of making other bankers nervous, however, the *Journal* would not publish it, even as an advertisement. Ball then sent squads of employees over the city to spread the $15-million news but, next morning, the door crowds were as big as ever. Yet, through a sort of crowd osmosis, the news of the $15 million took root and, by noon, the run had slowly petered out. Some months later, another crisis caused Florida National president Arthur Perry to panic. He suddenly resigned and, within 24 hours, joined rival Barnett National. Fearing Perry would take a quarter-chunk of deposits with him— about $5 million—duPont levered his full prestige into the breach and took the presidential reins himself. His customers stayed put.

The second siege came on duPont's St. Petersburg bank. In Florida, heavy tourist flows put banks, such as the one in St. Petersburg, through recurring summer crises, when tourists returning north took their hefty balances with them. By depleting often-bare reserves or by frantic out-of-state borrowing, banks usually survived. But the market crash succeeded in toppling four of five of these survivors. In those days, banks adhered strictly to a peculiar code of silence when their inner circles learned of a bank's impending collapse. The word was "do nothing, say nothing," and if a last-minute miracle failed to show, tough. This code often held up even if a personal friend had his life-savings tied up in the prospective failures. Thus, aside from Florida National, St. Petersburg's last survivor was unprepared for a sudden wallop of $40,000 in withdrawal checks one afternoon; next morning it closed its doors permanently. By the morning after, the run was on. Florida National now stood alone against a near-hysteric siege. Its astute and able president C. D. Dyal (hired away from his Daytona institution earlier by duPont) normally kept up to 30% over regular cash reserves, but even this could not stem the floodtide of withdrawals. Realizing cash on hand would be gone by noon, Dyal had director Dixie Hollins call Ball in Miami. Ball at once directed both the Bartow and Lakeland banks to send by automobile a total of over $128,000. The tellers had already learned how to slow down a run—meticulous verification of balances, counting money several times over, etc.—but it wasn't enough. By noon the cash had still not arrived. Then Dyal got an idea. At noon, he walked calmly into the lobby and cheerfully announced: "It's lunch time, but I know you don't want to lose your places in line. So we have sent for sandwiches and coffee, which will be served here in the lobby." It worked. Before the food was consumed, the Lakeland-Bartow funds arrived and, two hours later, Tampa-Jacksonville sources sent cash totaling $1 million. Just the sight of employees ostentatiously stacking piles of cash in the teller cages had a soothing effect, and the pay-out line slowly slackened. Next day the crowd was neither frantic nor as large, and they were paid off within an hour. The run was over. Within 30 days, deposits returned in record amounts and, thereafter, they stayed.

DuPont's sound banking methods, which had restored financial confidence throughout the state, drew national praise. Winthrop Aldrich, head of New York's powerful Chase National, declared duPont had given Florida "one of the finest phases of banking organization I have ever known." *Time* magazine effused: "When about two and a half years ago Florida's banking structure was toppling, a strong man came to save it [with] new sound banks." At home, Florida tycoon Barron Collier commented succinctly: "Alfred duPont's banks are liquid as the lakes."

Nevertheless, after fifty years, it seems curious that the lessons to be learned from duPont's keen fiscal policies were never more critically viable. Banks throughout the country today are attempting to withdraw in droves from the Federal Reserve System, mainly to dodge the mandate that they keep adequate portions of their cash deposits in noninterest-bearing reserves with the Fed. This might enable free-wheeling loan or investment policies and, hence, greater profits. But the trend harbors substantial risk not only to their own stability but in the potential to cripple seriously the Fed's ability to manage the nation's money supply and keep steady an already tremorous economy. If the lulling myth that the 1929–1930 disaster "can't happen again" still holds hypnotic sway, then Congress may have to act quickly to refresh short memories, even if it means resurrecting the ghost of the man who once taught bankers everywhere the purpose and function of a bank, and how best to execute both.

10.
Florida—A Wellspring for Delius' Music

Delius, one of the world's celebrated composers, let Florida inspire some of his greatest works.

He could not get music out of his soul, any more than his father could get "business" into it, and so, in 1884 at 22 years of age, he was packed off by Dad from England to faraway Florida for one last effort in the mercantile world—as a citrus grower.

Thus, fortuitously, Florida would become and remain the inspiration for one of the most creative musicians of the century—Frederick Delius, 1862–1935.

On arrival, young "Fritz" found the exotic flowerland even more enhancing to his musical aspirations than his native industrial Bradford, where Dad had his flourishing wool business. The son proved as allergic to grapefruit and orange picking as he was inclined to "wool-gathering" around the wool trade. And so, while the citrus lay rotting on the ground, Frederick banged away at the piano, listened fascinated to the hymns, chants, and folk tunes of local blacks and "crackers," and fell under an enchantment of nature amidst the woods, river, and wildlife of his "Solano Grove" on the St. Johns River, 35 miles south of Jacksonville.

Florida may have lost a citrus tycoon but it gained, inspired, and gave to the world one of its most eminent modern musicians, whose innovative compositions bore forever the birthmarks gestated in the wild tropical "mystery" of Solano.

Fred arrived in Jacksonville in 1884 with Charles Douglas, another "turned-off" Bradford businessman's son; the fathers of each had sponsored their partnership in Solano.

Traveling by riverboat, they arrived at the small cottage to find a dilapidated four-room structure in some disrepair, fronted by an immense live oak tree. The weed-choked grove behind gave off the rancid odor of rotting fruit; the men could only laugh at their disappointment. (The house stands restored today on the Jacksonville University campus.)

But within hours, a young black man turned up—Elbert Anderson, who lived with his wife, Eliza, and her sister, Julia, in a shack back further in the pines of the property. Anderson familiarized the novice growers with the area and then, over their first Florida dinner of pork and field peas, made hopeful plans to put the grove and house back into condition.

But on this same first night, this black family would innocently turn Fred's entire life in another direction—music—from which he would never veer. He would always recall this "state of illumination" as he sat alone on the porch, looking out over the glowing dusk on the St. Johns and listening to the chorus of insect, bird and wildlife in this mystical, isolated topic setting. For soon he heard another chorus drifting through the woods, the strangest he had ever heard—the Anderson family singing. He listened as if spellbound as the melodies, from note to note, rose and fell in shifting discords—sad, melancholy, old slave songs of sorrow at separated families and fears of being sold away. Then, suddenly the voices turned joyous, crying out the hallelujahs of spirituals into a mounting crescendo. When the voices had finally ceased and the echoes of jubilant sound had washed over him, Delius was almost exhausted by the intensity of feelings aroused in him. He believed he had heard the music of the universe in its most elemental celebration of the human spirit's renewal, and he knew he would not rest until he bore witness to it.

Charles was soon discouraged over his partner's neglect of the grove, for now Delius spent his days with the Andersons whom he had prevailed upon to teach him their hymns, chants, and the work songs of other pines-dwelling blacks. At night, Anderson would take him hunting for quail and alligator and, on one such outing, Douglas contracted malaria and Delius rushed to Jacksonville for a doctor. The doctor was out, so Delius wandered through the city until he discovered a piano store. Excitedly, he entered and at once sat down at a piano, trying to form the difficult notes of Anderson's melodies. A passerby overheard him, entered, and soon the two men were engrossed in a warm discussion. The man was Thomas F. Ward, a pianist, organist, and music teacher. The pair spent two more days discussing plans whereby Ward might come live at Solano and teach Delius, when the latter recalled, to his chagrin, his original errand. Hastily, with Ward, the doctor and a rented piano in tow, Delius hurried back to the grove. Under the care of Mrs. Montgomery Corse, of nearby Picolata Landing, a much disgusted Douglas had recovered, but he wasted little time investing his share of funds in another grove nearby and leaving his erstwhile partner for good.

Ward, an excellent teacher, saw at once the promise in his young charge and drilled the youth intensely in technique, composition, harmony, and counterpoint. Both admired the subtle tones of the black chants, the flatted notes—called blues, and the hymns. The blacks were often joined by banjo-picking poor whites (called "Crackers" because they ate cracked corn), and an occasional Seminole Indian family for woodsy songfests. They attended the small Negro churches—"praise houses"—and the outdoor worship times and dances at night around a pine-stump fire. Delius soon came to believe that he could translate the black and rural white psychology into pure music.

As Ward observed the vigorous artistic development of his pupil, he strongly urged him to study at the world's music center—Leipzig. (Delius would later discover that Ward's tutelage equalled or surpassed most of the best theorists of the great conservatory.) But the youth's stern father refused, and Delius would not leave the grove untended while trying to make his own way to Germany.

His answer came one day with the sudden appearance of Ernest, his brother, who had chucked his sheep-raising job in New Zealand and now needed a temporary refuge. Overjoyed at this chance to start working his way to Leipzig, he turned house and grove over to Ernest and headed for Jacksonville where he earned a few dollars teaching violin and piano. He later took a job teaching at an exclusive girls' school in Danville, Virginia, where he also was able to further study the unique styles and rhythms in blues, rag, and accented off-beats of black tobacco workers. Such self-reliance and the ability to earn his own way had by now brought a grudging response from the father; he would pay for Fred's study at Leipzig. Delius had won—and so had the world of music.

Throughout his long career, the deep and enduring baptism of nature that Delius so traumatically experienced in the lush wildland of Solano proved a wellspring from which the composer drew his finest achievements. Classics such as "In a Summer Garden," "Summer Night On the River," and even the poignant "Sea Drift" were inspired and informed by this mystique. Under the technical influence of men as diverse as Wagner and Debussey, Delius yet maintained his own unique style of composition. The seemingly discordant harmonies of his work were slow to be understood. He gave an over-all style of romantic impressionism but his peers were both startled and fascinated by the syncopation and blue notes.

His first full orchestral composition was heady stuff for the Leipzig of that day—like folk music wrought into a new symphonic form. It was almost a hymn of celebration of Solano, its people and the St. Johns—the "Florida Suite." "Florida" echoed the gaiety and melancholy of blacks like Anderson, their spirituals and joyous dances, such as "La Calinda," and the sombre woods, gay wild flowers, and dark, brooding river. Poorer students at the conservatory could hear their pieces played if they could summon enough off-hour players together and then only if they furnished them enough beer. Excitedly, Delius borrowed enough for a barrel of brew, and "Florida" had its debut. The innovations at first baffled some players but gradually they moved enthusiastically into the rhythms of each section— "Daybreak," "On the River," "Sunset Near the Plantation," and "Night." When it was finished, the players applauded the piece as wildly as did Fred's companion and partisan, the master musician Edvard Grieg. Delius was drunk, but not on beer.

New expressions were not confined to music in that day. Delius shared lively discussions over Parisian coffee tables with such trend setters in the arts as DeMaupassant, Zola, Rodin, Corot, Matisse, Monet, and Strindberg. He was glad to help pay the food bill of his friend Gauguin by purchasing the painter's invaluable, "Nevermore" for a generous 20 pounds.

The composer's next major work, the nocturne "Paris," had a similar rhapsodic pentatonic melody suggestive of folk music. An opera, "The Magic Fountain" celebrates a Spanish hero, Solano, and his Seminole Indian princess who perish together in the Everglades.

His great opera, "Koanga," the first Negro opera and first European opera ever set in America, offered blues, rag, chants, and those "strange" discordant notes on the grand tragic scale. To perfect it, Delius happily returned to Solano for a joyous reunion with the Anderson family, and a few weeks of working on the opera scores in the old cottage. He learned that Ward had since died and Ernest had long ago left for Australia where he later died of alchoholism. But the Florida visit brought refreshed inspiration and when "Koanga" played in London's St. James Hall in 1899, it won instant acclaim.

One of his most ambitious projects was the tone poem, "Appalachia" (the Indian name for America). A series of variations, it combined "cracker" folk songs with the haunting laments of black men, a panoramic canvas of the most imaginative nature music he had ever written. Of all these Florida-inspired pieces, one critic observed: "Though grounded in European art-forms, the works are saturated with a quality of sound not heard before in the orchestra, or rarely since, a quality derived from and redolent of Negro hymnology and folk-song."

Although Delius' recognition grew over the years only slowly, and often painfully, he lived—although paralyzed and blind—to see his career honored finally in his native England. At age 67 he was decorated by King George V with the order of Companion of Honor. In that same year, 1929, all of his achievement was crowned with a Delius Festival in London. Crowds packed the Queen's and Aeolian's Halls where the concerts were arranged and conducted by the famous Sir Thomas Beecham. The eminent conductor had been for years a champion of Delius' work and he had a share of his own in the composer's final glorious hour.

But the land of Florida could as easily claim him as its own, for the world might never have known his genius if the young Yorkshireman had not experienced his mystical "state of illumination" long ago in the flourishing wilderness of Solano.

11.
The Bohemian Birth of Coconut Grove

Early settlers stamped a slightly Bohemian personality on the Grove, some of which still exists today.

If Coconut Grove—that seaside village just south of Miami—is today a vintage blend of culture, counter-culture, and Bohemian schmaltz, an improbable sort of Gold Coast Greenwich Village, it is only because it was born that way.

The Grove was in fact the first winter resort on the lower east coast, well before Henry Flagler even thought of pushing a railroad spur to Miami or building the Royal Palm Hotel in 1896. The settlement was an unusual mix of "crackers" and "swells," the crude and the elegant, a frontier-cultural community that seemed as much out of place as did its uniquely individual residents.

Whether merchant, writer, farmer, teacher, titled nobility or Bahamian black, these early pioneers blended into a loose-knit camaraderie of free spirits in the wilderness, dedicated to the "simple and genuine life." And they stamped that indelible color into the area to this day.

Both the stimulus and the lodestar of this remarkable settlement were a young English couple, Charles and Isabella Peacock. They would build the lower Gold Coast's first luxury resort hotel, the Peacock Inn; its reputation for fine food was exceeded only by its warm informality as the lively center for Grove social activities.

The town's name apparently was a joke in the mind of one Dr. Horace Porter, a former Confederate doctor, who founded the first post office in the 1870s. For, at the time, there were only two bare and scraggly coconut trees in the whole area.

The Grove itself was a jungle wilderness when Edmund D. "Alligator" Beasley and his Bahamian wife, Anna, staked the first claim on a mile and a half of its shoreline in the 1850s. Beasley built a thatched-roof house from shipwreck salvage lumber and then hand-carved a fresh spring well out of solid coral rock. "Beasley's well" still stands today in the public park that was the former estate of Ralph M. Munroe. Munroe came to the Grove shortly after Beasley died in 1870 and was a major influence in the area. An amateur photographer, Munroe left a priceless treasure of early photographs of the virgin grove wilderness and Biscayne Bay. "Commodore" Munroe was also a devout conservationist who would join botanist Charles Sprague Sargent in discovering in a nearby swamp the towering Royal Palm trees. Munroe also contributed many valuable articles on native plant and sea life to scientific journals of the period.

Keepers of the famous Biscayne Light House (Cape Florida), and their families were also early comers to the Grove. These included John and Edward Pent, and Joseph and John W. Frow.

In the early 1880s, coconut trees almost came near playing a part in the Grove scene when Henry B. Lum devised a grandiose scheme to plant 334,000 coconuts along 65 miles of barrier beaches from Cape Florida to Jupiter Inlet. It looked like a windfall investment; when the trees grew in three years, all you had to do was gather the fallen coconuts and ship them off to lucrative world markets. The tender green shoots of the untended coconut plants proved a delicious fare for deer, rabbits, raccoons, and rats, while the massive maze of interlaced mangroves backed up the beach and choked out those trees that reached half-growth. Lum cursed his coconut "bonanza" and finally left the scene.

In the 1870s, a gregarious Englishman, John Thomas "Jolly Jack" Peacock became enchanted with the Grove and bay and built a waterfront home on the south Grove end called (after him), "Jack's Bight." Meanwhile, he barraged his brother, Charles, in London, with extravagant reports of the wonders of the Grove and the idyllic living. So much so, that Charles chucked his ham and beef warehouse business, packed up his wife and three young sons and said goodbye to London's dreary cold, rain, and fog, arriving at Biscayne Bay in 1875. But his first sight of the wild overgrown frontier sent his stout English heart down to his boots, and for several disenchanted years he rented quarters in a building at the old Fort Dallas.

However, by early 1880, the Peacocks had become acclimatized and when Munroe offered to help them build a hotel in the Grove, they bought 31 acres of Grove seashore from John Frow and built a two-story rambling structure that was actually only a large home with extra guest rooms. But the Peacock Inn would literally "make" the Grove in the following years. And its hostess, Isabella—mother, nurse, friend—would earn the title, "Mother of Coconut Grove."

In a short time, the Inn began to attract winter visitors who were drawn as much by the rarity of this hideaway resort in the midst of a wilderness as by the excellent fishing, hunting, and climate. The Peacocks soon had to add a complex of buildings to handle the overflow. They built dressing rooms at the bay's edge for swimmers, rented sailboats for $2 a day and $50 a month. The food was both bountiful and excellent, and, with a room, all for $10 a week, this "bargain" resort was irresistible. Many who came to visit only, stayed to settle the area—and they were a varied lot.

E. A. and Thomas Hines, who stayed at the Grove and later bought Long Key just offshore, would later form the original Biscayne Bay Yacht Club. Kirk Monroe, a nationally-known young people's writer for *Harper's* came with his wife, Mary Barr, a headstrong Scotch girl with voluble opinions which she freely expressed in the Peacock's rustic "salon" atmosphere. She was often joined by a bright and articulate schoolteacher, Miss Flora MacFarlane, who would later form the "Housekeeper's Club," a cultural and social group that left a vital stamp on the Grove's character. And visitors were always ready to help the neophyte village, as when Mary Barr, who had been decrying the lack of cultural needs, received from Mrs. Andrew Carnegie, wife of the steel king and a former yacht visitor, enough bundles of books to begin a library.

Another settler was Count James L. Nugent, a tall, black-bearded Frenchman whose Irish grandfather had been one of Napoleon's generals. Nugent took the informal life-style literally, as when he showed up at a wedding once in full formal dress, but barefooted. But when he married Miss Florence Baldwin, head of Baldwin school at Bryn Mawr, he reluctantly shod his feet for the occasion. The count attracted another fellow count, Jean d'Hedouville, to the area. The latter spent his time collecting old treasure maps for buried sea treasure that he never got around to salvaging. But the land he bought up left his heirs treasure for generations.

One remarkable woman was Dr. Eleanor Galt Simmons, a Bryn Mawr graduate who had brought her lawyer husband to the Grove for his health. Dr. Simmons made her rounds by sailboat and pony, and Seminole Indians often camped outside her door, eager to try out her "wonder medicines." There wasn't much practice for either medicine or law in the Grove then, so she and her husband created the modestly successful business of making mango jam and pineapple wine which was a lucrative hit in the Northern exotic food markets.

Dick Carney, a roustabout who had helped Lum plant his coconuts, was sort of a rustic bon vivant who served for a while as sheriff in the area. But he devoted almost as much of his time to practical jokes. Once he painted stripes on a lost mule so realistically that the owner kept driving the "zebra" off for a week while he looked everywhere for his lost mule.

Black people also numbered among the Grove's first families. Miss Maria Brown, a Bahamian, came to help Isabella organize the hotel and then created the settlement of "Evangelist Street," near the Peacocks. She brought in other black settlers—the Stirrups, Burrows, Roberts, and Andersons—whose descendants still live in the Grove today. Miss Brown's original home still stands on Charles Street.

Isabella began a fund drive for the area's first church and Sunday school which, in the late 1880s, would also be used as a school building. Blacks and whites worshipped together at Union Chapel and its first preacher was a winter visitor named Charles E. Stowe, whose mother, Harriet Beecher Stowe, had written a book of some consequence years earlier.

But the democratic and distinctive spirit of the Grove gestated at the Peacock Inn. Here both natives and "swells" gathered to discuss and debate every topic from fish and the weather to world affairs. Those with no formal education jousted with and shared ideas with the sophisticated and well-traveled new arrivals. Those who had grown up in the shadow of the Cape lighthouse discovered that they could teach as well as learn from those who had been tutored at expensive private schools. Afternoon tea at the Inn became a daily ritual and dinner was a bountiful, ceremonious, but unhurried affair. The crux of such evenings was the spirited, animated gusto of earnest conversation on a variety of subjects, whether cultural or mundane, as the townspeople gathered on the cool, outdoor verandas. Picnics, boating, and shell-gathering were also major pastimes. When Monroe and the Hines brothers formed the yacht club, they began, in 1887, to celebrate Washington's birthday with a regatta, topped off with a feast of the Peacock's famous fish chowder. This annual event proved so popular that it is celebrated to this day, albeit with more formal fanfare.

Thus, it was this unusual hybrid of frontier-cosmopolitan roots which even today marks the Grove as a world apart from its gaudier big sister just northward. There are differences, of course. The high rises and condos overshadow the numerous wonderland parks named after some of these pioneers. But, according to one *New York Times* writer, it is still a refuge for the cultural offbeat, artists, stockbrokers, career loafers, hippies with Ivy League accents, the new rich, and the deliberate poor, plus the oldest streets and 19th-century buildings in Dade County.

It was a unique community then, but even now, a century later, the Grove retains its aspect of "different." And on today's Gold Coast, that sounds like a commendable distinction of sorts.

12.
T. T. Fortune: Florida's Black Militant

T. Thomas Fortune was born a slave near Marianna. He grew into one of the nation's most able black leaders and journalists.

It seems grittily ironic that Florida—and especially the hard "Cracker" Panhandle country around the town of Marianna—should have spawned America's first and most prominent black militant over a century ago.

T. Thomas Fortune was a born (1856) and bred Marianna boy—and a slave. But he was to become the country's most zealous crusader for the rights of his people as well as the dean of American Negro journalists, during a long dim time in history when it was a very unhealthy prospect to be either.

Raised during the most fiery and turbulent period of Florida's history, the Civil War and Reconstruction, he has been cited as the most influential black to arise between the eras of Frederick Douglas and Booker T. Washington.

He gave first impetus to a movement that would grow into the NAACP and he charted far in advance the course to be taken in the civil rights struggles of the 1950s and 1960s. In articles, lectures, and scathing editorials, he courageously demanded full rights for blacks, at a time when their legal and political status was at the lowest ebb. He defended the right to use force in the face of lynchings and other atrocities, and he assailed the Supreme Court for decisions adverse to Negro rights. "There are some laws which no self-respecting person should be expected to obey," he once wrote. "No man is compelled to obey a law which degrades his manhood and defrauds him of what he has paid for."

Fortune was a complex man—fearless, sensitive, humane, but sometimes arrogant and seemingly paradoxical. Ideologically, he was closer to W. E. B. DuBois, but he heatedly defended his close, personal friendship with the more moderate Booker Washington. He held strong religious beliefs and was an active African Methodist Episcopal Church leader, but he often castigated organized religion: "The white minister who finds it uncomfortable to sit in the church . . . with a colored minister may just as well make up his mind now that God will make no special provisions for him in Heaven on account of his tallow complexion." He lashed at the sham of "separate but

50

equal" school systems and scored the white South for thinking it "a sounder principle of government to equip and maintain vast penal systems—with chain gangs, schools of crime, depravity, and death than to support schools and churches."

Like a later educator, Mary Bethune, he stressed the desperate need for practical and rudimentary education for blacks. "Many a colored farmer boy or mechanic has been spoiled to make a foppish gambler or loafer, a swaggering pedagogue or a cranky homiletician. Men may be spoiled by education, even as they are spoiled by illiteracy." He believed that talent or genius would take care of itself but that the great number of blacks needed "instruction for the work to be done" in the fierce competition for daily economic survival.

Timothy Thomas was the first born son of Emanuel and Sarah Jane Fortune, slaves of Ely P. Moore, in October, 1856, in Marianna. His heritage was strongly mixed. Emanuel himself was born in Marianna in 1832, his slave mother the daughter of a mulatto slave and a Seminole Indian, his father a white Irishman, Thomas Fortune. The latter died, when Emanuel was an infant, in a duel with a local planter. Emanuel learned to read through the close friendship he had with the son of his early owner, a Mr. Russ. He also learned a trade—shoemaker and tanner—before Russ arranged for him to be sold to Moore, in order for Emanuel to marry his slave sweetheart, Sarah Jane. Besides Tim, the couple had three daughters and a son, Emanuel Jr.

During the Civil War, the boy enjoyed a childhood almost unaffected by the struggle but, at war's end, he was aware of a new order by the presence of a garrison of blue uniformed troops, blacks among them. The Union soldiers were socially scorned by white Marianna residents but the newly freed slaves almost idolized them. Union officers, along with the federal Freedmen's Bureau, legalized marriage unions for slaves, formerly denied them, and distributed Bibles. Teacher-soldiers gathered a motley lot of both children and adults into classrooms to help them master the mysteries of Webster's speller, and arranged for employment conditions with their former masters, and otherwise protected them from exploitation.

Emanuel was able to rescue land from his white boyhood friend, Joseph Russ, and soon prospered with a modest living. In the revolution that swept the region under Republican Reconstruction, Emanuel was elected to the Florida Legislature. He steered a balanced coursé between extremists in the semi-chaotic government but would later find his life threatened due to the rise of Ku Klux Klan "regulators" who were laying a violent groundwork for the counter-revolution by the Bourbons in 1874. This effectively ended the exhilirating climate of freedom, and Emanuel was forced to flee to Jacksonville where he lived the remainder of his life as a modestly successful businessman.

Thomas served as a legislative pageboy while he furthered his schooling in Tallahassee. He then went to Jacksonville and served as a printer's devil on the *Daily Union*. Printing and writing were his first loves and he became an expert compositor. Later, W. J. Purman, a Union freedman and a U.S. Congressman from the Marianna district, secured for Fortune a customs position in Delaware. While there, the youth was able to obtain part-time work on a local newspaper and earned enough to continue his studies, this time at Howard University. But he could not forget a girl back home, Carrie C. Smiley, and he returned home to marry her. When Fortune's school savings were lost through a bank failure, the couple obtained work again on the *Daily Union*. But he found the "poisonous" oppressiveness for an educated Southern black, under the Bourbon reaction, too heavy. In 1881, he took his wife and young child (they eventually had a son and a daughter), to New York City. His career would now begin, on the renowned *New York Globe*.

The *Globe* would prove the most illustrious—and enduring—of scores of black newspapers burgeoning over the North in the late 19th century. Fortune soon became editor, and his editorial acumen and pungent clarity of style in treating major issues of the times, rapidly fixed his reputation as the country's foremost crusading journalist. His intellectual growth was also greatly influenced by the white journalist, John Swinton, as editorial chief at Dana's *New York Sun*. Swinton was a major force in the great progressive-reformist movements of the period and Fortune's own trenchant prose style bore colorful traces of his white colleague's caustic polemics.

The *Globe's* aim was to supply "a national journal" for America's blacks, since white newspapers were primarily "by white men, for white men." This aim was razor-honed with Fortune's militant and uncompromising position on civil rights, his attacks on federal courts for decisions that increasingly began to abridge those rights, and his advocacy of the use of force to resist lynchings and shootings. He outraged white Americans (and many blacks) when he defended the marriage by the eminent Frederick Douglass, to a white woman, surprised, he wrote, over the "gush" from white or black over intermarriage, "a personal matter." It was, he found, "in strict keeping with all the sophistries kept alive" by white society, "the ceaseless but futile effort to show that the human nature (of black and white) differ in some indefinable way" when, in fact, "human nature . . . is the same wherever mankind is found."

The death of the *Globe* several years later was attributed by a peer to Fortune's "brilliant, fearless, and uncompromising" editing. But Phoenix-like, the *Globe* soon reappeared as the *Freeman*, with Fortune now the sole owner and his crusading continued even stronger.

In ensuing years, Fortune was much in demand as a speaker on the lecture circuit and, to devote more time to speaking, writing a book, and diversifying himself in other civic pursuits, he left the paper, leaving his brother, Emanuel Jr., as business manager. The paper's name was again changed—to the *New York Age*.

Fortune now plunged actively into educational politics, exhorting blacks to think independently about both the major parties. He also formed the National Afro-American League which anticipated the NAACP and promoted Negro civil and political rights, focusing on the Deep South. He toured the South extensively, observing and writing on race conditions in the 1890s. During this period, his close friendship began with the Wizard of Tuskegee, Booker T. Washington. Both men—born in slavery, succeeding against great odds, both Southerners at heart—felt they worked toward the same goals. But while Washington believed that "brains, property, and character" would settle the civil rights question, Fortune felt that stronger measures under law, along with bolder political and economic programs, would be essential. They would correspond often and, in later years, when stresses and political attacks induced in Fortune a sometimes acute drinking problem accompanied by severe nerve relapses, Washington helped him over a long period of illness and poverty. But Washington also mismanaged some of Fortune's newspaper interests and this gravely hindered Fortune in recovering both his health and his professional career.

Fortune was not, as sometimes portrayed in the white press, a one-issue, one-sided firebrand, for he saw clearly that the interests of blacks and whites were "one and the same," and "the man who lifts a finger to disturb the good relations which should exist between them, who would put neighbor against neighbor . . . is a common enemy to the state and to the nation."

After recovering his health, Fortune resumed a successful career in writing free-lance editorials, columns, and features. More effectively, he served in the 1920s as editor of Marcus Garvey's renowned paper, *The Negro World,* until his death, at 71, in 1928.

Two years before, at a convention of the National Negro Press Association, he was hailed as "the beloved dean of Negro journalists" and "the ablest and most forceful editorial writer" ever of his race. At his death, Kelly Miller, dean of Howard University, eulogized: "His pen knew but one theme—the rights of man. [He] represented the best developed journalist that the Negro race has produced in the Western World."

It wasn't a bad tribute, (for Timothy Thomas or the state), that a small-town Florida Panhandle boy should rise from slavery to become, for nearly half a century, the conscience of the race of man, and the scourge of his injustices.

13.
Sidney Lanier: A Poet Turned Promoter

Lanier's sickness and need for money overrode a stricken conscience. He agreed to write promotional material about Florida for a railroad. He disapproved of his product, but it has merit today.

The job of selling Florida has never wanted for publicists—from Ponce de Leon hawking its rejuvenating waters down to the genteel pitch of Harriet Beecher Stowe and, finally, the hard sell of the land speculators. No state has been more celebrated in prose and puff for its natural assets.

But one of Florida's most renowned promoters was also, undoubtedly, one of its most reluctant. The famous Southern poet, Sidney Lanier, embodied almost that classic prototype of a sensitive writer, struggling to maintain his artistic integrity against the grim necessities of survival, and the abhorent possibility of compromising his talent to the demands of the material world.

In fact, Lanier shuddered at the prospect of doing a promotional guidebook for a railroad company, with a special spiel about the fine townsites that lay along the railroad's line. It was during the post-Civil War years, when railroad companies and other promoters and developers were saturating the country with an increasing volume of printed matter designed to sell land to prospective settlers as well as lure the wealthy winter tourist.

But to the man who immortalized the Florida Mockingbird, whose "Marshes of Glynn" would one day become a standard school-book recitation, the young heir-apparent to Bryant, Longfellow, and Lowell, this idea of writing a commercial guidebook for Atlantic Coast Railway, in a sales pitch for the Yankee dollar, was downright painful.

With a helpless sneer, Lanier would describe himself to a friend as the "Poet-in-Ordinary to a long line of railroad operations."

But poets—then as now—were never exactly the rage of the common marketplace, and though their verse might prove immortal, their bodies definitely were not. So, as often true in history, a minor classic scribbling might be bartered gratefully for some nourishing bread and butter.

In Lanier's case, this job vexation was compounded severely by two other millstones. He had a growing family to support and, at the same time, he was afflicted with chronic tuberculosis, often rendering him semi-invalid with excessive expenses for travel to various states in search of "cures," or at least relief.

Under such conditions, the work that would later become an historical collector's item—"Florida: Its Scenery, Climate, and History"—was born.

Sidney Lanier was born in Macon, Georgia, February 3, 1842, to a prosperous family. His father was a partner in a successful law firm and afforded to his son those advantages of classical tastes in music and literature. In his genial temperament and charm, Sidney perhaps epitomized the chivalric tradition of a Southern gentleman, (but he would later repudiate its conservation orthodoxy). He only dabbled in poetry in his student years at Oglethorpe University but he was already an accomplished musician on the flute. After graduation at the top of his class, in 1860, he was able to enjoy a brief season to indulge "friends, books, music, wine, hunting, fishing, billiards, ten-pins, chess, and serenading ladies," before the scourge of Civil War would darken his life permanently.

Simply out of a curious mix of duty and destiny, Lanier, at 21, joined the Confederate Army and distinguished himself in several battles, but was captured late in the war while on special assignment with a blockade runner. He ended up in one of the worst of the Union prison camps. Crowded into an unsanitary tent, fed the barest rations, and constantly exposed to severe winter cold, he contracted first fever and, finally, tuberculosis. Although infected with the youthful—and often mindless—enthusiasm of his peers at the outset of the war, he had some reason to later make the bitter postwar comment: "What fools we were!"

The next year saw Lanier teaching school, writing poetry, and publishing a book, "Tiger-Lilies," in 1867, a more rambling, somewhat autobiographical characterization of his earlier days in war and peace than the novel it purported to be. But reviewers—even the prestigious *Atlantic Monthly*—labeled it "promising." He was more successful with the poetry he submitted to the distinctive *Round Table,* but efforts to earn a livelihood in the poverty-ridden South were restrictive at best. Moreover, he had suffered his first severe lung hemorrhage from consumption in this period. He had married an earlier wartime girlfriend, Mary Day, in 1867, with whose family he had boarded at Wesleyan College in Macon. This tall, attractive, dark-eyed girl very probably prolonged Lanier's life more than any medicine or cure. Through illness, poverty, and disappointment, it was a rare idyllic marriage, a love affair that many compared to that of Elizabeth and Robert Browning.

With a household now, Lanier finally consented to work in his father's law firm. He worked competently, but exhaustively, for several years, but the law proved as harmful to his health as it was to his temperament and, in 1872, he left the practice. His expertise on the flute enabled him to win a seat on the famous Peabody Symphony Orchestra at Baltimore and, although he relished the work (while writing his poetry on the side), the $60 per month pay was hardly adequate to meet growing family needs. By 1873, Mary had given birth to her third son and she was often forced to stay behind with her family at Brunswick, Georgia, while Lanier went off to New York and Baltimore, barely able to sustain himself with his music and occasional "pot-boiler" magazine articles.

Ironically, Lanier had just written one of his better-known, abler poems, "The Symphony," a lyrical tirade against the spirit of the age—trade, the commercialism that he felt was destroying the social harmony of America—when A. Pope, an ACL railroad executive, sought to commission him to write the Florida guidebook, in early 1875. Debt-ridden and nearly-destitute, Lanier struggled painfully with a prospect that, superficially at least, seemed repugnant to his artistic and social temperament, if not his writing abilities. But his family's pressing needs, plus the generous terms of the contract were enough to tip his decision: he accepted.

Nevertheless, the strain seeped through a bantering letter to his wife:

"Here hath come a letter from one A. Pope, the same being a high functionary in the network of railroads . . . the Great Atlantic Coast Line . . . but he wisheth me to write,—by Homer and Lucretius, by Dan Chaucer and John Keats and Will Shakespeare—he wishes me to write a ____, a ____ (Choke, choke, choke) a ____og ____(gulp, gulp, gulp) a Guide book to Florida Travellers. He proposeth, By Pegasus, to pay my hotel-bills and travelling expenses, and to give me one hundred and Twenty-five dollars a month—by Croesus, in addition thereto: and I am to take from April to the last of June for the work."

Ever conscientious, however, Lanier plunged into the work, going first to Jacksonville, Palatka, St. Augustine, then along the St. Johns and Indian Rivers, and over to the Oklahawa by steamer to the Silver Spring. Moving north he visited Lake City and Tallahasee where he was the guest of ex-governor David Walker. His wife joined him at Gainesville, thence to Cedar Keys and from here, a southerly journey as far south as Manatee County. The book was completed by June but Pope continued Lanier on salary until revisions, editing and final proofs were finished.

Working under painful illness and strain, Lanier was not free of the work's "dreadful bonds" until it was published that November. "It is," he noted, "very handsomely printed, bound, and illustrated—but I hate It . . . [it] has been a wound to me ever since I was engaged to write it . . . like being stabbed with a dull weapon. I did not wish ever to appear before the public again save in the poetic character." He was even more disappointed in the book's reviews—or lack thereof. *Harper's* and *Atlantic Monthly* ignored it, and the best that *The Nation* could observe was that "Mr. Lanier's poetic licenses in prose are accordingly fewer than usual." But the Boston *Literary World* called it "an uneasy and sometimes brilliant" work; all reviewers agreed that it was at least what it professed to be—a competent, serviceable, and interesting guidebook to Florida. Some chapters such as "The Oklawaha River" and "St. Augustine in April," were given special critical praise and published again as single pieces.

Had Lanier earlier heeded his own advice in one of the book's chapters, "For Consumptives," he might have greatly benefited because his hemorrhages became more frequent and his doctor ordered him to Florida. Leaving the children with her family, Lanier and Mary went to Tampa that winter, 1876, where they found "perfect summer" and a restful, healing time. As a small boy, the late historian D. B. McDay recalls being "enthralled" by the enchanting music Lanier often played on his flute for guests in the parlor of the old Orange Grove Hotel. Here also Lanier was inspired for his poems on the mockingbird, "Shakespeare on the tree," "Tampa Robins," and his poignant "Evening Song." It would also instill within him the inspirational tone and mood background for his later "Marshes of Glynn" and the popular "Song of the Chattahoochee."

Lanier might have recovered from his wracking illness, or at least prolonged his days considerably, had he remained in the state he had so recently celebrated to a nation, a land justly famous for its healing sun and climate. But hard economics, and his own chronic restlessness, sent him scurrying back to the big city, New York, armed with writings in poetry and music with which "to fight the Wolf." For a flute composition, he won high praise from the great Leopold Damrosch, father of the modern master, Walter Damrosch, and for a volume of collected poems, he won beneficient acclaim from Lowell, Longfellow and the New York literati generally. But the praises of men proved sorely unequal to the demands of rent, food, utilities, and clothing for his family in their Baltimore home.

His illness also grew progressively worse in the hard, unaccustomed climate and, in 1881, he was forced to move with his family to the home of a friend in Lynn, North Carolina. On September 7th of that year, he died, at age 39.

Thus, the American poet who was Florida's most reluctant promoter (but who incidentally, enjoyed every day of his reluctant travelogue sojourn) rendered the state a unique historical and descriptive guide that is still of value today. Nevertheless, he might have rendered himself—and posterity— an even more vital service had he come to Florida, not as the Tampa robin, for a season, but like his Shakespearean mockingbird, a permanent resident.

14.
Horticulturist Dr. Perrine's Senseless Death

Dr. Perrine's work could have meant much to Florida's economy, but greed and stupidity killed him.

The massacre at Indian Key in 1840, in which the renowned horticulturist Dr. Henry Perrine and six others perished in an Indian raid, was one of the most senseless tragedies to occur among Florida's early settlers.

And it might never have happened but for the personal greed and the political duplicity of a Florida Keys "wrecker" captain and a secretary of war, respectively, not to mention a U.S. Navy guard post that wasn't around to guard anything when the critical time came.

Captain Jacob Housman profited hugely in the Key West wrecker business, although his high-handed and often illegal methods did not endear him to other Keys salvagers. He solved this by purchasing rights to the 11-acre islet of Indian Key in 1825, an almost solid rock with a fine deep harbor, located halfway between Key West and Cape Florida. Here he located stores, a hotel, cottages, customs and post offices and, at one time, even made the key, through political sway, the seat of Dade County. With almost total jurisdiction over his own wrecker operations, he prospered greatly until the 1830s, when a U.S. court pulled his license after he was caught red-handed trying to divert salvage goods from their legal jurisdiction. He now faced hard times financially, being dissatisfied with his modest island income.

Meanwhile, horticulturist Dr. Perrine had been given a U.S. land grant near the present site of Miami to study and experiment with tropical and semitropical plants that might benefit the nation's agriculture. The doctor was given a temporary residence and station on Captain Housman's Indian Key until the mainland could be rendered safe from marauding Indians, still on the warpath from the Second Seminole War. White settlers had fled Dade for Key West, following several deadly Indian attacks, while cries for the government to "do something" were mounting.

The government finally acted on the suggestion of one Lieutenant Colonel William S. Harney, a wise and able soldier who fully understood Indian character. Under authorization of Joel R. Poinsett, Secretary of War, Colonel Harney pow-wowed with various chiefs and soon an agreement was reached giving the tribes a vast reservation in the Everglades on which they would remain and, in turn, the army would keep white settlers out of the reservation. The treaty was formally ratified in Washington and peace at last seemed assured.

But a few violent and influential Floridians stormed at Poinsett—they wanted complete removal of the Indians from Florida, by extermination if necessary. When Poinsett gave in and wrote one protester that the treaty was only a temporary placebo, the public learned of it—and so did the Indians. They vented their rage at this double-cross by attacking Colonel Harney near Ft. Myers, killing a number of his men. Harney, who had not yet learned of the secretary's bad faith, barely escaped with his own scalp.

Adding fuel to this perfidy, Captain Housman, hoping to bolster his thinning purse, offered to "contract" with the government, at $200 a head, to kill or capture every Indian in the 'glades. The preposterous offer was ignored, of course, but not by Indians who were led by the astute Caloosa warrior chief Chekika. The captain was marked for special attention—and it soon came.

When Chekika learned of the departure on patrol of both of the war cutters at the Tea Table Key Naval station—less than a mile from Indian Key—he saw his chance. Usually, one or the other boat was required to be on patrol guarding Perrine's station. Now there were temporarily only one officer, five men, and a few patients at Tea Table.

Shortly after midnight, in the humid early hours of August 7, 1840, James Glass, a ship's carpenter, awoke restlessly and stepped to his porch for some fresh air. He was startled to see on his beachfront a row of large empty dugout canoes. Cautiously, he awoke another carpenter, George Beiglet, and together they set out to warn Housman and the others, a total population of 35 whites and 10 blacks. But suddenly an Indian came at him from the darkness and Glass felled him with his shotgun. The blast, and the ensuing war cries, awakened the island; pandemonium spread as the redskins headed straight for Housman's dwelling while other villagers scurried for refuge.

As they battered down the captain's front door, he and his wife raced barefoot out the back door, cutting their feet on the knife-sharp coral as they plunged into the water. As his two dogs came barking in after them, a frantic Housman grabbed their heads and held them under water, drowning them to keep them quiet. Then he untied a skiff nearby and the pair escaped/to the government supply schooner Medium anchored a half-mile away.

Failing to find Housman, the raging Indians plundered his warehouse, home, and retail store, loading their canoes with valuable goods and barrels of shot and gun powder.

Many villagers had escaped by this time, mostly by swimming out to the Medium and a few by hiding up to their necks in the huge water cisterns.

The Perrine house, which rested partly over the water, had a bathing cellar beneath it which was refilled at every tide through a tunnel leading from under the porch all the way out to the wharf's end. The tunnel had originally been constructed for just such escape purposes in early days but had recently been partially blocked off with pilings to use as a turtle crawl. As a group of Indians approached his home, Perrine hustled his wife, two daughters and son into the cellar, closing the trapdoor and covering it with a large chest. He then raced out on the upper porch and hailed the Indians. Speaking in Spanish, he told them he would treat any of their wounded and give them medicine later if they went away. They went. Perrine knew of their awe of the white medicine man.

But mere awe could not compete with demon rum and the Indians soon became saturated with kegsful from Housman's store. They soon came shrieking wildly back to Perrine's house. They rushed in and chased the doctor up into the rooftop cupola, smashing the door in and beating him to death. They then dumped the doctor's fine library and valuable manuscripts out the window into the water. After smashing everything breakable, they set the house afire.

The horror-stricken family, having heard the calamity taking place above, now faced a fiery death as cordwood stacked on the wharf overhead caught fire. Young Henry made his way through the pilings to the wharf's end and spotted a small launch being loaded by the Indians. When the latter went back inside the warehouse, the boy raced over and pushed the boat off, reaching the wharf where his mother and sisters had climbed out of the burning wharf section, their faces and shoulders seared. They all piled in and poled the craft straight for the schooner. The Indians were yelling and shouting at the launch while another canoe nearby set off in pursuit. But a rowboat launched from the schooner caused the raiders to turn back and the Perrines were soon safely aboard.

Elsewhere on the island, a few had not been so fortunate. The drunken redskins confronted Captain John Mott, his wife and two small children. They were all beaten and shot to death; Mott's mother-in-law escaped by hiding under a house. The Indians had set fire to every main building on the key except one—this was the home of postmaster Charles Howe. The Indians had found Howe's Masonic apron, with its emblems, in a closet. Whether from superstition or some other omen, they laid the apron neatly on the table and left the building untouched.

The 12-year-old son of Captain Elliott Smith died of burns received while hiding in a cistern beneath a burning building, while Smith, his wife and another child were severely injured. James Sturdy was parboiled to death in the large cistern beneath the flaming warehouse. Four of the blacks were abducted and carried off to be slaves.

Meanwhile, the officer and five men from the schooner Medium rowed toward the besieged key in a gun barge. They had mounted a four-pound cannon but, in their haste, had picked up charges for a six-pounder. Within 200 yards of the Housman wharf, they fired at a group of Indians but the overcharged recoil kicked the cannon overboard while the Indians whooped with drunken laughter and fired one of the wharf's cannons in return. The barge was forced to retreat.

By late morning, the raiders had left, bearing away 28 canoes and six of Housman's boats laden with booty. Aboard the Medium, the captain stared in disbelief as his last possessions billowed up in smoke. The next day, as the Perrines sifted through the ashes of their home, they uncovered the skull, a few ribs, and a thigh bone. These remains of the good doctor were buried on Lower Matecumbe near one of his prized experimental sisal plants.

A great uproar followed on this tragedy, with black-bordered, front-page national editorials lamenting the eminent doctor's fate, the negligence of the Navy, and the need for drastic action.

Ironically, the responsibility fell on the shoulders of the one man whose wise and humane counsel—if the vengeful had only heeded it—would have prevented the tragedy beforehand. But Lieutenant Colonel Harney knew what had to be done. With 90 picked men painted and dressed up like Indians, guided by a runaway Indian slave, he canoed deep into the Everglades. Within 12 days, he had wiped out most of the warriors and recovered a large part of their booty. Chekika was shot while chopping wood and his body was strung up in a tree as a warning to the few remaining braves. This permanently ended any further Indian hostilities.

Captain Housman, whose bloody avarice had cost him everything, now had to go to work as a lowly deckhand on a salvager. One year later, this once king of the Florida wreckers lost his footing while trying to board a wreck. He fell between the two heaving vessels and was crushed to death.

The people of Key West did not soon forget Indian Key, if only because they had at least one poignant and tragic reminder in their midst. A Mr. and Mrs. Williams barely escaped death in the raid, but their young son, James was driven insane. He was called "Crazy Jim" and for many years he wandered the streets of Key West uttering harsh cries and at times screaming, "The Indians are coming!"—and people remembered.

15.
Marjorie Rawlings Portrays Florida to the World

Marjorie Kinnan Rawlings came to Florida to write and this she did, producing one of the most successful novels of all time.

It seemed so baldly improbable, this sophisticated, college-bred Northern city girl suddenly transplanting herself into the Deep South wildlands and Cracker country of north central Florida.

And yet Marjorie Kinnan Rawlings, a newspaperwoman-cum-frustrated-writer, already had a flinty streak of pioneer stock in her veins, and it blended mystically with her root-love of this strange earth, flora and fauna, its people. So much so that, within a decade, millions of people in America and in over a dozen foreign countries would come to know—and love—this robust, witty, humane woman, as well as the "invisible country" she wrote about.

And invisible it was, even to most Floridians then—a primeval, semitropic garden, its pristine beauty still unscarred by "civilized" tentacles, a land of swamp, hammock, lakes, rivers, scrub pine forests, gators, snakes, panthers, possum, bears, cooters, wild fowl, and exotic flowers, known only to its odd inhabitants, the proud, taciturn, poor-white Cracker who loved and respected this wildland even as he fiercely wrestled it for marginal existence, for field peas, bacon fat, grits, and corn liquor.

Her portrayal of one of these poor-white families and its 12-year-old protagonist in "The Yearling" has now become a literary classic to millions, both children and adults, strongly in the Mark Twain tradition. And her powerful, sensitive, and warm depiction of the land and people of "Cross Creek" has made this book one of the finest pastoral allegories since Thoreau's classic, "Walden Pond."

Still, her arrival into this moss-draped hinterland was sort of chancy, even desperate. As she recalled later: "When I came to Florida I was in despair about my writing. I had tried to write on the job but could not. When I came here I put all thoughts of popular writing behind me. I was determined to try and interpret the people whom I had come to love. If I failed, I would write no more."

But writing was a first love to Marge Kinnan. At age 11 she won a $2 prize for her first short story published in the *Washington Post* under the pen name, "Felicity." Born in the capitol to Arthur F. and Ida May Traphagen Kinnan, he a U.S. Patent Office official, she and her younger brother, Arthur, moved to Wisconsin with her mother when her father died in 1913. She attended the University of Wisconsin, earning a Phi Beta Kappa key and graduating with a BA degree in English in 1918. On campus, she excelled in dramatics, short stories, and poetry, but upon graduation, she married class-mate Charles Rawlings and both chose the bread-and-butter job of newspa-pering. In their spare time, both tried, unsuccessfully, to write fiction. Then, in 1928, they took a brief respite from their frenetic pace with a leisurely cruise down the St. Johns River.

Enchanted by this virgin stillness and beauty, especially the wild Okla-waha river country, they decided almost at once to carve their own Eden out of this lush and primitive garden—and write freely. That same year they bought some 72 acres of woods and farmland, including 40 acres of citrus groves, plus an old rambling farmhouse located on Cross Creek, near Island Grove. The creek, connecting two large lakes, Lochloosa and Orange, lay about midway between Ocala and Gainesville.

They pruned trees, fought storms, frosts and fruit flies, planted the fer-tile hammock in truck crops, but Charles soon tired of the life; he left the Creek and returned to the urban fold. The two would later divorce, with ami-cable understanding. But Marjorie had found "home." With part-time help she struggled with the farmwork and also began writing copiously as she explored the land and people around her, even living for short periods with neighboring Cracker families, listening, learning, coming to know them intimately. They soon came to understand the warm, sympathetic, generous-hearted nature of this "outsider" and they responded in kind; the "outsider" was taken in.

Frosted crop failures and desperate poverty haunted her the first two years, but her writing "crops" finally bore fruit. In March 1930, she sold her first story, "Cracker Chidlings," to Scribner's for $150. Nine months later, Scribner's bought, for $700, a second, longer story, "Jacob's Ladder," a tale of a young Cracker couple eking an existence in the wild country. This time she got an unexpected bonus as well; she became a protégé of Scrib-ner's editor, Maxwell Perkins. Perkins, already nurturing young writers like Thomas Wolfe, Scott Fitzgerald and Ernest Hemingway, would become her closest and most valuable mentor, guide, critic, and friend. Her response to him was joyful: "I am vibrating with material like a hive of bees in swarm." She was indeed.

While continuing to publish short stories, she finished her first novel, *South Moon Under,* about Cracker life in the Big Scrub, a wild, thick stretch of pine woods skirting the Oklawaha River. Scribner's published it in March 1933, and it won immediate critical acclaim—"fresh, honest, poetic . . .

rich in the humor of natural man . . . a great new talent." Also that year, she won the $500 O. Henry Award for her short story, "Gal Young Un." A lesser work, "Golden Apples" followed; a cut version of it sold later to *Cosmopolitan.* But the author had now won, and secured, her literary beachhead.

While healing from a broken neck in a fall from a horse in 1935, she traveled, visiting her brother Arthur in Seattle, touring Alaska by boat, returning home to hunt bear with Barney Dillard, and meeting Hemingway at Bimini Island. Marjorie wrote Perkins of her apprehension about meeting the now famous writer. She had heard tales of "a fire-spitting ogre . . . who went around knocking people down" and perhaps especially female novelists. "Instead, a most lovable, nervous, and sensitive person took my hand in a big gentle paw and remarked that he was a great admirer of my work." Hemingway's simple, declarative writing style would also show its influence in Marjorie's later work.

Finally, in late 1936, she went to a mountain cabin in North Carolina to begin writing *The Yearling.* While there, she called on Scott Fitzgerald who was "drying out" at a rest home in nearby Asheville. She felt him to be "a true artist" who had been conditioned to false values but, knowing the values to be spurious, was yet unable to disconnect from them.

The Yearling was published in February 1938. It became Perkins' favorite personal book—and a triumph. For months it rode the crest of best-sellers, MGM bought the movie rights to it, and Marjorie became a national celebrity. It was acclaimed a literary masterpiece and won her the Pulitzer Prize for fiction in 1939. It was soon translated into 13 languages. One critic best summed it: "It has the warmth and humor and understanding, the feeling for drama and for human verities, the earthy richness and stylistic beauty which a book must have [to be a classic]." And it remains one today.

Her next work, *Cross Creek,* not so much a novel as a biographical chronicle of the creek country and people, a pastoral idyll, light, comical, serious, reflective, using real names and true events, became an immediate success with both critics and the public when it appeared in 1942. She had crammed her 13 years of creek existence into one masterful achievement.

In all her work, the much-maligned Florida backwoods Cracker, depicted by writers for years as slovenly, backward or degenerate, is given a truer and more sympathetic appraisal. These tall, lean, gaunt descendants of poor farmers from Georgia and the Carolinas had, to her, a primal quality enabling them to live in the closest harmony with their wild environment. With a "spiritual eye" she saw a beauty in their repose, their dignity, their self-respect, even a certain graciousness in the midst of hard impoverishment. She was surprised to find them gentle, honest, with a warm self-effacing wit and elemental ingenuity, a zest for living in the bleakest conditions. From these people she learned the arts of hunting, fishing, logging, and moonshining "an excellent corn liquor," a cask of which she kept on her closet shelf. She knew them and ardently defended them to one and all "outsiders."

In her heady celebrity days, Marjorie was often hostess to a variety of the famous at her rustic farmhouse—Robert Frost, Wendell Wilkie, Sigrid Undset, Wallace Stevens, A.J. Cronin, Dylan Thomas and many others. She even had been wined and dined herself by Eleanor Roosevelt at the White House. In 1941, she married Norton S. Baskin, a St. Augustine hotel manager, and she would move to that city soon after to live.

Her departure from Cross Creek—aside from later brief and periodic visits— would also curiously mark a decline in both the quality and output of her later work. Perhaps erringly, she felt she had to shed the label of being only a "regionalist," a "Florida writer," and she embarked on a Great-American-Novel-type project, *The Sojourner.* Set in Michigan and the midwest, the book embraced a grand sweep of time, characters, and themes, but critics found it flawed with woodenness and stereotypes, lacking both the earthy vitality and the universal conviction of her earlier works. This ten-year effort also greatly taxed her already failing health and on December 14, 1953, she died of a cerebral hemorrhage at Crescent Beach near St. Augustine. Another work, a biography of the noted writer, and her personal friend, Ellen Glasgow, was never finished. She was buried in a cemetery near her beloved Cross Creek.

Unlike her contemporaries of the thirties—Faulkner, Hemingway, Dos Passos, Fitzgerald, Steinbeck—Ms. Rawlings' work contained none of the pessimism, or social consciousness of the period, and she made little use, if any, of sex, violence or sensation. Her themes, characters, and places affirmed old virtues and old values, combined with the harmony and timeless relation between man and his earthly setting. And yet she wrote with an earthy candor, lucidity, pungency, and crispness, a great-hearted zest that made her books enormously popular with millions of men, women, and children, in every walk and station of life.

She once said that her Florida writings were "a love story" for a land and a people. If so, then Florida was fortunate to have this remarkable woman share that story with the world, as one of the country's most distinctive writers.

16.
Educator Holt Remakes Rollins College

The president of Rollins College abhorred "lock-step" mass education, the lecture system, and prevailing research mania.

Back in the 1920s, education was something of a mystery in Florida. It was a process whereby "the contents of the professor's notebook are transferred by means of a fountain pen to the pages of the student's notebook without passing through the mind of either." So said Hamilton Holt, the father of modern education in Florida.

Holt hated the old "lecture system" of teaching which was so prevalent in the early party of the century, and he wasn't above criticizing it—or trying to change it.

In just that spirit nearly 60 years ago, the 54-year-old Holt assumed the presidency of small, struggling Rollins College at Winter Park. It was 1925. Soon, Holt would turn the school into an experimental "adventure in common-sense education" that would excite national interest and remain a usable teaching tool for a quarter-century. In fact, in the ferment of educational reform sweeping the country in the 1930s, the little college would be at the vanguard with such university innovators as Wisconsin, Antioch, Swarthmore, Chicago, and Bennington.

Holt was convinced that American higher education was rent with failure—the "scandalous scramble" for students and physical expansion, the "assembly-line" techniques of dehumanized "lock-step" mass education, and the glorifying of research at the expense of teaching. So, with idealistic zeal, he set about to reverse the process with a series of bold experimental programs that would transform Rollins' sleepy little campus and leaving a lasting and singular impact upon American higher learning in general.

First, to counter those educators who confused "bigness for greatness," he set a cap on school size (Rollins enrollment never exceeded 700), and, to complement its physical plant needs, he stressed "beauty and utility" in architecture and landscape, convinced of the psychological importance of an attractive academic environment.

More importantly, he sought out the best professors with the "gift of teaching" and earmarked funds to pay them the highest salaries necessary. Scorning the research mania prevalent in so many schools, he insisted that a teacher's duty was primarily to teach. Deriding the "publish or perish" syndrome, where uninspired men engaged in the "arid and unprofitable task of writing weighty papers [on trivia] . . . trying to know more and more with less and less," he declared that colleges needed "not more information but more inspiration, not more profound scholars but more great teachers . . . who can touch the lives of their students." Holt strongly believed that a teacher must stimulate the student to think as an individual and not force him to learn by rote processes. He lambasted the lecture and recitation systems which merely crammed facts into "passive receptacles," later to be squeezed out, spongelike, onto paper and quickly forgotten. Too often, he claimed, this left a student with the only aim of guessing enough right answers to get a decent mark. Such a system, he declared, "puts a premium on bluffing."

But Holt's primary aim was to "individualize" education by fostering a close, informal, intimate classroom relationship between student and teacher. To this end, he kept the teacher-student ratio as close to one-to-ten as possible. He then threw out the hourly class for a "conference plan" whereby teacher and students met in regular two-hour sessions for a more personal interplay in the learning process. This new experience elicited the enthusiasm and support of faculty and students. From here he moved swiftly into other innovations. Students were allowed to go as fast as their abilities would take them, without regard to calendar time, toward their degrees. He shocked some educators by abolishing exams. When Harvard President Abbott Lowell once asked him how a professor could evaluate a student without exams, Holt quietly asked him whether he examined his secretary every six months to see if she deserved a raise. Lowell, somewhat subdued, replied in the negative. Holt staunchly believed that teachers in daily sessions with a relatively small number of students could easily determine the quality of their work without resorting to written probes.

Perhaps few men could have ventured such radical departures from conventional education—especially with unquestioned support from trustees and students and faculty—but Holt, with his idealism and driving energy, was steeped in the tradition of reforms. For almost 25 years he had edited and published one of the most influential voices in the progressive movements in America in the early century, *The Independent* magazine in New York City. He also had a life-long devotion to causes of world peace and world government which drew him into close working relations with presidents from Theodore Roosevelt to Woodrow Wilson and, later, the League of Nations. He was born into an affluent Connecticut family whose reformist ardor dated to pre-Revolutionary days. Fortunately, this "true Yankee" innovator's impact on the mostly Southern conservative residents of the Winter Park-Orlando area was beneficently softened by his charming and gracious wife, Alexina "Zenie" Crawford Smith, a descendant of an old Baltimore family. They married in 1899 and had four children.

Holt himself was a complex man. He was said to be shrewd and salty, with a droll, dry wit plus a moral stamina that reinforced his reformist ardor. Yet he had a natural human warmth and friendliness, and a sentimentality that was leavened with an irrepressible boyish and even mischievous streak. Once when a visiting Yale team came to argue that "women in politics are a fiasco," he made a last-minute substitute of a squad of girls to answer them. He nonplussed one graduating class by informing them: "You came here as young undeveloped, untrained, and mostly devoid of what—even by stretching the point—might be called intelligence. Little you have experienced here has changed you in this respect."

He was the strongest defender of intellectual and academic freedom, once hotly rebuking some powerful alumni who expressed concern about "reds" on the faculty—two socialist professors. But an otherwise excellent record here was severely marred with his dismissal in 1933 of the brilliant classics teacher, John Rice, in what was essentially a personality confrontation, causing Holt, for once, as one critic noted, "to lose his perspective." Rice set out to form his own experimental college at Black Mountain, North Carolina, taking a few Rollins faculty and students with him.

Throughout the 1930s and early 1940s, Holt continued to innovate and search for more efficient educational methods, calling on leaders like John Dewey, James Harvey Robinson, and others to help formulate new courses and programs. Some of his pioneering programs were later changed or modified, and some even abandoned by his successors. But most educators agree that Holt succeeded admirably in his singular goal of humanizing the classroom and individualizing the learning experience to draw out the best in both teacher and student—especially in an age of mass educational techniques.

At his retirement in 1949, he could look back on one of the most exciting experiments ever conducted in education—one that would make Rollins one of the ranking liberal arts colleges in the nation, even though he had to turn a campus upside down to do it.

17.
The Greeks Conquer the Sponge Industry

For 40 years Tarpon Springs was the world's sponge capital until red tide killed its trade.

The Greek was certain of it. He knew it. So on weekends he would quietly slip off with his brothers and row out to the islands at the river's mouth and then beyond into the Gulf.

There they would peer intently through glass-bottom buckets, scanning the exotic undersea garden of sand and coral. And each trip it was always the same—a profusion of sponge beds plushly carpeting the sea floor as far as the eye could see. It was a bonanza strike: massive fields of "golden fleece" awaiting only the harvest.

But 26-year-old John Corcoris said nothing of it. He waited and planned. It was the early 1900s and Tarpon Springs was just a frontier village of several hundred souls. But it was on the verge of a revolution. The American sponge industry would soon make it the sponge capital of the world.

Corcoris had arrived in New York City from his native Greek island of Peloponnesus in 1895 and worked as buyer for a Greek sponge firm. Sponging in America in the 19th century was a somewhat primitive, indolent industry, dominated by Key West "Conchs" who harvested sponges from the coastal shallows, rarely deeper than 25 feet. They worked from dinghy "hook" boats, hooking the sponges with long fork-tined poles. Corcoris had heard about the sponge beds discovered off the coast of Tarpon Springs. But he was certain that, in such climate and waters, the thicker sponge beds, and, hence, those of the best quality like the durable sheepswool, lay in deeper waters.

The Greek knew sponges; his family had been in the sponge trade for centuries. The eastern Mediterranean was then the sponge capital of the world and the world's best divers came from the Greek islands where they had been gathering the sponges since before the days of Homer.

In New York, Corcoris met John K. Cheyney, who needed help in his small wholesale sponge business in Tarpon Springs. Corcoris quit his job to go to work for Cheyney and, soon after, sent for his brothers—George, Louis, Constantin, and Gus—who were also employed by Cheyney. Corcoris then returned to Greece briefly to marry his fiancee, Anna, and bring her back. After buying and converting a fishing boat, the *Elpis,* which means hope, he bought some secondhand diving equipment, including a futuristic diving suit, in New York and sent an agent to hire an experienced sponge crew in Greece. He then confided his secret to Cheyney and convinced him of the practicality of deep-diving for the valuable sponges. The diving suit, which was equipped with steel and glass helmet and air hose, had been successfully introduced in Greece in the 1880s, but American sponging was still done in shallow waters by the primitive "hook" boat method. Corcoris then entered a business arrangement with Cheyney, who put up some funds of his own, and ads were placed in newspapers in key Greek ports and islands.

Meanwhile, Corcoris' first crew had arrived and, on a clear, sunny day in June 1905, history was made when America's first mechanized sponge diver, Demosthenes Kavasilos, went overboard from the *Elpis.* Within ten minutes he returned with a bagful of the best known sponges, the sheepswool, and exclaimed, prophetically enough: "There's enough sponges in these beds to supply the whole world."

By the end of 1906, some 1,500 Greek Spongers had arrived—and the streets were suddenly filled with swarthy dark-haired men uttering the musical, staccato cadences of a strange language. In the evenings they would noisily gather in the small cafes to sip their rich black coffee or native wine, *Retsina,* or smoke water pipes, while the rhythmic strains of *buzouki* music would send them leaping and twirling in the native folk dances. The rich aromas of Greek cookery—spiced lamb, pickled grape leaves, pignolia nuts, feta cheese—would one day transform much of Florida cuisine and add a landmark to the west coast, with the opening of Louis Pappas' first authentic Greek restaurant in the 1920s.

Some townspeople resented the "foreigners" and moved away, but most, somewhat apprehensive at first, began to warm to the good-natured gaiety and sober industry of these Hellenic invaders, especially when the sponge boom began to infuse the town with jobs and prosperity. By 1908 sponging was a million-dollar industry and Tarpon Springs was indeed the new world sponge capital. Cheyney opened the first Sponge Exchange on Spring Bayou, and the fleet harvesting the sponges averaged 200 boats through the next three decades. Festivals and religious rites still mark the gaily colored boats' departure each January. And they still return to port in June and go out again from July to Christmas just as they did at the turn of the century.

At Epiphany, early each new year, the annual dive by Greek boys to retrieve a golden cross from Spring Bayou has become a national event attracting thousands of viewers.

The sponge divers of the early 1900s—tough, cool, resourceful men—were the "elite" of spongers and, literally, the industry's lifeline. One diver's work provided 15 other jobs at sea and on shore because harvested sponges had to be washed, dried, and sorted before they were sold at the Sponge Exchange. (In later years the workers' diminishing numbers would mark the industry's sharp decline.) But theirs was a taxing, hazardous occupation. If a diver stayed down moments too long or came up too fast, he would get "the bends," an excruciating and often fatal condition caused when the blood bubbles with nitrogen; the limbs can become paralyzed and the skin often turns blue-black. Often, on removing the helmet of the diver surfacing with the bends, the crew would quickly throw him back into the sea to restart his circulation when they saw his ghastly color. But sometimes this cure failed and he either died or was crippled for life. Sometimes he would drown or suffocate when he was deprived of air due to cuts, tears, or kinks in his air hose. There were always a few casualties each year.

Violence, too, marred some of the early years when the Key West Conchs—an often clannish, sullen and volatile people—resenting the transfer of the nation's sponge-buying market to Tarpon Springs, attacked the Greek spongers and burned their boats. But the Greeks fought back in the streets and the courts and eventually the Conchs returned to their native Key West waters.

The multimillion-dollar sponge industry thrived and prospered through the 1920s and 1930s even while Florida suffered during the Great Depression. But in the early years of World War II, disaster struck. A massive silent undersea killer, the red tide, enveloped nearly all of the Gulf coast, lingering throughout the 1940s and destroying from 70% to 90% of the sponge beds. The industry lay almost dormant through the 1950s until the beds could recover and regenerate.

But by this time, most spongers had sold their boats and drifted into other occupations. The divers had become a vanishing breed, and a third generation of young Greeks, Americanized and better educated, disdained this hazardous calling for an easier life on shore. Today sponge harvesting has virtually dwindled to a cottage industry, displaced largely by a tourist business of curio shops, restaurants, and diving exhibitions at the site of the original sponge docks.

But veteran spongers say the rich beds are still there, awaiting only skilled men and boats. They say the world demand for natural sponges is still eight times greater than the supply and that the industry could be in for a great revival. That sounds a lot like the message of John Corcoris, another Greek who, three-quarters of a century earlier, was convinced of a similar dream—and saw it develop into a colorful and unique industry.

18.
St. Petersburg's "Romanov Connection"

When terrorists killed the czar, Peter Demens, a Russian nobleman, moved to Sanford. The railroad he built to Pinellas County opened the Gulf coast to development.

If some nihilistic terrorists had not bombed the imperial dining room of the Winter Palace in St. Petersburg, Russia, in 1880, the city of St. Petersburg, Florida, might never have been born.

One might call it "the Romanov connection," for had it not occurred, a dynamic Russian might not have left his country to come to Florida and build a railroad from the St. Johns River near Sanford to Pinellas Point in St. Petersburg. And in frontier Florida, only a railroad could create or make a town.

Of course, Piotr Alexewitch Dementier (who Americanized his name to Peter W. Demens) was hardly a terrorist. He was an educated Russian nobleman, a prince from an ancient landed family and he served as a captain in the Imperial Russian Guard. But, like many of the educated men of his day, including novelists Turgenev and Tolstoy, he held liberal and reformist views of government. Ironically, the Romanov czar himself, Alexander II, held similar views and won renown as "The Liberator" for emancipating Russian serfs in 1861. The beautiful but deadly fanatic terrorist leader Sophia Perovskaya missed killing the czar in 1880 when he delayed entering his dining room by half an hour. She succeeded, however, in assassinating him the following year in March 1881. Thus began a wave of repression in which even liberals like Demens became suspect. So, at age 30, Piotr moved his family to America, settling in Longwood, Florida, near Sanford, where he built a makeshift ten-mile railroad to haul timber for the sawmill he operated.

Demens' chance to become a railroader came in 1885 when he took over the charter of the financially ailing Orange Belt Railroad—from Lake Monroe on the St. Johns River to Apopka—in settlement for a debt of $9,400 worth of crossties. With a railroad but no funds, he took in three partners: Josef Henschen, a New York visitor, Henry Sweetapple, a Canadian, and A. M. Taylor from Virginia. Together they invested $37,000 to form the Orange Belt Investment company. They laid out the town of Oakland, west of

Orlando, managed to get land donations for a right of way and had the first train rolling into the new town by November 1886.

But Demens was already dreaming of a line to the Gulf, at Pinellas Point 120 miles away, where he hoped to see "a city of international importance" built. He secured the charter for it, plus permission to issue and sell $700,000 in bonds. But New York bond brokers were skeptical of the "wilderness railroad" and refused to handle the sale.

At this point, in walked wealthy Philadelphian Hamilton Disston, who had just bought a huge chunk of the state (four million acres at 25 cents each), and offered Demens some 60,000 acres for right of way and townsites if Demens could push his line to the southern section of Pinellas, of which Disston owned about three-fourths. He also helped the Russian secure some state land grants. With this in hand, a jubilant Demens returned to New York where he found the firm of Griswold and Gillett eager to sell his bonds.

Disston had wanted Demens to run the railroad to Disston City (Gulfport) but, unexplainably, Disston's board of directors turned the arrangement down.

This time another developer stepped in to rescue Demens' plan. John C. Williams, a Detroit realtor who owned much of what is now Gulfport, offered Demens a half-interest in 500 acres of it, including a mile of bay frontage, if Demens would run the railroad to Paul's Landing, near the area of the old Vinoy Hotel. It would include construction of a 2,000-foot wharf running out to 12 feet of water in Tampa Bay to accommodate larger ocean-going vessels.

But a desperate Demens was hitting financial snags elsewhere. Anticipated funds from the bonds had not arrived, and brokers were blaming a "poor bond market." But Demens had already called for 600 laborers. He had also accumulated a stack of bills for construction materials, and his creditors were besieging him. A frantic Demens had to rush once more to New York and put most of his railroad in hock at a high interest rate to obtain a $100,000 loan from H. O. Armour & Co. The creditors were paid off, and grading and tie-laying began again. But the funds were soon exhausted, and no bond money had yet materialized, nor had the vital rails, which were ordered from London. Other crises quickly followed. Demens stayed in the field with his workers night and day to keep them from quitting due to a nearby yellow-fever epidemic. When this threat subsided, his creditors once more began to clamor angrily. When a few of them chained the engines to the tracks, partner Sweetapple was so shocked he suffered a stroke and died. Meanwhile, an angry mob of 100 workers threatened to lynch Demens if they did not receive three weeks of overdue pay by eight o'clock that night. At the last minute, a sweating Demens was reprieved when local friends came up with the amount needed.

Finally, the first shipments of rails began arriving. As fast as they were laid, Demens was able to secure more loans, another from Armour and one from a Philadelphia syndicate. Working his crews overtime, Demens finally caught up to his construction schedule and, on June 8, 1888, the first train from the eastern terminus on Lake Monroe chugged into the new town of St. Petersburg.

Demens' wish to have the town named after his own hometown had been granted. But "town" was still an overstatement. When the first—and sole—passenger, a shoe salesman from Savannah, stepped onto the platform that summer, he looked around in bewilderment. "Where's the town?" he asked the conductor. "I don't see anything but a couple of shacks and lots of woods." "You've got me, mister," the conductor answered. "This is my first trip here."

In that first year, the only buildings in St. Petersburg were the railroad depot, the Orange Belt office building, and the Detroit Hotel, an ornate three-story structure that would remain a landmark for nearly a century. Williams named it after *his* hometown. Williams would also lay out the broad 100-foot-wide streets and the park which still bears his name. The 2,000-foot rail pier was completed the next year and by 1890 the town would boast 273 inhabitants, most of whom arrived by rail.

The tiny train itself, resembling some "early Toonerville Trolley," was often ridiculed. Occasionally it would jump its narrow-gauge track, at least when it tried to exceed 20 miles per hour. And when its pine wood fuel got wet, it would crawl at the walking pace of two miles an hour. Worse yet, it was a losing operation, and Demens and partners were forced to sell it to the Philadelphia syndicate. Demens, who later moved permanently to California, received only $14,000 for it, a fraction of all he had invested.

But the man who worked so long and hard against hopeless odds, even after all hope of profit had vanished, to put a railroad to a town that could not have been created without it, deserved to be honored, according to historian Karl Grismer. Although a loser to its owners, Grismer concludes, the Orange Belt was a "glorious success." It brought in the first settlers, gave them access to outside markets, boosted land values, and brought prosperity to other towns along the right of way, like Tarpon Springs, Dunedin, Clearwater, and Largo.

Villains and Characters

19.
Banker Ed Romfh: Supreme Iconoclast

E. C. Romfh was one of Florida's finest bankers. He survived both the bust of the 1920s and the Great Depression.

E. C. Romfh: a very paternal employer.

Bankers as a breed evoke a fairly static image—staid, low profile, impeccable propriety—but now and then a financier comes along who shatters all the stereotypes and leaves a unique and colorful mark of his own on the financial history pages.

Such a figure was E. C. Romfh, who founded the First National Bank of Miami (plus a few others) at the turn of the century and who, when he died in 1952, was hailed as one of the giants in Florida's financial annals.

He was a mixed man; combining traits of the elder Pierpont Morgan with perhaps a bit of Ebenezer Scrooge, yet leavened on occasion with a dash of pure P. T. Barnum. He could be personally explosive, whether smashing his bank's front window over some employee's error or defying a president (F.D.R.). With employees, he was the stern Biblical patriarch—often to a fault—right down to prescribing their dress and even their choice of mates! But for all of that, he was a financial genius.

With the canny, keen eye of an early Yankee trader he could sense financial storm clouds even on the clearest day. As a result, he was able to steer his holdings through boom, bust, panic or depression with relative ease, even as mighty houses toppled around him.

Edward Coleman Romfh was born at Camden, Arkansas, February 8, 1880, to a Florida citrus grower and merchant, George Boddie and Virginia Romfh. Due to ill health, he had little formal education and, at age 13, went off to Nacogdoches, Texas, to work for several years before coming to Miami in 1898. Here he began as a clerk at the Bank of Bay Biscayne and moved quickly up to assistant cashier. Within only four years, the apprentice moneychanger had parlayed his financial acumen into the organization of the First National Bank of Miami and became president in 1902, a post he held until retirement.

During this period, his shrewd foresight and talents were not confined alone to banking. For example, in 1904, he and some associates bought up the state's existing telephone facilities for $2,000; in 1917, they sold this interest to Southern Bell Telephone Co. for $1,750,000. The golden touch was evident early.

For the next two decades, First National saw only a steady upward progress under Romfh's guiding hand as the little "Indian trading post" town of 2,000 grew to bustling city stature. By 1922, when the original tiny building was razed to make way for Miami's first steel skyscraper, deposits had soared to over $7 million. (At his retirement 24 years later, they would be over $100 million.)

During this period, Romfh also found time to marry Marie Antoinette deCamp, in 1905, and they had three sons; two are still living and residing in Miami. He also served as a Miami city councilman for 12 years, including four years as mayor. He found time to dabble in the booming hotel industry and operated several such luxury resorts, and was an original founder of the Miami Jockey Club later renamed the Hialeah Race Track.

Finance, however, was his forte. By the time the 1930s had rolled around, Romfh had added the First Trust & Savings Bank and the Little River Bank & Trust Co., in Miami, and the Coral Gables First National Bank, to his Miami First. He was also co-founder in 1920 of the Miami Beach First National Bank. And he kept a tight rein, especially during the runaway excitement of the giddy Florida land boom of the twenties and its spectacular bust. "His were the only banks in the area that weathered the bust," one veteran banker asserted. Immune to the fever, he kept a tight fist on every dollar while other lenders shelled them out like tipsy sailors. He simply refused to extend credit for what he believed, accurately, were abnormally inflated real estate purchases.

This judgment proved even sounder in the soon to follow Depression. While others tottered and fell, First National remained open throughout the dark decade, closing only for the Bank Holiday in 1933. Even here, Romfh attempted to defy President Roosevelt's order, keeping his bank open 24 hours after all others had closed, until the federals finally moved in and forced him shut.

As one house after another failed, Romfh was not above resorting to the flamboyant and sensational to head off panicky runs on his own First National. Once he sent to the Jacksonville Federal Reserve Bank for $8 million in cash which he stacked in huge piles on the balcony surrounding the bank lobby. As fearful customers came in to withdraw deposits, he stood on the balcony shouting down, "Come on in . . . don't worry about your money, there's plenty here!" Pure corn—but it worked.

Veteran employees recall him perhaps with some mixed feelings—stern, unpredictable, a father figure both harsh and humane. He might fire a high-ranking officer on the spot for a minor infraction, or demote him to "warehouse" level. A mistake by one employee prompted an angry Romfh to smash one of the bank's huge plate glass windows with his cane. Arthur McCormack, a 44-year employee recalled Romfh's sister, "Miss Mildred," who ran the bank's administrative functions for some 20-odd years. The short, heavy-set spinster regulated employee dress and once bought McCormack a new suit to make him get rid of a pair of pants she thought offensive.

Tully Dunlap, a recently veteran Florida banker, spent the first five years of his career at the "Romfh School of Banking" in the 1930s and offers some discerning glimpses into both man and banker. It was a time, he recalls, when the five-day, forty-hour week was unheard of. You worked from 7:00 or 7:30 a.m. to 7:00 or 7:30 p.m., plus eight hours Saturday. Starting salary was $50 a month straight, no deductions then.

"No one ever quit, but it was unusual for anyone to stay a lifetime," Dunlap related. "When you reached the top of the pay scale, the slightest mistake became grounds for discharge. A teller who was short or a book-keeper who paid a forged check was likely to be fired without getting a second chance. I remember hearing Mr. Romfh remind an employee, who thanked him for a promotion, that 'the higher you get, the harder you fall.'

"Mr. Romfh's personal policies were very rigid. His permission was required to buy a car, a house, or to get married. He wanted to make sure that each one lived on what he earned at the bank. If a person got into debt and couldn't pay his creditors, he might be tempted to steal from the bank."

When Dunlap once wanted to buy a used car for $300, Romfh gave his permission only after thoroughly itemizing all the maintenance expenses Dunlap would have, as opposed to riding the bus, and whether he could meet them on his salary.

Romfh's marital views, which would surely appall a modern couple, were equally strict. In 1939, when Dunlap married a bank employee, Mary Doughton Miller, he recalls that he had to ask Romfh's permission even before he asked Mary's father!

"Later, 'Miss Mildred' (Romfh's sister), personally inspected the house we proposed to buy. It was a new two-bedroom, one-bath frame house on a 50-foot lot for $2,500—$300 down payment and a $2,200 FHA mortgage. This was actually our second choice as 'Miss Mildred' disapproved the first one. We were thrilled when she gave us approval to proceed with *her* choice!"

But, on occasion, employees might also view a sympathetic niche in the flintlike figure, especially in the hard Depression years. One retired employee recalls Romfh standing in the bank's lobby at closing time, handing silver dollars to employees as they left; another remembers the banker strolling through all the offices leaving bus tokens on every desk. He might surprise a teller or a bookkeeper with a special gift or favor, for no apparent reason.

Dunlap notes that Romfh's tight money policy on loans (he made very few) was more than made up for by his success in buying and selling bonds. "The first thing he did each morning was to review the daily statement. Next, he called me to his office to bring him the big loose-leaf bound book. He would then get Chris Devine (a New York bond specialist) on the phone, thumb through the bond book, selling one issue and buying another. This would go on for an hour. He was recognized as one of the most astute bond traders in the country."

His educational deprivation of early years may have spurred him in later years to broaden his perspectives for he would spend a late evening hour with Dunlap often, conversing on every subject but banking. "He was a well-read man, very knowledgeable on many subjects, especially history, theology, and the Middle East," Dunlap recalls. In fact, his two foremost hobbies were collecting rare books and old maps. He was also a golf and yachting enthusiast, dividing much time in later years between Palm Beach's Everglades Club and the New York and Biscayne yacht clubs.

When he died in 1952, the institution he had spawned and nurtured through stormy decades of financial stress and turbulence was thriving as heartily as ever; it ranks today among the nation's top 100 commercial banks. But it might have been otherwise without the dynamic single-mindedness of a banker who was almost an institution himself.

20.
"Bone" Mizelle Was a Cowboy's Cowboy

Palmetto scrub was the range and a rifle was the law, and
"Bone" Mizelle was a tough, impish cowboy equal to both.

Most Americans think "out West" when they think of cowboys, but Florida's last frontier in the late 19th century spawned a breed of cowpoke every bit the equal of the Western counterpart.

In fact, the intensely individual, free-wheeling stylist who herded the ancient Spanish stock of hardy beef over the scrubland and piney woods of Southwest Florida's sprawling flatlands, often made his Western brother look like a mere comic strip Tumbleweeds. Zane Grey's purple sagers had nothing on Florida's palmetto cabbagers. And even though cow-stealing, then as now, was strictly a no-no, this rule was more often honored in the breach by the early Florida cattle baron. In the vast open fenceless ranges stretching for miles south, north, and east of Arcadia and DeSoto County, herds often got "mixed up" and both baron and his men "plumb swore they couldn't tell one from another." Those who thought they "could tell" also swore, usually on a stack of Colts and Winchesters, blazing mightily. They were, as noted, a free-wheeling lot.

One of the best known and most colorful of these punchers was a long, lean saddle-reed named Napoleon Bonaparte "Bone" Mizelle born in 1863 at Lily, on Horse Creek near Arcadia, to Morgan and Mary Mizelle. And, until his death in 1921 (greatly hastened by a generous consumption of strong waters the night before), Bone was revered as a cowboy's cowboy; he rode hard, drank hard, lived hard, was a crack shot with rifle or six-gun, and yet had a temper generous to a fault, leavened somewhat by an impish prankster spirit that enlivened many a dull long drive—he is still very much part of West Florida folklore today.

Bone had little if any formal education; he was literally raised in the saddle, bred to the hard, strenuous lot of the cowhand. Yet he had a firm but easy way in working with men and became one of the youngest foremen for the King Brothers, progeny of Judge Ziba King, one of the most powerful cattle barons of the era. Only in his twenties, he earned a statewide reputation as the top rounder, "lightning fast at roping and branding, an expert horseman, and a remarkable memory," recalled a contemporary. "He could

81

remember almost every cow or steer in a thousand head by their flesh marks."

"No four-legged critter could daunt him," recalls another who was present when Buck King, an owner, and Bone came upon an especially wild, pugnacious cow one day at the edge of a thorn-bush thicket. "Rope her and put your mark on her and you can have her," King challenged Bone. Bone accepted and soon had a rope on her horns. But as he dismounted with his knife to mark her, the old beast reared forth and dragged Bone into the thicket, causing him to lose his knife and half his clothes. A disheveled Bone finally emerged and King chided him for letting the animal best him. "But I put my mark on her," protested Bone. How could he when he lost his knife, King inquired. "Marked her ears with my teeth," Bone replied. They soon ran the cow out of the brush and, sure enough, firmly etched teethmarks adorned both ears.

Bone's disregard for money was notorious, especially his penchant for lighting his pipe with dollar bills, usually when he was drunk. He once had a horse and buggy and fell out of it one night while in his cups, the horse continuing on to town. Many buggies later, they finally identified his— strewn with scorched dollar bills. Often at the end of a market drive to Tampa, he would treat his hands to a steamboat ride for several days, footing the bill for food, drink, and extras himself, without asking the price. One such spree took his entire cattle profits but he just shrugged and headed home, poorer but no wiser. His arrival in Tampa was usually heralded with some prankish behavior, such as riding into Pomp Gibson's saloon at the corner of Kennedy and Ashley, reining up to the bar and ordering a shot or two, still mounted, then clattering out again.

One of his more celebrated, if dubious, pranks was a corpse switch. The wealthy Vermont parents of a young man who was stricken and died while on a camp hunt near Arcadia requested Bone to send the body back to that state for burial. Bone agreed. But after pondering it awhile, he exhumed the corpse of an old cowhand friend and sent it instead, reasoning that "the poor devil hadn't ever traveled none" and "it wouldn't make no difference to the rich boy nohow." The incident inspired a local school teacher to write a short "Ballad of Bone Mizell," the last quatrain of which read:

So instead of that Yank with his money and rank

Who had been round and seen lots of fun,

I jes' dug up Bill Red and sent him instead,

For ole Bill hadn't traveled round none.

Occasionally, Bone was the subject of a practical joke himself. Once, after having passed out from too much of his favorite firewater, Jamaica ginger, his cronies built a circle of fire around him, poked him with a stick, then hid behind some shrub. Bone raised up, looked dazedly around, then remarked: "Dead and gone to hell. No more'n I expected."

But he foiled another joker. While on the range, each cowboy took turns cooking for a week, with the strict rule that anyone who complained of the chow had to serve that cook's week out, plus his own. One miscreant thought he would let Bone fill in for him, whereupon he served Bone's portion to him first, after saturating it with salt. Bone took one mouthful and almost exploded, then caught himself, "This shore is good," he said tightly. "I always like plenty of salt on my victuals, this is just right," as the camp roared with laughter.

Like many another—whether baron or lowly cowhand—Bone, too, was infected with the sometimes lawless spirit prevailing in the wide open country. This took the form of misbranding cattle—his own, his employer's or someone else's. Mrs. Robert H. Roesch, wife of a pioneer judge, reported that Bone's name rarely failed to appear on the annual circuit court docket and that, after many efforts, he was finally convicted of cattle stealing. Bone was something of a folk hero to many of the early settlers and the "general feeling" was that the cattle kings themselves should be the ones on trial since Bone, if guilty, was stealing for his boss. But the trial began and the jury locked in for a night, after efforts by Bone boosters to sway the jurors with liquor, food, and cigars through a jury room window, failed. Found guilty, the judge delayed setting the time to begin serving the sentence. Meanwhile, a petition bearing the names of people along the entire Peace River Valley requested a pardon for him. They hit a legal snag when it was learned Bone could not be legally pardoned until he had served some time in the pen. But—no problem. Cow land ingenuity proved equal to the occasion.

Mrs. Roesch reports: "He [Bone] was dressed up in the best the Arcadia stores afforded, and escorted to the train by a large group of friends. At the penitentiary station he was met by an official, escorted through the prison buildings, given a banquet and made a speech in which he found no fault with the management. Having [now] 'served time' in the pen, Bone was then given the pardon which was waiting for him, and boarded the train for the return home."

About the time he reached age 40, Bone decided that he just wasn't making it as a foreman and he would go into the cattle business for himself. He had already acquired a government homestead earlier, although he never did build a home on it. And thus, true to the enterprising spirit of the day, he boldly announced to any within hearing that from here on, "instead of marking every fifth calf for my old boss, I'm marking them for Mr. Napoleon Bonaparte Mizelle." With the few head he already owned, Bone decided, he would build up a large herd simply by using the methods he had been employing for other cattle owners for years. Such frontier initiative seemed commendable but, as he knew from previous days, these "methods" were not always tried and true and could even pose sticky legal obstacles.

Sure enough, the first "obstacle" proved to be a little heifer calf upon which Bone had put his brand, "since it didn't have no brand at all." The irate owner of the calf's mother disagreed. Upon his arrest and conviction, Bone protested, "'Tain't fair, Judge, I have done the same thing for several of the men who testified against me and now they're sending me to prison for taking one little scrawny calf for myself." Whether he actually served time on this occasion is not known but, if so, it was brief enough, for he was soon back on the range again, "developing" his business.

Over the years, his herd slowly grew to sizeable proportions and he enjoyed a modestly prosperous cattle business. One contemporary friend and admirer observed that, whatever his attitude toward his former baron bosses, Bone was scrupulously honest with the smaller ranchers of the valley. For example, he recalled once when one of Bone's boys got someone else's year-ling "mixed up" with his own herd, he came straight to the owner to make good. "The boys drove your yearling with our cattle across the river. What's it wuff?" He then wrote a check on the spot for the amount named.

Bone never married, and he lived, worked, played, and drank as hard as he ever did right up to later years. But the rugged life—and especially the Barley-corn binges—took their toll by the time he was 58.

He died in his sleep in 1921, while sitting in the Atlantic Coast Line depot at Fort Ogden. The somewhat informal listing of the cause on his death certificate read simply: "Moonshine—went to sleep and did not wake up." Bone probably would have enjoyed that line himself.

21.
The
Notorious
Ashley Gang

Tough killers and bank robbers, the Ashley gang had few Robin Hood-like impulses. They died in their boots.

John Ashley, right, with prison officials as he prepared to enter Raiford to serve sentences.

Kansas had its Jesse James and Dalton gangs, but early in this century, Florida boasted a family troupe every bit the equal of those marauders—the notorious Ashley gang, scourge of Southeast Florida for a decade.

Young John Ashley, a one-eyed sharp-shooter with the cunning of a swamp rat, led his motley members on a spree of bank robberies, shootouts, bold hijackings in the lucrative rumrunning trade, and sundry other forms of larceny and mayhem before the gang's demise in a bloody ambush at Sebastian Inlet in 1924.

The elusive bandit king, with his bawdy mistress, Laura Upthegrove ("Queen of the Everglades"), reigned almost unmolested over the wild woods and swamps stretching from Fort Lauderdale up the coast to north of Lake Okeechobee. There was John and Laura, Ma and Pa Ashley, brothers Ed, Frank, Bob, and Bill, a host of relatives and "friends and neighbors," plus a variety of lawless characters who sought a natural refuge in the vast and obscure Okeechobee regions.

But the family began as just plain Cracker folks when Joe Ashley brought his wife, five sons, and four daughters from Fort Myers to the lower east coast to help Henry Flagler lay his railroad to Miami. Joe and the older boys chopped railroad ties while young John became a skilled hunter and trapper. They were soon close neighbors with the sparse lake and coastal settlers and their lives passed uneventfully.

Then, on December 29, 1911, a dredge in a lake canal churned up the body of a Seminole Indian, DeSoto Tiger. Investigation showed that John Ashley was with Tiger when the latter was on his way to Miami to sell otter skins belonging to his tribe, skins that John later sold to Girtman Bros. in Miami for $1,200. The Indian nation raised an outcry, the federal government stepped in, and John skipped the state, working in the Northwest awhile before returning to give himself up in 1914. He was jailed in Palm Beach County (where he feared no jury), but when the state attorney had the trial site moved to Miami, John broke through the chicken wire fence one night and escaped his unusually lax keeper.

His formal debut in crime began the next year, 1915, with the robbing of the Stuart Bank of $4,300. He escaped, but by a bizarre fate a confederate, Kid Lowe, accidentally shot John in the cheekbone causing him to lose his right eye. Lingering in the area to seek treatment, John was caught and taken at once to the Miami jail for his murder trial.

An incensed brother Bob Ashley decided to rescue John and, on June 2, 1915, broke into the home adjoining the jail of jailer Wilbur Hendrickson, fatally shot Hendrickson and took his keys.

An ensuing commotion in front of the jail forced him to flee to a nearby garage, where, failing to find a driver for the car left for him, he jumped on a delivery truck. With police in pursuit, when the truck stalled he shot it out with the officers. One officer was killed, and so was Bob Ashley. His body was shown to an angry mob of citizens to assuage them from seizing John. Later, a note signed by "the Ashley gang" was sent to the Dade sheriff warning that if John was not released they would "shoot up the whole . . . town."

Whether this threat had any effect or not, John's lawyers got the case abandoned the following November. John was then moved to Palm Beach County where he pleaded guilty to the robbery and was sentenced to Raiford for 17 years. After being sent to a road camp in March 1918, he escaped.

With prohibition now in effect, the rich field of rumrunning was now wide open. John, his brothers, and gang made frequent runs to West End, Bimini, in the Bahamas. They also ran three huge liquor stills in north Palm Beach County. Then they learned of an even more profitable venture—let the rumrunners do the work and then relieve them of their cash or cargo on sea or land. The rummies soon were forced to flee to other landings farther south as the gang hijacked them at leisure.

They had not neglected their other business, banks, and they earned such a horrendous reputation that witnesses report they could merely walk into a bank in a small town like Fort Meade, Avon Park or Boynton Beach, simply announce the name "Ashley," and tellers would frantically scoop their cash drawers obligingly. The gang could even afford to indulge a quirky sentiment, such as the time "Wild Bill" Henderson persuaded his colleagues not to hit the Pahokee Bank because he recognized the president as a close boyhood friend.

Ashley's arch foe, Palm Beach Sheriff Bob Baker, once sent two reluctant deputies after John. The latter, spotting them coming down the road, simply walked up to them and ordered them to drop their weapons. They did. He laughed, and then sent them back to Baker, unharmed but red-faced.

Whenever Baker sent a posse out into the swamps and woods, an ingenious "grapevine telegraph of the 'glades" went into operation at once and the gang simply vanished. The Ashleys had accrued a sizeable but undetermined amount of wealth in a few years and they didn't spend it all unwisely. They had "bought" at least two deputy sheriffs and a police chief, in three different counties. Other officials also reportedly were blinded by the glitter of tainted gold.

A vital force in the gang was Laura Upthegrove, John's mistress and confidante. She exerted much influence over the gang and also served in "casing" banks and driving the getaway car. She often carried a .38 revolver strapped to her hip while directing bootleg loads. She was formidably Amazon in size, but her dark unkempt hair and squinty, sharp black eyes made her something less than the beauty the press painted her. However, throughout their infamous careers, they were as devoted a couple as any newlyweds.

But fateful incidents began to unwind, starting in June 1921, when John was caught while delivering a load of liquor in Wauchula. He had given an alias to the sheriff but his identity was disclosed by another prisoner and he was soon Raiford-bound again. That same year, in October, Ed and Frank Ashley sailed to Bimini with $18,000 cash to buy liquor. They paid no heed to storm weather warnings and left Bimini in an overloaded craft. Neither boat nor men were ever seen again.

In John's absence, and even with Ed and Frank now gone, the gang still carried on its prolific activities, with John's young nephew, Hanford Mobley, in charge. Operations went well, as usual, until Mobley decided to revisit the Stuart Bank again in September 1923. The gang escaped with several thousand dollars but Mobley and Clarence Middleton were tracked by Sheriff Baker to Plant City and apprehended. Baker housed the pair in the Fort Lauderdale jail (assuming it safer than his own), but a lax jailer allowed their escape shortly after. In the same month, John Ashley escaped Raiford (in what manner was never explained although his numerous cash "deposits" may have helped considerably). The gang was in full swing by November when they raided the Pompano Bank for $23,000 in cash and securities, leaving a bullet with one of the victims to give to Sheriff Baker, in case he "gets out to the 'glades." That did it.

"This bunch of desperadoes cost me many thousands of dollars and many restless nights," Baker later explained, "but after they sent me the message with the bullet I was determined to get them . . . and I left no stone unturned." Baker borrowed rifles and ammo from the local National Guard unit, deputized numerous citizens and sent a large posse to a camp and still that was discovered two miles south of the Ashley homestead.

Baker's cousin, deputy Fred Baker, led his men right up to the edge of the camp early in the morning of January 10, 1924. As they slowly moved in, a dog barked and lead flew from both directions.

Pa Ashley, in one tent, was shot and killed instantly. Albert Miller escaped with his arm broken by gunfire but was caught a day later. John and Laura were asleep in a third tent. She was wounded by buckshot and captured, but John escaped.

"I grabbed my rifle and got behind a forked tree . . . in my underclothes," he later told a friend. "They poured enough lead at me to kill ten men. I noticed a palmetto move and I let fly a bullet in short order. A man toppled from behind the palmetto." John then escaped into the woods and the firing ceased.

The man he killed was deputy Baker. News of Baker's death caused an angry crowd to burn Joe Ashley's and Hanford Mobley's homes, plus a small grocery owned by Miller. But, failing to find John or other gang members, the posse gradually dispersed.

Ashley hid out and brooded for months with plans of vengeance for his father's death. Finally he decided to take his top gang lieutenants with him to Jacksonville and plot an attack on Baker at the courthouse after the latter's election in November. Baker, learning of their plans to go to Jacksonville, saw his chance. "I knew that they had relatives and friends all along the highway as far north as Fort Pierce and for that reason I decided to attempt the capture at the Sebastian River bridge, 28 miles north of Fort Pierce," he related.

Reportedly, a disgruntled brother-in-law informed Baker on the day of John's departure, November 1, 1924, and Baker sent some of his deputies to join St. Lucie Sheriff J. R. Merritt in the ambush.

Merritt drew a chain, with a red lantern attached, across the bridge, and the lawmen did not have to wait long before Ashley, with Mobley, Middleton, and Ray Lynn drove up, stopping at the chain. Within seconds, they were surrounded by deputies and then lined up in the car's headlights for searching and handcuffing.

At a signal from John, the foursome all went for pistols held in their waistbelts—but not fast enough. The lawmen fired point blank and all four men fell dead.

The Ashley gang was wiped out. The few remnants of the gang were killed, captured, or run out of state during the next few years. Only about $32,000 of gang loot was recovered, and this through the aid of former gang member Joe Tracy. But a reported cache of $110,000 somewhere in the 'glades, plus other sums were never located.

A somewhat disturbed Laura, grieving over John's death, spent most of the next two years in and out of jail on liquor violations until one day, after an altercation with a customer at her gas station home, she snatched up a bottle of Lysol and drank it—foaming at the mouth in agony until she died ten minutes later.

Ma Ashley died a few years later and only Bill Ashley, the "straight" son who survived the family's lawless propensities, lived a modestly successful life and died a natural death.

22.
Miami's Horrendous 'Guest,' Al Capone

Things were hot in Chicago for Al Capone, so he sought sanctuary in Miami and laid the foundations for the legalized gambling there during the 1930s.

In the desperate efforts recently by certain South Florida interests to bring casino gambling to Miami Beach, ostensibly to revive its ailing economic vitals, the ensuing furor seemed to evoke a strong sense of déja vu—another time half a century ago when another proponent of casino gambling came to reside in Dade County and threw the Biscayne Bay folk into an uproar that left civic scars to this day.

Of course Alphonse Capone, better known as Scarface Al Capone, "Public Enemy No. 1," did not exactly come to Miami Beach in 1927 on business. In fact, he came incognito, in temporary exile from his Cook County, Chicago, empire where a rash of gangland slayings and political violence prompted him to vacate the scene until a brief spurt of civic reformist heat could cool somewhat.

But his search for a quiet hideaway proved difficult. His infamous reputation as America's top hood caused civic doors to slam on him across the land—from Los Angeles to Baltimore, from New Orleans to St. Petersburg. This honcho supremo of the world's most notorious underworld, who could riddle a competitor's body with bullets one day and send truckloads of flowers for his funeral cortege the next, was experiencing for the first time feelings of downright rejection.

Didn't mayors and city hall heelers snap at his command? Couldn't he buy judges, like his silk monogrammed pajamas, in lots of a dozen? Didn't he control a major city's police department?

At 28 he was a multi-millionaire czar who directed a syndicate that owned or controlled breweries, distilleries, speakeasies, warehouses, boat and truck fleets, nightclubs, gambling houses, horse and dog races, brothels, labor unions, business and industrial associations, and other interests which together yielded hundreds of millions of dollars annually. In his lavish headquarters room at Chicago's Lexington Hotel he kept stacks of cash packed in padlocked canvas bags, awaiting transfer to various banks under ficticious names.

But now, outside his barony, he found the Capone persona painfully non grata. What was a poor, hard-working, successful businessman (as he fancied himself) to do? Thus desperation proved equal to guile and Capone turned another tack.

First, he rented a beach bungalow from an absentee owner, using the name of "Al Brown." Soon after, he cultivated close rapport with 24-year-old Parker Henderson Jr., son of Miami's former mayor, and leased a top floor suite in downtown Miami's Ponce de Leon Hotel from the young playboy. Henderson was fascinated by the affable gangster with the swarthy, sinister mien. He went out of his way to serve Capone, such as collecting money order wires from Chicago for him, under different aliases, when the exile needed quick cash. He later helped Capone secure his Palm Island estate in Biscayne Bay.

The solid citizens of Miami and its beach were now aware of the identity of their latest resident and their reaction was . . . somewhat schizoid. The *Miami Herald,* if forced to refer to him at all, called him Alphonse Capone; the *Daily News,* published by former Ohio governor James M. Cox, kept up a barrage of editorials against "Scarface Al Capone . . . the notorious beer and brothel baron of Chicago."

But privately, many civic and social leaders were perversely attracted to this dark, colorful, demonic presence and, particularly, to the fabulous wealth he so lavishly displayed, often on mere whim. Dade was in the post-boom depression. Banks had failed, business was bad in general, and the tourist trade was almost zero. Capone and his sizeable entourage of henchmen spent generously at local stores, such as Ev Sewell's haberdashery, and local politicians found him to be liberal with discreet contributions.

An incisive illustration of this schizoid attitude was Miami mayor John N. Lummus Jr. Under pressure from publisher Cox and city councilmen, Lummus conferred briefly with Capone and then announced that the gangster was going to voluntarily leave Miami Beach after deciding it would be "to the best interests" of all. Lummus became a comedic butt when Capone announced that he intended to stay put. Privately, however, Lummus, a realtor, later worked with young Henderson to secure the two-story villa estate on Palm Island, the former home of brewer Clarence Busch, for Capone for $40,000. When the *News* exposed the transaction, a citizens' group demanded the mayor's resignation, but Lummus weathered the blast and finished out his term.

Meanwhile, Capone, his demure and attractive wife, Mae, and their 11-year-old boy, Sonny, moved into the Palm Island villa, around which Capone erected a concrete wall, with a guardhouse at the high wooden front gate. He actively curried Chamber of Commerce favor with eulogies over Miami, "the garden of America, the sunny Italy of the new world." Sixty business and professional men attended a special banquet given by Capone and one Miami elder rose at table to introduce the racketeer as "the new businessman of the community."

Roddy Burdine, the department store head, soliciting a Community Chest donation swilled champagne with the gangster for several hours one morning. He left with a $1,000 check and a pointed suggestion from Capone that Burdine "arrange a little party" for the new resident at the country club of which Burdine was president. But indignant charity board members forced Burdine to return the check; he also quickly forgot "the little party."

Scarface Al would find his new haven a fitful one for some time. When the notorious gangster Red McLaughlin was killed in Chicago and dumped in a drainage canal, a Miami Beach Police courtesy card was found in his pocket. The incident triggered a storm among Dade interests who had hitherto ignored Capone's presence. Led by Miami Beach developer Carl Fisher, protesters screamed that the bad publicity would "hurt the real estate values." Governor Doyle Carlton labeled Capone as "undesirable" and urged Dade officials to arrest him, which they did numerous times but each time he was freed when his clever and able Dade lawyers, Vincent Giblin and J. Fritz Gordon, got him off.

Finally, the city brought a circuit court suit against Capone to padlock his island estate, asserting it to be a harbor for gangsters, racketeers, and assorted fugitives and a "menace to the safety and well-being" of residents. Fifty witnesses, led by Fisher, testified that nearby residents feared the gangster's presence, but Fisher could only name two persons, Mrs. Earl Kiser and Harvey Firestone, as complainants. Most of the trial was a duel of "glares" between Capone and Fisher, each of whom detested the other, but the vague charges were ultimately dismissed.

Meanwhile, Capone's periodic visits to oversee his Chicago dynasty were becoming aggravated. He had already wiped out rivals like the Aiello gang, the Terrible Gennas, Dion O'Banion, and Hymie Weiss. Now he had to contend with O'Banion's successor. George "Bugs" Moran, and he did so, from his Palm Island refuge, with brutal vengeance in the 1928 St. Valentine's Day massacre. Then, in May 1929, returning from an Atlantic City conference of 50 gang chiefs to sign new "peace" treaties, he was arrested in Philadelphia for carrying a gun and sentenced to one year. At the same time, a zealous young prohibition agent, Eliot Ness, was wreaking havoc on Capone's breweries and distilleries, and tax authorities were nearing completion of their enormous file on the gangster's "business" enterprises.

Yet during these years, Capone had not only won his "squatter rights" on Palm Island, he would lay the foundation for casino gambling on the Beach. Previously, most illegal hotel games were operated by local people, but all this changed when Capone brought in colleagues like Jake Guzik,

Frank Nitti, and Tony Accardo, followed soon by Frank Erickson, Meyer Lansky, Frank Costello, Joe Adonis, and Vincent Alo. These men would make Dade County the Las Vegas of the 1930s, and the Beach would revive its depression-wrecked economy—at least for some individuals. The racketeer soon controlled most law enforcement and many area political leaders. Capone himself threw lavish parties for local bigwigs and winter visitors. He especially favored star entertainers such as Harry Richman, Joe E. Lewis, George Jessel, Al Jolson, Eddie Cantor, Sophie Tucker, and Helen Morgan.

Otherwise the family lived quietly. Al Jr., a shy, semideaf boy, attended a local parochial school on the Beach. He would later marry a high school sweetheart, father four girls, and live in relative obscurity in the area in later years. He was studious, conscientious, the ethical antithesis of his father; he later found his name a handicap when he sought to earn an honest living.

But the axe was about to fall on Capone's empire, and what the good citizens of Dade had failed to accomplish, the government was about to do for them. Indicted on charges of income tax evasion, Capone was tried in Chicago and convicted in October 1931. Bribes of thousands of dollars, threats against tax investigators, even bought jurors, all failed the czar. A stunned Capone was sentenced to serve 11 years, most of it at the tough, disciplinary federal island, Alcatraz.

His fortune mostly depleted, his health and nervous system shattered from a venereal disease contracted from his blonde teenage mistress, and his old organization destroyed, Capone was released from jail in 1939. He returned to his wife at the Palm Island home, remaining here in almost total isolation—a virtual mental and physical invalid—until his death, at 48, on January 25, 1947.

The most brutal and ingenious criminal organizer in U.S. history had finally succumbed, his passing almost unnoticed. But the ghost of Al Capone seems at times to still haunt Miami Beach today as other "boosters" also seek to "revive its ailing economy." One can almost see the perennial sardonic smile on the late czar's visage.

On August 7, 1965, Albert Francis "Sonny" Capone, while shopping in a Kwik Chek market at Hollywood, Florida felt a sudden impulse to pocket two bottles of aspirin and a box of radio batteries, value $3.50, items he neither wanted nor needed. When queried by the judge, after his arrest, the saddened Sonny could not explain why he took the items, except to say: "Everybody has a little larceny in him, I guess."

The following year, Albert Francis Capone, only son of Alphonse Capone, officially changed his name, and has not been seen in the area since.

23.
He Narrowly Missed Killing FDR

Giuseppe Zangara tried to kill President Franklin Roosevelt. But a larger crime may have been committed against the justice system.

His ailing stomach was acting up again, but, even so, the thin, small figure strode purposefully down North Miami Avenue, as if under a compulsion that hardly seemed his own.

He finally turned into a pawn shop and briefly scanned the lethal items on display. Then he laid eight dollars on the counter and walked out with a "Saturday night special"—a .32 caliber pistol that would indeed mark a special day in history.

Nevertheless, 33-year-old Giuseppe Zangara would miss his momentous target—U.S. President-elect Franklin D. Roosevelt—in Miami's Bayfront Park nearly half a century ago. Instead, his frantic shots would claim the life of Chicago Mayor Anton J. Cermak, and wound five others.

Providentially, the nation was spared a tragic calamity that February 15, 1933. Yet the event itself would overshadow, even as it generated, a somewhat grimmer epilogue. This was the "lynch mob" atmosphere in which this obviously possessed and demented little man was rushed to the electric chair at Raiford after two hasty, somewhat cursory, trials, leaving a stain on Dade County's justice system that lingers yet. It also still poses a provocative case study of the "stress point" of a democracy's judicial system, to wit: under an irresistible force of inflammatory mob pressure, at what point does the immoveable object of judicial integrity give way and dissolve into the very state of mind it has vitally sworn to resist. It is a question that has challenged legal minds perhaps since the days of Hammurabi but it is as viable as ever today.

It was a pleasant, almost summery night that February 15, and by 9 p.m. some 20,000 persons—sitting and standing—were crowded around the bandstand shell at Miami's downtown Bayfront Park. FDR, who would take office March 4, had just returned from a fishing vacation. He would speak briefly and then ride in a motorcade to the train station for a scheduled trip home to New York. About 160 lawmen dotted the park and parade route and 20 motorcycle policemen surrounded FDR's open-topped car parked in front of the bandstand. The polio-crippled President-elect gave his brief talk sitting on top of the back of the seat, using a hand-held mike.

Among notables on the bandstand was Mayor Cermak who on a reform ticket had just defeated Chicago's notorious William "Big Bill" Thompson. Though on vacation, Cermak hoped to talk briefly with FDR, a personal and political friend, before the latter left. Cermak had recently vowed to destroy Al Capone and his gangs and, consequently, had ordered a bullet-proof vest to be ready on his return home. He cold not foresee that the vest might have saved his life that night.

Zangara was a tiny man (five feet, one inch, 105 pounds), and few noticed him burrow his way into the second row of bench seats and sit next to Mrs. W. H. Cross, a Miami doctor's wife. He was exactly 30 feet from Roosevelt's car.

His talk ended, Roosevelt chatted briefly with his friend, Cermak; then the latter turned to leave. Bob Clark, chauffeur and secret service man, then started the engine, preparing for departure. Suddenly Roosevelt bent far over from the back seat to examine a telegram just brought to him. It was a fortuitous change of posture for, at that moment, he heard what he mistook for "firecrackers."

When Mrs. Cross had stood up on the bench to get a better view, Zangara had quickly stood up also and fired his first shot. Seeing the gun, Mrs. Cross screamed for help and then grabbed Zangara's forearm, pushing it upward. But the assailant turned his wrist downward and continued firing until the last bullet was expended. By this time, a host of lawmen and bystanders were on top of him. One grabbed his pistol; others tried to choke him. People clawed most of his clothing away as he was dragged to a motorcade car. In the pandemonium of shrieks and sirens, men and women screamed: "Kill him! Kill him!"

Two persons were slightly grazed by the bullets, but Cermak and Mrs. Joe Gill, wife of the president of Florida Power & Light Company, were struck in the abdomen. William Sinnott, formerly a personal bodyguard for then-Governor Roosevelt, had a bullet partially lodged in his head. Clark, the driver, had his hand skimmed by a shot that might have struck Roosevelt had he not bent over. Mrs. Gill and Sinnott recovered but Cermak would die 19 days later, March 6, from peritonitis and complications.

Roosevelt himself displayed the calm executive presence that would so reassure a troubled nation in the austere years ahead. When Clark started driving away after Secret Service men shouted at him to "Get out of the crowd," Roosevelt, who had turned to see Cermak doubling up and Mrs. Gill collapsing, ordered Clark to stop. The President-elect then refused to leave until Cermak had been placed in the back seat with him and the other injured put in another car. He then ordered the motorcade directly to the city hospital. Roosevelt later related: "He [Cermak] was alive, but I was afraid he would not last. I got my hand on his pulse and found none." But minutes later the pulse returned. "For three blocks I actually believed his heart had stopped. I remember, I said, 'Tony, don't move. Keep quiet.' It seemed like 25 miles to that hospital." Roosevelt stayed at the hospital, visiting the injured persons, each of whom—except Cermak and Mrs. Gill—were only slightly hurt and released soon after. He would not leave for New York until next day, after learning that Cermak's condition was "stable."

The prisoner, meanwhile, had been whisked to a private 24th-floor cell in Miami's skyscraper jail downtown. Sheriff Dan Hardie, who spoke some Italian, had ordered the prisoner stripped naked during his night-long interrogation. A sketchy portrait of the excited, often incoherent, assassin emerged.

Zangara came to the United States from Calabria, Italy, in 1923. He had served in the Italian army, on the Austrian front, in World War I. THere he developed an intense hatred of the army, which he later transferred to "all ruling figures." He said he once tried to shoot Italian King Victor Immanuel, at Naples, but a packed crowd blocked his access. Later, in the U.S., he briefly plotted an attempt on President Herbert Hoover but changed his mind when he learned that Roosevelt would be coming to Miami. A now naturalized citizen, Zangara came to Miami in 1932. Outwardly, he led a quiet life, working at his bricklayer trade. Though he expressed also a hatred of "capitalist crooks," he had no affiliation with any radical groups. In fact, he was a registered Republican. But his demonically-tortured mind continued to seethe with hatred toward "ruling figures," an obsession which in some twisted fashion he related to his chronic stomach pains. (Later, his autopsy revealed a diseased bladder, with complications.)

Zangara displayed every classic symptom of a deranged man—a mental incompetent who legally should have been committed under statutes relating to the criminally insane. Yet out on the city's street corners, ugly rumblings of "lynch talk" bandied freely about, even from respectable sources. A prominent ex-mayor's wife boasted she would gladly shoot Zangara personally, and even the staid *Miami Herald* shrieked editorially: "Get his kind off the earth." Yet at times, some of this crowd rancor seemed more concerned with how this wretched figure had sullied the city's "image" than with any administration of justice per se.

The judge in the first trial appointed three reputable local attorneys to defend Zangara. They filed routine, technical motions, relating only to the degree and definition of his crimes, but made no moves to examine him. They themselves ruled their client "sane." Zangara pleaded guilty to four counts of attempted murder and was sentenced to 80 years, 20 years on each count, consecutively. In an unusual move, the judge had appointed a commission of psychiatrists to examine Zangara, but with the odd stipulation that they were to make no determination of his competence. Nevertheless, the doctors did describe the defendant as a "psychopathic personality."

The judge even refused at first to question the defendant prior to sentencing, until one defense attorney persisted. As to his motives, Zangara replied: "All the time my mind is in my stomach . . . . When I get in trouble in my stomach, when it come, my head look like I am gone. You see I suffer all the time and I suffer because my father send me to work when I was a little boy—spoil my life. If I no suffer, I have no trouble. I kill no President. It get in my mind—capitalists make trouble to the poor people." Again: "I decide to kill him (FDR) and make him suffer. I want to make it 50-50 . . . I got to kill, that is all." After sentencing: "Judge, don't be stingy. Give me hundred years."

Justice—within five days—had never moved so swiftly; it would move even more swiftly. The morning Cermak died, an autopsy was quickly performed, a coroner ruled, a grand jury convened, and an indictment was returned and filed in the clerk's office, all before 5 p.m. that same day. Zangara pleaded guilty to first degree murder and Judge Uly O. Thompson sentenced him to the electric chair March 9. At the sentencing Zangara said: "Well, I no scared of electric chair because I was thinking I was right to kill the president, . . . and you is a crook man because the crook man put me in the electric chair."

Sheriff Hardie (who later was removed from office for some extra-legal activities), insisted on taking Zangara to Raiford and remaining to watch his execution. He also insisted on taking a state National Guard detail of machine-gunners to guard the tiny prisoner. Governor David Sholtz had hastily signed a death warrant (without any review) and Zangara was executed March 20. This swift sequence, from Cermak's death to execution, took only 14 days.

Entering the execution room, Zangara shook himself free of his guards, saying "I no scared of electric chair. I show you," and walked swiftly to the chair and sat down. A steady rain beat on the room's gray windows and, while strapped in, Zangara stared at the 30 spectators outside and taunted: "No movies, hey? Where the camera to take my picture? Lousy bunch crooks." And then, his final words: "Addio to all the world. Pusha the button."

One may or may not conclude today that Zangara's trial and execution constituted a hasty "legal lynching." Nevertheless, the questionable legal processes, the inflammatory influences, and the rush to execution, all must certainly render the case a classic study for those legal minds concerned with searching out the "stress points" in the judicial fabric of any free society.

24.
The Denouement of "Bloody" Ed Watson

His hired hands were paid off with a knife in the back— until angry neighbors shot him down.

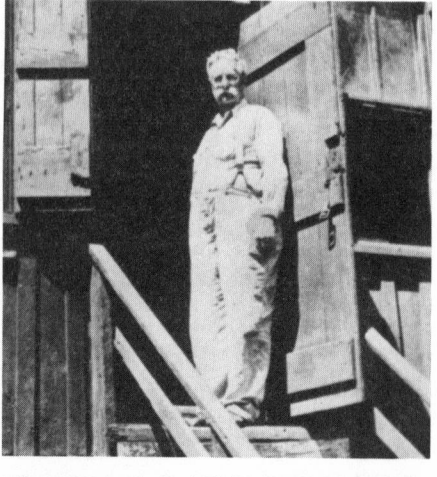

Postmaster C. S. "Ted" Smallwood on the steps of his postoffice/store where Bloody Ed got his supplies . . . and finally got his due.

Folks who lived around Chokoloskee in southernmost Collier County back in the 1890s always thought it strange that Ed Watson's hired help rarely seemed to return at the season's end from his Chatham Bend island plantation, one of the Ten Thousand Islands.

Stranger still, he seemed to have quite an employee turnover through the years. But then, Watson was a stranger sort himself, and in that wild, isolated frontier country, it was never healthy to inquire too closely of a neighbor's business, especially in the area that attracted so many of the fugitive and lawless types.

But when "Bloody" Ed Watson died in 1910 at the hands of those same neighbors, about 50 skeletons were uncovered near and around his island home (no count known of watery Gulf graves), and the strangeness became grimly less so.

Watson, one of the most notorious figures ever to haunt Florida's west coast, had devised a unique "payroll savings plan" for his employees—he would simply withhold their pay and save it for himself. After all, they would not need it, since he had also instituted a sort of mandatory "early retirement plan." When all the produce had been picked and packed, when all the cane had been cut and boiled in his 80-gallon kettles and the syrup packed in tins for his lucrative cane syrup commerce, Watson would just quietly and methodically "do in" each worker, by knife or gun, bury them, and then get a new crew. The NLRB today would certainly frown upon such labor relations but Old Ed found it very convenient; in fact he prospered mightily for almost 20 years in this manner.

Born in Edgefield County, South Carolina, Edgar J. Watson possibly inherited his savage nature from his father, "Ring-Eye" Lige Watson, a one-time penitentiary warden who came by his nickname from a circular knife wound around his eye incurred in one of his many fights. The mother fled the brutal husband, taking young Ed and his sister Minnie to relatives in Columbia County, near Lake City, Florida.

Here Ed later married, rented a farm and then lost it after being disabled with a busted kneecap after a tavern scrape. The disgruntled youth then took his wife west to Arkansas and, reportedly, met the bawdy female outlaw, Belle Starr, with whom he had some dubious "business" dealings. But they soon became bitter antagonists. Shortly afterward, the lady was fatally "bushwacked" on a lonely trail, in February 1889. Her assailant was never known, but Watson was rumored to be one of those under suspicion.

His wife having died previously, Watson soon returned to Lake City and remarried. He got into a few scrapes again and finally wandered down to the Ten Thousand Islands where he was able to purchase the Chatham Bend Key for $250 from the widow of an outlaw who had recently been shot.

Charles S. "Ted" Smallwood, postmaster and owner of the general store at Chokoloskee where Watson got many of his supplies, recalled first meeting Watson at nearby Half Way Creek in 1891. Watson had just fled from a murder scene, himself unscathed and unidentified, after knifing a man named Quinn Bass at Arcadia.

After settling in at Chatham Bend, Watson returned briefly to Lake City. Here he got into a quarrel with a Sam Toland. He shot him. Ed narrowly avoided a hanging party on this occasion and his trial had to be moved to Jacksonville. He was acquitted, mostly for lack of evidence. But Captain W. H. Towle, who helped pick the jury, reportedly warned Watson: "Now you get back to the Ten Thousand Islands as fast as you can—and stay there."

"Bloody" Ed did just that, and it was not long before he had his fertile little island lush with cane crops, produce, and the valuable buttonwood, cords of which he shipped to Key West. His cane syrup was a popular product and he shipped tons of it in his 70-foot schooner to Fort Myers and to dealers such as Bryan and Snow of Tampa.

Although his peculiar labor practices were still of a covert nature, such a demonic proclivity could not always be concealed, such as in one violent encounter with Adolphus Santini, a member of a pioneer Collier County family. The pair met in an auction room in Key West one day and exchanged heated words; whereupon, Watson attacked Santini and cut his throat. Bystanders finally got Ed's weapon away before he could further display his knifemanship and, Smallwood recalls: "I think that scrape cost Watson nine hundred dollars."

Another time, two "squatters" who balked at moving from a small key owned by Watson were found dead one day near their camp. No one knew the culprit but, by this time, area settlers just naturally suspected Watson.

Watson was, naturally, very cautious in hiring help, usually going long distances to Fort Myers or Tampa. One scribe recalls: "He evidently picked his labor with an eye to whether or not they had anyone who would inquire too closely about them." They were usually transient men, and only single or widowed women. Then, either when the work was done or they became too insistent about their wages, he would kill them, mostly alone and singly. They were then buried either near the mangroves or, often, dumped into the Gulf. Those curious about the irregular labor turnover just remained silent, due either to the mind-your-business code of the area or else to reluctance to tangle with one of the trigger-temper and pure meanness of "Bloody" Ed.

Some early Tampans remembered Watson, not always pleasantly.

A drunken Watson one day wandered into Tampa's old Knight and Wall hardware store and overheard John T. Campbell, the bookkeeper, relating an anecdote to fellow workers about a recent incident at a dancing school. Suddenly Watson drew a large pistol from his belt and fired a shot near Campbell's foot, exclaiming: "Well, let's see how nice you can dance." One of the scattering coterie quickly summoned police, and Watson was jailed overnight.

Early Tampan W. Fred Ferman recalls a less comical episode when G. W. Dean, a Tampa postmaster and real estate dealer, met Watson at Sanibel Island to inspect some large land tracts in Collier County that Watson was offering at attractive prices. The pair set out by boat to inspect the tracts and, when some distance offshore, Watson asked Dean if he had brought his money with him, Dean replied that he had all his money in a Fort Myers bank and would pay for the property by check if he thought it a good investment. On pretext, Dean then told Watson to take him over to Fort Myers and he would draw out his cash for any purchases. But, once ashore, Dean made a rapid departure for Tampa. He later told Ferman he was convinced Watson would have killed him and dumped him overboard had he taken his money with him.

And yet Watson could apparently turn on the charm when he so chose. A Punta Gorda pioneer, J. F. Corbett, met Watson and his wife once on a train trip to Tampa and briefly recalled: "They seemed to be delightful people, sharing a fine lunch with us."

But finally the days were numbered for Watson's evil island of horrors. As if in some wrathful portent, the great hurricane of 1910, which sideswiped Collier County and caused no little flood and rain damage, signaled

the end. It came shortly after when a young black boy fled the island in terror, racing over river, swamp, and sawgrass, to reach a group of farmers,
clamdiggers, and herdsmen near Chokoloskee. The frightened boy bore witness to a gruesome murder by Watson, after which the boy had been threatened also, but managed to escape. The boy's story seemed to galvanize at
once all the long-smoldering distrusts and suspicions of Watson into a tight
resolve by the settlers. Watson was not on the island when a "posse" of the
men arrived at the scene: the boy then guided them to a freshly dug grave
from which protruded an unusually large human leg. Watson apparently had
difficulty managing the huge 300-pound frame of the woman known as Han-
nah Smith. Either he did not see the leg uncovered in the darkness or else
rigor mortis had somehow raised the limb. The men brought the body back
to Chokoloskee—and waited. They figured Watson would be coming into
Smallwood's store next day, his routine supply day.

It is not known whether, upon his return, Watson discovered the disin-
terment of his last victim. But he headed for Smallwood's store next day on
schedule, a loaded shotgun lying in the bottom of his boat. (Watson did not
realize that, the day after the storm, Mrs. Smallwood had sold him, wit-
tingly or unwittingly, some water-damaged shells, useless). Previously, during the tense hours, Mrs. Watson had come in to stay with Mrs. Smallwood.

Smallwood himself recalls that he went up to his house behind the store
to look after the two women. "There was a crowd gathering at my landing
and I supposed there would be something doing when Watson got there," he
later wrote. "I could hear his boat coming down the pass and I did not want
any [part] of it." Later, "we heard guns going off and I heard Mrs. Watson
say, 'My God, they have killed Mr. Watson!' "

A witness reported that Watson, when informed that they were going to
"take him in" for murder, cursed them and came forward with his shotgun.
But the dampened shells failed to fire in the seconds before a flurry of gunfire
felled "Bloody" Ed.

Watson's body was carried to Rabbit Key and buried there, and the settlers involved were all summoned to Fort Myers for an official inquiry. They
were all released without charges and, a short time later, Watson's grisly
island graveyard was uncovered.

"Bloody" Watson had indeed earned his nickname—and his fate as
well.

25.
Eccentric Prince Murat Dazzles Tallahassee

Forced to flee the royal French courts, Napoleon's nephew found his place in the rude huts of the Florida frontier.

The prince found Miss Kate's slipper a convenient cup.

From the glittering courts of Europe to the muddy, mosquito-ridden log cabins of frontier Florida in the 1820s came Napoleonic exile Prince Achille Murat, to dazzle, eccentrically bemuse, and somewhat honor ante-bellum Tallahassee society for nearly a generation.

Finding room for a "free spirit" in his newly-adopted land, the 22-year-old prince disdained comfortable refuge for the pioneer existence of the Tallahassee frontier when it was little more than "a few Indian hog-pens." And, as if to seal the devotion he felt to the young republic, he soon after married the great-grandniece of that country's "father," George Washington. But he never quite severed his Old World loyalties from the New World's promises, and this star-crossed allegiance would plague him until his death in 1847.

When Murat's Uncle Napoleon was toppled at Waterloo and the oppressive forces of reaction under the iron hand of Metternich began to recarve the continental kingdoms like so much royal pie, Bonapartists of any kind were lucky if they escaped the fate of some like Achille's father, the renowned Napoleonic General Joachim Murat, King of Naples, who was shot. It was only because of his exiled mother, Queen Caroline, Napoleon's sister, that Metternich (a former lover of Caroline), allowed the young prince to leave Europe.

Two other Bonapartists, Murat's uncle Joseph and cousin Jerome, had wisely slipped away from the continent earlier to settle in affluent, if not baronial splendor in New Jersey. But, after a brief sojourn in St. Augustine, and at the insistence of his friend, General Richard Keith Call, Achille entered into a land partnership with another friend, Colonel James Gadsden, and set up his first plantation, "Lipona" just west of Tallahassee, in 1825.

He cleared the land, built a one-room log house in which he slept on a moss mattress and, in spite of privations, delighted in the primitive backwoods living and its freedom. His enthusiasm for America was unabated. "It is the American Union which gives us the best model of government . . . a nation the most reasonable, the most sensible," he would write to European friends. "What astonishes me is that every other nation is not governed in the same manner."

Area citizens such as Territorial Governor William P. Duval, Call, John Gamble and the Bellamy brothers had been disappointed that Murat's fellow countryman, General Lafayette, had never settled on the township grant the U.S. had given him in the Florida capital to reward his services under General Washington. But they felt that Murat's famous name would certainly help lure a few new pioneer settlers. They delighted in the young prince's energetic bouyancy, intelligence, and eccentric humor. He was equally amused to describe his new life to friends in Europe, imagining their chagrin at describing, in contrast to their marble halls of state, a high meeting of state between Governor Duval and Gadsen, dressed in coarse deerskin, seated over a rough table and dining on salt pork and apple jack as they discussed Indian problems.

But by this time, the area already had over 100 houses, 300 inhabitants and a newspaper, where 18 months before it was only a forest. As with any frontier, the feminine element was sparce but soon enhanced by the arrival of a 23-year-old widow, Catherine Daingerfield Willis Gray, great-grand-niece of George Washington, with her parents and family from Virginia. A close friend attributed to Kate a "noble, generous, and gentle heart, enchanting face and form . . . modest in demeanor and gifted with a readiness of wit," charms that could hardly elude an ardent Gallic temperament. During their first meeting, alone beside a spring at a picnic, Murat toasted his suit for her hand by removing her slipper, filling it with wine, and draining it. The social world buzzed over the courtship; many approved but some felt a "first family" lady was marrying down into "dubious royal status." Even Achille's personal habits entered assessment. He seldom changed clothes and boasted of rarely removing his boots. He had unusual culinary tastes and once served some unaware guests a roast buzzard. His untidy tobacco chewing was hardly less obnoxious for his using a large, shaggy pet dog for a spittoon.

But true love prevailed, and the heirs of the two most popular French and American heroes of the time were wed in July 1826. The pair were "extremely happy," Murat wrote. As mistress of "Lipona," Kate made the plantation one of the most popular in Tallahassee with dinners and other socials. The crude log home was greatly enlarged but still the silken linens with coats of arms and the golden spoons with Napoleon's crest must have struck a bizarre note in the primitive setting.

The prince soon picked up a new title—Colonel—after joining an expedition with General Call against some marauding Indians, even though they captured no Indians in this "petty parody of war." Later, he journeyed to New Jersey to introduce his wife to the other Bonapartes. On the way, he met and became the friend of a young American philosopher, Ralph Waldo Emerson. Although an atheist, so taken was Murat with Emerson's Unitarian doctrine that he invited the latter to set up such a church at Tallahassee. Their friendship would later fall out in the gathering storm over the slavery issue. For all of his vaunted belief in human freedom, Murat found slavery too convenient and remunerative to expand his egalitarian empathy to a black brother. He believed the "natural altruism" of the master would gradually remove this condition. (But he drew no lines at egalitarian intimacy with his black sisters, and so demonstrated on more than one occasion.)

While his cotton and cane were growing, Murat studied law and was admitted to practice, accepting the crudities of frontier justice, so often determined by knife and gun, for the "pure theatre" of the courtroom with its "tragedy, farce, and comedy." He once also dabbled in a more dubious pastime of the day—dueling. In a tiff over a hog theft with a Judge McComb, the Prince got half his little finger shot off while Murat's own bullet merely passed through the Judge's shirt "and scared out the lice."

The Colonel's general appearance to his neighbors seemed less than royal if one accepts a description of the time in the *New Yorker* magazine. "He [Murat] might be met in the woods, on a lean horse, dressed in the common homespun of the country, with a long whip in his hand, hunting cattle, with the outward style of what is known in that country as a Cracker."

But, in reality, this "Cracker's" heart had never left Europe and when, in 1830, it seemed that France's monarchy might tumble, Murat hocked his plantation and with Kate in tow, hastened to London. Although he echoed romantic sentiments of liberating France with democracy, his more realistic interest lay in pressing his mother's claim against that government to release their impressed fortune of several million francs. But Metternich was still in tight control and every continental door was barred to him. After nearly three years of frustrated political effort, in which his only success was the publication of his very perceptive but often highly prejudiced sketches: *America and the Americans,* he returned to his neglected plantation; it had gone to seed and would mark his downward turn in fortune.

Over the next years, he served by appointment as a Jefferson County Judge and also sought election to the territory's Legislative Council. He lost, after collapsing into fever from days of horseback politicking under the blistering August sunshine, plus an overdose of his favorite "health diet" of milk and whiskey.

He also joined the wildcat financial speculation that swept the country during President Jackson's second term. He again hocked his properties to buy stock in the newly-formed—and ill-fated—Union Bank of Tallahassee and became giddy at the prospect of "paper riches." He even wandered over to New Orleans, bought a large sugar plantation "on paper" and even sought to speculate in Texas real estate, expecting, erroneously, its early admission to the Union which would rocket its land values. Then came disaster.

The great Panic of 1837, which devastated the country's business, banking and factories, also wiped out the Murats. Tallahasseeans even faced a real food shortage and were fortunate to come by a little "black bread and stinking shoulders of wire-grass beef," as one of them put it.

The prince was forced to move to a smaller plantation and, when his Queen Mother died in 1839, he once more went to Europe to press his claim to the Bonaparte fortune, and once more failed. His remaining years passed uneventfully and at subsistence levels. He was often forced to depend on help from close friends up until his death, from a chronic recurring childhood illness, at age 46, in 1847.

Ironically, a political crisis in France months later restored the Bonapartes to rule again, when Achille's first cousin, Louis Napoleon Bonaparte III, became Emperor. Louis did not forget the good and fair Kate and bestowed upon her all of the claims her husband had so vainly sought, along with the title of "Princess." She remained a prosperous, successful, and popular plantation owner in Tallahassee until her death in 1867.

And this at least would surely have pleased the Cracker-Prince, whose torn loyalties to two different worlds left him successful in neither.

26.
Florida's Dubious Dynasty: The Porkchop Gang

For generations, a feudal patronage system made lawmaking a futile business.

They were like latter-day feudal barons, spawned in the red clay of North Florida's cotton country, where, amid tobacco, pork back, and moonshine, a half century ago they commenced a reign over the rest of the state that any medieval monarch might have envied.

They were "the Pork Chop Gang"—truly a mutation of representative government—for they represented more pine trees than people and, with control of less than 15% of the state's population, they could elect and control a majority of the state legislature. Once in place, their colorful, turbulent—and devastating—grip on state government would not be entirely broken for nearly four decades. Meanwhile, they ladled out the "red-eye" gravy of patronage and politics with brazenness and flair, while their "lamb chop" counterparts in the more populous southern counties fumed in frustration as they watched their share of state needs getting pickled in the North Florida pork barrel.

It was all made possible by an archaic constitutional Catch-22. Florida's antiquated 1885 constitution (revised only in the last decade) decreed that, regardless of population, each county could have no more than one senator and no more than three representatives, and that the Legislature alone had the power to apportion either house's districts. Naturally, the "good ole barons" were not about to vote to unseat themselves or lessen their power. Thus, the undisputed pork chop king, Senator Scott D. Clarke, a Monticello banker, could perpetuate his oligarchy, often with fewer than 400 voters in his tiny, single-county district of Jefferson. Dade County, with more than 100 times that number of voters, still had one senator.

Nor were pork choppers unduly timorous about wielding their golden keys to the state coffers, especially during the Great Depression when they found ample means to console suffering friends and relatives. Highway monies were poured into capacious road building projects even though those roads might often lead only to swamp or a crossroads hamlet. A state hospital would find its convenient way into the Senate president's district (far from the population centers), and other critical funding needs would emerge suddenly somewhere within that 400-mile North Florida strip during annual legislative sessions.

Indeed, more often than not, pork choppers awaited the spring sessions as fun time as they flocked into the stately halls of the antebellum-style old Capitol. Amid the festooned mounds of Cherokee roses or waxy camellias, they eagerly anticipated the ritualized rounds of free meals, thoughtful gifts, free-flowing liquor, the rollicking "caucus" weekends at private resorts and the usual stable of comely Cuban girls imported for the session, all generously provided by a host of special interest groups.

The pork choppers in turn proved duly grateful for these thoughtful attentions by providing thoughtful legislation on behalf of these interests. This was never more graphically revealed than in the state regressive tax structure, as one historian noted. There was no income tax, no state property tax, no corporate income tax, and no severance tax on natural resources. There were few, if any, demands on taxes from paper mills, banks, insurance, citrus, mining or timber companies. Yet hardly a voice dissented when a three-cent sales tax was imposed on the general public.

Any "lamb chop" bills designed to reform or change social and fiscal inequities rarely survived a pork chop "killer" committee. Here a "killer" chairman like, say, Marion B. Knight, merely had to sit alone in a room, his pockets stuffed with proxy votes from absent members and quietly vote such legislation into oblivion. Dempsey Barron once expressed the chopper social conscience on a critical urban renewal bill by claiming "you could make a good argument that we need some slums in America" to give people an idea of what they could "work up to."

It seemed significant, too, that demands for reapportionment reform never came from industry or big business, even though most of them were based in populous metro areas. But the prevailing credo here might have been summed up by the late Ed Ball, trustee of the billion-dollar du Pont empire. Asked why he opposed reapportionment, Ball replied: "Suppose you get a governor with a lot of hog-wild schemes—you've got to have a legislative block that will keep a check rein on the big counties."

Yet one colorful pork chopper took memorable exception to the pine-tree-power code. Beneath a folksy exterior enriched with Elizabethan eloquence and humor, Fuller Warren, a Rooseveltian populist, possessed a dedicated and cosmopolitan political instinct. Becoming governor in 1949, he enraged chopper colleagues by courageously endorsing "fair reapportionment" and strongly castigated that "band of willful men" who blocked it. He fought the sales tax (unsuccessfully) and instituted a number of reforms over powerful opposition from citrus, cattle, and timber interests. To historian Gloria Jahoda, he brought to state government "an innocent and honorable joy that antedated the present era of country-club candidates."

But the end of the pork chop reign did not come suddenly. It was a slow, often bitter, piecemeal struggle, beginning with untiring efforts in 1955 by one of the state's most distinctive governors, LeRoy Collins. Legislators so diluted his reform amendment, however, that it was defeated at the polls. Nevertheless, his efforts gave rise to several redistricting efforts until the U.S. Supreme Court's "one man, one vote" ruling in 1967 forced a massive statewide reapportionment. This finally gave the large counties an effective voice in both houses and ushered in a decade of progressive reform culminating with Governor Reubin Askew's two terms in the 1970s.

Still, many authorities, like Manning J. Dauer, political science chairman at the University of South Florida, today question the effectiveness of reapportionment and see a reassertion of economic dominance by special interests in Tallahassee. Dauer notes that the rise of two-party politics has initiated a new kind of polarization, along with a strong conservative shift, notably in the "urban conservative horseshoe" (up the East Coast and then across the state at Orlando to St. Petersburg and down the West Coast to Naples—excepting Miami and Tampa). Since pork-chopism is not rural in character but only in origin, Dauer believes it may have simply assumed a more urban guise. A combination of high mobility, rootlessness, and fragmentation by thousands of mini-incorporated areas induces a kind of "alienation" among citizens from the larger urban needs around them as well as the broader common needs of the state in general, he believes. This absence of common public voice in government leaves the legislative doors open to the old rule by special interests.

The truth of these observations, of course, may await more definitive evidence. Nevertheless, even though the colorful, high-rolling days of pork chopism supposedly are gone forever, many observers insist that the pork chop spirit is still very much around, haunting both the Florida House and Senate, simply awaiting to reappear with a brand-new image.

27.
A Florida Boy Joins Lincoln's Assassins

Lewis Powell, known as Lewis Payne, was recruited by John Wilkes Booth in the conspiracy to kidnap President Lincoln. Powell-Payne was hanged for trying to kill Secretary of State Seward.

He was a rural boy from the rolling hills of Live Oak in north Central Florida. Local folks described him as a nice, well-behaved boy. None could have imagined that before he was 21 the boy would bring infamous attention to himself and to Live Oak, Florida, by sharing in a conspiracy that would stun the world, or that he would end up on a gallows.

Lewis Thornton Powell was the youngest son of a respectable Baptist minister, George Cader Powell, a farmer-blacksmith who had brought his wife, six daughters, and three sons from Georgia to a farm at Live Oak in the 1850s. They were a solid, industrious family. They were also pro-secession when the Civil War erupted. Young Lewis, over six feet tall, strapping and 17, joined with his two brothers in the Confederacy's Second Florida Infantry.

During his war service, it is believed Lewis first met John Wilkes Booth by invitation backstage after seeing the popular young actor in a play in Richmond. The war had induced in Lewis a sullen and taciturn nature, but the semiliterate youth was captivated by Booth's impressive manner and especially the actor's impassioned espousal of the Southern cause. They would, fatefully, meet again.

In 1863 Lewis was captured at Gettysburg, but he escaped shortly afterward, crossing Union lines to join Mosby's Rangers. Then, for unknown reasons, he deserted the Rangers and rode into Union lines. He swore allegiance to the Union under the newly assumed name of Lewis Payne, received parole and, garbed in civilian clothes, went to live in Baltimore.

In February 1865 Powell, now Payne, heard a familiar voice hail him. It was Booth. So mutual were their sympathies and attraction that Booth soon informed Powell of his daring plan to kidnap Lincoln and several cabinet members, whisk them to Richmond and ransom them for a peace settlement favorable to the South. At the Baltimore boardinghouse of Mrs. Mary Surratt, a widow, Lewis Payne finally met his co-conspirators: Mrs. Surratt, her son, John, Michael O'Laughlin, Samuel Arnold, George Atzerodt, and David Herold.

But the kidnapping plans were snagged several times, and by the time Lee surrendered to Grant in early April an enraged and frustrated Booth had decided he would simply kill the President. When he learned of Lincoln's forthcoming attendance at Ford Theatre, he summoned Payne to the boardinghouse and handed him a pistol and a bowie knife. At the moment Booth would approach Lincoln's theater box, Payne was to assassinate Secretary of State William Seward at his home, where Seward lay in sickbed recovering from injuries received in a carriage accident.

At 10 p.m. that fateful night of April 14, Payne, with Herold tending their horses a short distance away, knocked at the Seward residence and informed the servant, William Bell, that he had a package of medicine for Seward which he must deliver to the ailing man personally. Payne then pushed past Bell and stomped up the stairway where he was met at the top by Seward's son, Frederick. When the latter informed Payne that Seward was asleep and could not be disturbed, Payne turned, feigned to leave, then wheeled around with drawn revolver and fired at Frederick's head. The gun misfired, and Payne began to pistol-whip his victim, severely fracturing his skull. He then rushed into Seward's room, sent sprawling a soldier-nurse, George Robinson, hurled aside Seward's daughter, Fanny, and rushed to Seward's bed, slashing the prostrate man about the face and neck. Seward managed to roll off the bed, momentarily out of Payne's reach. Seward's other son, Major Augustus, was awakened in a nearby bedroom, rushed in and, with Robinson, grappled with the thrashing Payne. The excited assailant gave the Major's forehead several knife slashes before twisting free and dashing down the stairway. At the door Payne bumped into a messenger, Emerick Hansell, whom he stabbed in the back before racing to his horse. (Fortunately, all the victims recovered.)

Confused and lost on his way to the rendezvous with Booth, Payne was forced to hide in the woods for three days before he decided to head for Mrs. Surratt's boardinghouse. Disguised as a handyman laborer, he knocked on her door late on the night of April 17. He was met by federal officers who had just taken Mrs. Surratt and several others into custody. His excuse—that he had come to "dig a drain gutter" for Mrs. Surratt—was exposed when the widow, surprisingly, denied even knowing him. Payne was arrested at once and taken with the others to the provost marshal's headquarters where, several hours later, the servant Bell identified him as Seward's assailant.

John Wilkes Booth was later caught in a Virginia tobacco barn and fatally shot. Of the others, only Mary Surratt, Herold, Atzerodt, and Payne were found guilty of conspiracy and murder; they were given death sentences. The four were hanged together in Washington on July 7, 1865.

Powell's grief-stricken and ailing father had been unable to reach his son before execution day. In mournful humiliation he abandoned his Live Oak farm and removed his family to the then-remote wilderness of Jesup Lake near present-day Orlando. He would later establish several Baptist churches in the area. Gradually the Powell family overcame the tragedy and began to thrive; they would leave many descendants around Florida over future generations.

After their hasty departure from Live Oak, only one encounter with the Powell family is recorded. This was by popular historian Susan Bradford Eppes of Tallahassee, who found herself sharing a train seat one day with a sobbing elderly lady. As Mrs. Eppes attempted to comfort her, the lady turned a saddened, querulous face to her consoler and asked: "Chile, ain't you read the papers? Don't you know how them devils hung poor Mrs. Surratt and my boy, my baby boy? They said he had plotted to murder President Lincoln, my baby chile, who never had the heart to hurt nothing."

28.
When Palm Beach Courted Royalty

The titled heads of Europe found South Florida a whimsical wonderland in the twenties. So they moved in, in droves.

Of all the lavish social rituals and preoccupations that characterized that gold-plated barrier reef, Palm Beach, during the madcap Roaring Twenties, perhaps none was as excessive as its unabashed pursuit and acquisition of royalty.

The scramble for titled blue bloods—dukes, counts, princesses, lords or ladies—quickly became the touchstone of social supremacy among the gilded titans of oil, pharmaceuticals, corn flakes, soap, and railroads as they flocked each year to Henry Flagler's fabulous playground. No party, banquet or guestbook, however glittering, was complete if not graced with a baron, prince or duchess. Indeed, cultivation of the linear progeny of Bourbons, Hapsburgs, or Hohenzollerns became *de riguer* for any socially aspiring host or hostess. And to marry such a personage—one's name thus acquiring an instant royal prefix—was the pinnacle, the social *ne plus ultra*.

The twenties, of course, were propitious times for such courtier mentality. The "proud towers" of Europe's royal houses had toppled everywhere after World War I's devastation. Hard times fell painfully on royal heads; they suddenly found themselves to be quaint if superfluous pariahs (a few even reduced to waiting tables in the elegant restaurants in which they had once sumptuously dined). In short, it became increasingly difficult to strike a royal stance with your morning coat frayed at the cuff and collar or your bright medals and jewelry in hock.

But the international grapevine was as fast as Marconi's wireless telegraph; titles, it seemed, had become "collector's items" of a sort at an extremely wealthy American Riviera off the Florida coast. Thus was churned up a miniwave of immigrants who came to Palm Beach with their titles and manners intact, hoping to restore their lifestyles, if not their gold.

Soon enough, social fetes within the island's stately mansions were speckled with monocled, heel-clicking scions and imperious scionesses. By the mid-20s, Florida publisher John Perry Sr. would enthuse in print that there were "more titled people in Palm Beach than were ever concentrated in one spot before."

According to Palm Beach chronicler Alva Johnston, Joshua Cosden, the former streetcar-conductor-turned-oil-millionaire, was the first to discover the "one great social secret"—titled nobility. Cosden set out at once to "corner" the market on titles, wining and dining the Prince of Wales, Lord Louis Mountbatten and the rest of the Buckingham Palace set. His mansion, Playa Rienta, soon became the center of the social whirl. Thereafter, the market for titles became positively bullish; royal refugees found carte blanche favor waiting in every gilded foyer. As Princess Rospigliosi (herself elevated from plain Cincinnati-born Laura Stallo) said at the time: "They [royalty] just come down here, select the house they like, meet the hostess and move in." Pampered though they were, even "royalty" could be occasionally irksome. Palm Beach's social queen emeritus, Mrs. E. T. Stotesbury, for instance, became annoyed at the esoteric daily personal menu drawn up by her guest, Bulgarian Prince Cyril. He complained that she never had what he ordered. She is said to have replied with a smile, "Prince, you never order what I have." Mrs. Stotesbury's disdain for courtly fawning once left peers aghast when she refused to curtsy to the Earl and Countess of Athlone.

But generally the hospitality for the titled could be even more than effusive. In *The Last Resorts,* Cleveland Amory reports of one Palm Beach matron who, upon meeting a penniless marquis off the boat, inquired with unadorned directness the purpose of his visit. Nonplussed at first, the marquis admitted to his insolvency and frankly confided he had come over to look for a rich widow. "Look no further, Marquis," Amory quotes the lady.

The exclusive Everglades Club, not above shunning membership to even the wealthiest Palm Beach regulars, boasted such titled members as the Prince of Monaco, Prince Philip, Princess Alexandria, Grand Duke Nicholas, and the Duc du Richelieu. In time, the integration of the emigrés into the social milieu seemed complete when one observed at the clubs and salons such notable Palm Beach playgrounders as Tony Biddle, Peggy Joyce, Dudley Field Malone, Nancy Harriman, Bill Rockefeller, and even Flo Ziegfeld and "Hizzoner," dapper Jimmy Walker bantering amiably with regular luminaries like Countess Salm, Lord Ivor, Countess Bracatti, Princess Bibesco or the haughty Baroness de Cartier de Marchienne.

To lesser mortals dwelling on the mainland, however, much of this royal gushing somehow seemed ludicrous. In a then popular book on the land boom, *Florida,* author Kenneth Roberts deftly parodied Palm Beach social columnists: "Mrs. Lipstick Bubblewit was hostess to . . . the Princess Glukhose of Ptomania . . . Countess Blorp (whose father was L. Bunner Streek) . . . His Grace the Duke of Clutterfloor . . . etc."

But Palm Beach courtiers, unaware of or unfazed by such coarse jibes from the lower orders, eagerly embraced and patronized the newly adopted bluebloods. Once they even "retitled" one of their favorites when his government abruptly removed his title. While basking in the Palm Beach sun one day, the Maharaja of Baroda, who was forced to make do on a mere two million tax-free rupees a year ($400,000), decided to organize all the princes of India into a trade union. His Palm Beach social consorts thought it a splendid idea. Indian authorities did not. They took away his title and gave it to his son. Empathetic Palm Beachers promptly promoted and thereafter called the Maharaja, "Major General."

Curiously, despite the age-old magnetic orbit of power, wealth and nobility, many of the Palm Beach social set seemed hard put to explain the island's attraction to the titular personalities. Almost naively, social charmer and American-born Countess Dolly Dorelis (more exactly Countess Dolly Hylan Heminway Fleischmann O'Brien Dorelis) could remark: "Foreigners are irresistibly drawn here. I never could figure out why."

But if she herself did not personify an answer of some sort, one of her more authentic peers managed to summon up a forcefully explicit explanation. The seemingly sedate Rumanian Princess of Ghika was hired by flamboyant Palm Beach architect Addison Mizner to peddle real estate in his lavish boomtime Boca Raton project. She did well; sales at the project were brisk and her commission reached six figures. But payday was inexplicably delayed from week to week. Fuming, chomping at the royal bit, and doing so in a manner that seemed somewhat less than regal, she finally burst into Mizner's office one day and shouted: "Where's my money? If you think I'm in this goddamn plebian swamp for my health, you're crazy as hell!"

Crazy, indeed.

Heroes and Heroines

29.
The "Little Alamo" at Cape Florida

The Cape Florida Lighthouse at Key Biscayne was the scene of fire and violence in Florida's past.

Burned and wounded so painfully he tried to commit suicide, the lighthouse keeper held off a marauding Seminole war party.

The Cape Florida lighthouse still stands today on the southeast tip of Key Biscayne, its towering antiquity preserved to the memory of stormy and perilous early 19th-century seafaring.

Its beacon once guided many a storm-tossed bark past the treacherous Florida Reef—and away from the locustlike Florida "wreckers" who anxiously waited ashore to hear the eerie screech of splitting timbers, heralding another "salvage" prize. The silvery beam also led many a tempest-threatened vessel into the safety of "Hurricane Haven," as Biscayne Bay came to be known then.

But its most memorable and unique distinction in all the annals of American lighthouse history had nothing to do with wreckers, reefs, or the distresses of men and ships at sea—although its services here were certainly of measureless value.

The scene of its finest hour was on dry, sandy land, within the very tower itself, and one might view that concrete sentinel today as a monument to an unforgettable true tale of human suffering, endurance, and courage, when the Cape Florida lighthouse became Florida's fiery "little Alamo."

The decade following construction of the lighthouse, in 1825, was relatively peaceful for the handful of settlers who lived in the swamp and scrubland that is Miami today. The tower itself, standing 65 feet high with solid brick walls five feet thick at the base and two feet thick at top, seemed to hover over the area like some peaceful guardian for those on land or sea.

117

(Much later, a contractor's fraud would be discovered showing the walls to be hollow from top to bottom!)

But in 1835, the Second Seminole War had begun and Indians were on a rampage throughout the state, sharply focused by the tragic massacre, in December 1835, of Army Major Francis L. Dade and all but three of his 110-man contingent on their way to relieve Ft. King near Ocala. (On February 4, 1836, Dade County was officially created by the bay settlers.)

But aside from sporadic harassments, the Dade settlers had experienced no heavy attacks until March of that year when a savage assault was made in the area, with many killed. Lighthouse keeper William Cooley returned to the mainland to find his entire family massacred. The surviving villagers, some 60 souls, were all removed to an area near the lighthouse and, soon after, evacuated to Key West, a bereaved Cooley included.

However, two men volunteered to stay and maintain the lighthouse; assistant keeper John W. B. Thompson and his elderly Negro companion, Henry, who now comprised the only two residents in the entire county.

It was a quiet, peaceful afternoon that July 23, 1836, as Thompson stepped away from the kitchen of the keeper's dwelling house to return to the tower. Suddenly, from the corner of his eye, he caught a movement in the brush ahead and, turning quickly, spotted a band of Indians crouching barely 80 feet away. He called to Henry and the two dashed for the tower's entrance building, slamming and barring the door just as the marauders piled up against it. He then grabbed one of his three muskets and, while Henry loaded them, fired continuously from shack and tower windows until the horde—some fifty in all—scattered for cover. Thus he held them at bay until nightfall while an uneasy quiet ensued.

But the quiet darkness was shattered suddenly when the Indians poured a withering hail of lead into the wooden structure; the bullets pierced the tin tanks containing 225 gallons of whale oil, completely dousing the two men and their clothing while spreading over the wooden flooring. The Indians then set fire to the door and the oil-fed flames spread rapidly through the small building.

Thompson quickly grabbed a musket, some balls and a keg of powder and, with his friend, dashed to the top of the tower. He then went midway back down and hacked away at the lower half of the wooden staircase to prevent the savages from coming up. The section collapsed and he returned to the lantern room. The flames were roaring beneath but the pair had a temporary respite from the inferno.

But soon the crackling flames burst into the lantern room. The tower had become like an enormous flue and a solid pillar of flame shot upward.

"The savages at the same time began their hellish yells," Thompson recalled. "My poor friend looked at me with tears in his eyes but he could not speak." The two men then crawled out to the two-foot wide gallery platform. Here, crouched against the increasing heat of the metal rim, with bullets flying up from below and the lantern flames sending the lamps and glasses bursting and flying in all directions, the men faced the grim prospect of being literally roasted alive.

Moments later, the old man caught a bullet from below and, with a whispered cry of "I'm wounded," fell dead. Thompson, his clothes afire, and his "flesh roasting," decided to "put an end to my terrible suffering." He got up and heaved the keg of gunpowder down the scuttle, hoping to blow the tower to pieces and perhaps take a few savages with him, but the explosion merely shook the structure momentarily. "It had not the desired effect of blowing me into eternity, but it blew down the stairs and all the woodenwork near the top of the house and damped the fire for a moment."

But soon the flames blazed as fierce as ever. By now Thompson had received a half dozen wounds in his feet and leg from gunfire. His hair was afire and he had to beat it out with blistered hands. Half-crazed from the tortuous pain, the man soon had one thought only in mind. "I got up, went inside the iron railing, recommending my soul to God, and was on the point of going head foremost on the rock below, when something dictated to me to return and lie down again. I did so." Providentially or not, within moments, the flaming wood inside fell to the bottom of the tower and a sudden cool breeze wafted over the platform, giving merciful relief to a pain-racked body. Determined now to survive, the keeper found strength enough to take a piece of the blood-drenched trousers of his friend to erect a crude signal and then he lapsed into comalike sleep.

By morning, the Indians had given the stubborn white man up for dead and after looting and burning the keeper's house, some of them sailed away in the lighthouse sloop. The others left by foot up the beach as Thompson, now awake, watched them hazily through his fire-blurred vision. Attesting to the keeper's marksmanship, a good number of the group remained behind permanently.

Nevertheless, he related, "I was now almost as bad off as before, a burning fever on me, my feet shot to pieces, no clothes to cover me, nothing to eat or drink, a hot sun overhead, a dead man by my side, no friend near nor any to expect, and placed between 70 and 80 feet from the earth with no chance of getting down." He then passed out again and slept until late afternoon.

When he awoke, he dimly made out the image of two boats coming toward shore, one of them filled with a party of men, the other, somewhat resembling his sloop, towed behind. For one horror-struck moment, he thought the Indians were returning; but this feeling soon changed to a flooding joy as he made out the U.S. naval uniform.

Within a short time, a Captain Armstrong and his crew from the U.S. schooner *Motto* were busy trying to rescue the stricken keeper. After many attempts, however, it was not until the next morning that, by firing twine, attached to a ramrod, from a musket, they managed to get a tail block to Thompson. With much effort, he was able to secure it to a tower stanchion. Soon two seamen were aloft and, with a makeshift stretcher in tow, they managed to lower the keeper safely; he was soon on his way to a military hospital at Key West.

The captain explained that they had heard the powder-keg explosion 12 miles away; they later sighted the drifting sloop which the Indians had abandoned after stripping its sails. Thus the blast that had failed to end his torment, succeeded instead in saving his life. He also learned how close his foe had actually come to him. One of the raiders had decided to ascend the tower by inserting sticks horizontally inside and across the lightning rod which went up to the roof. He had gotten to within only a few yards of the platform when his weight pulled the rod out and away from the tower, sending him to his death.

Months later, the 42-year-old Carolinian had recovered enough to be moved to his home in Charleston, but not without lasting scars from his ordeal. He was last heard from at his home where he wrote: "Although a cripple, I can still eat my allowance and walk without the use of a cane."

Congress authorized rebuilding of the lighthouse, with most of the original foundation and structure intact, but due to continual Indian harassment, the work was not completed until 1846. Later, in 1855, the tower's height was increased from 65 to 95 feet. But it was after the blaze that officials discovered the hollow walls and how the contractor, Noah Humphreys, of Massachusetts, after swearing in statement under oath contrarily, had made a 50 per cent extra profit with the absent bricks.

The lighthouse was finally discontinued on June 15, 1876, when the deeper draft modern vessels required a lighthouse further out. Iron piles were driven right out at sea into the jagged shoals of Fowey Rocks, four miles southeast of Cape Florida, and the Fowey Rocks lighthouse came into operation.

But the original lighthouse has been preserved and the keeper's house restored in the present Cape Florida State Park, a fitting memorial to an heroic saga, written in blood and fire, by two dauntless keepers of the light.

30.
Peggy O'Neale:
"Scandalous" First Lady

*She may have been a First Lady, but gossip nearly ruined her
reputation in two cities.*

As first lady, she reigned over Florida with the same sprightly zest and informality that had won her the admiration (and unmerited censure) of the
nation's capitol city.

And yet, had she not been the wife of the state's territorial governor,
John H. Eaton (1834-36), she might have been about as welcome to Tallahassee social circles as Hawthorne's doubtful lady Hester Prynne.

For Mrs. Eaton was none other than the attractive, witty, vivacious former Peggy O'Neale, a vibrant figure in Washington circles before she was
30; she had also been the object of gossip so scandalous that it caused a vice
president to fall, a dark horse to succeed him, a national party to split, and
an entire cabinet to resign. Disconcerting affairs, to say the least. Moreover,
one prominent Tallahasseean (a future governor) must certainly have had
mixed feelings about her arrival, for he had once pressed his rough and ardo-
rous attentions upon the fair Peggy—and received not only her tearful rebuff
but a scorching rebuke from no less than the president of the United States,
Andrew Jackson.

Thus it was a delicate atmosphere for Florida's third First Lady, but the
city and the territory received her politely, and even warmly, and so especially did the wife of the aforementioned gentleman and would-be dallier.
But a few citizens still had reservations about Peggy and maintained a cool
and sniffish petulance where social amenities were concerned. Peggy herself
recalled her time in Florida as "beautiful." She wrote later: "My neighbors
were pleasant. I had no ugly passages . . . and I was away from my husband's
political persecutors. God help the woman who must live in Washington. To
me, Florida was the land of flowers as Washington had been the land of
briars." Her distinguished husband, too, may have prevented any briars from
blooming, for his vested powers were such as might silence wagging
tongues.

But what was the truth of Peggy Eaton's dubious reputation, one that
had stirred a furor of national proportions even as it altered the course of
history?

121

Margaret (Peggy) was born in Washington, D.C., in 1799, to William and Rhoda O'Neale, she was a devout Methodist and he a shrewd business-man whose Franklin House, offering rooms, food and drink, became almost a second home for members of Congress and other dignitaries. Conse-quently, the lively, attractive, flirtatious young woman grew up among some of the great and near-great of her day. After receiving formal education at an exclusive New York finishing school, she returned to Franklin House. She had developed a sharp, incisive mind and could argue politics with the kee-nest wits. She knew by name every man of consequence in Washington and soon became a confidante of senators, congressmen, and cabinet officers. Ultrafeminine, she yet preferred the company of men which, along with her presence in public houses (forbidden to women in those days), arched the eyebrows of the city's good ladies. Even though it was after all, her legiti-mate home, it did naturally give rise to every manner of bawdy speculation in a town where gossip and politics were almost synonymous. But under the watchful eye of her parents and taking full advantage of the obvious preven-tive of "safety in numbers," Peggy could easily deflect an untoward advance.

But at age 18, Peggy met John Timberlake, a tall, dark, and handsome young purser in the U.S. Navy, and her parents approved her marriage, in June 1817, to him. Meanwhile, two O'Neale house visitors were becoming good friends of the family—Andrew Jackson and John Henry Eaton. Jack-son, aware that unfounded gossip had plagued Peggy even after her mar-riage, praised her virtues in writing to his wife, calling her "kind, sweet, amiable . . . and much maligned," noting that "her grasp of the human nature is surprising in one so young." Eaton, too, was fascinated with Peggy and aided her husband in securing a purser's position on the *U.S.S. Consti-tution*. The couple by now had two baby daughters.

Eaton, Jackson's closest political confidante and friend, was one of the country's most distinguished senators (Tennessee). He had fought with Jack-son in the Indian Wars but was one of the most progressive men of his day—an Indian sympathizer, anti-slavery, free trade advocate, prison reformer, etc. While Timberlake was at sea, Eaton often escorted Peggy to official functions and occasionally took the entire family on carriage rides. Although this relationship was strictly proper, it only fueled the more salacious town gossipers. And this would give rise to the sordid incident involving the Tallahasseean.

Captain Richard Keith Call, a Jackson friend from the Indian Wars and now Florida's territorial delegate, was also a visitor at the O'Neale inn at this time and, incited by the gossip, formed a hasty opinion of Peggy. He was far removed from his future wife, Mary, whose parents had frowned on the captain's suit, and, finding Peggy alone in the parlor one day, seized her in his arms and tried to force her onto the settee. Peggy struggled in vain, but finally managed to grab some fireplace tongs with which to strike him and drive him from the room. Jackson returned later to find Peggy in tears. At last he forced the reluctant woman to tell him what had occurred. It was a grim Old Hickory who summoned Call to his suite that evening to proffer the man a stinging censure. Call admitted the incident, saying he thought her "a woman of easy virtue and familiar with others." What others, the general demanded. Eaton, Call replied. Did he have "any evidence" of this? The unhappy captain had none. Jackson later wrote his wife: "I gave him a severe lecture for taking up such ideas . . . unless on some positive evidence; he also felt sure that 'sober reflection would guard him [Call] from like improper conduct.' " But the humiliated captain was still quietly seething over both rebukes and later compounded his mischief, unbeknownst to Jackson by writing a friend, William B. Lewis, accusing Eaton again of having an affair with that "notorious" woman.

Later, Timberlake died at sea of a pulmonary disease and, a year later, just before Jackson's first-term inauguration in 1829, Eaton married Peggy.

Meanwhile, two factions with Jackson's party were beginning to draw lines in rivalry over the vice presidency in Jackson's second term, an almost guaranteed succession to the presidency. The rivals were John C. Calhoun, already vice president, and Martin Van Buren, secretary of state. Eaton, who had been named secretary of war, and Van Buren, were much closer to Jackson, while Calhoun's cabinet allies were navy secretary John Branch, treasury secretary Samuel D. Ingham, and attorney general John M. Berrien. Although the Calhouns had been socially cordial to the Eatons earlier, the climate had changed and the cabinet members' wives, influenced largely by Calhoun's patrician wife, Floride, suddenly found it politically advantageous as well as morally proper to snub Mrs. Eaton at all social functions. The gossip relating to the Eatons' adultery—even though unfounded—had now become intensified as Calhoun's partisans set in motion a complicated intrigue, through slanderous whispers, to discredit Eaton and, therefore, any influence he might have with Jackson that could favor Van Buren. But this devious plan backfired.

Jackson was ever-sensitive to such calumny; he had always believed that his beloved Rachael's death in December, 1828, was hastened by the vilification campaign against her over the technical legality of her divorce from her former husband. He leaped to Peggy's defense, challenged her detractors to offer evidence of her waywardness and, when they could not, soundly rebuked them. Jackson later initiated a full inquiry, in which the Eatons were finally cleared of any charges of misconduct, but not before he arranged to have Eaton and Van Buren, by agreement, resign their posts, making it easier for him to force the resignations of Branch, Ingham, and Berrien, which he did. In one stroke, a bitter Calhoun saw his ambitions doomed; Van Buren would now get the vice presidency and, later, become president.

This, then, was the background of Eaton's appointment to succeed Florida's governor, William P. Duval, who was returning to his Kentucky home after 12 turbulent years in the post.

Although she could be candid and forthright, it is indicative of her generosity and tact that Peggy, now a first lady herself, did not take advantage of her power over her former vilifier. In fact, when Call's wife, the former Mary Kirkman, first called upon her, she made every effort to leave her bed, though slightly ill and exhausted from her journey, to greet her, in order to avoid even a semblance of vindictiveness. Soon the two women—both young, attractive, bright, and spirited—became close friends. Call must possibly have been no little disturbed by this friendship at first, but Peggy kept her silence, Mary was none the wiser, and Call became duly grateful. Eaton, however, had to strain his forebearance. He maintained correct relations with Call, but the two never became friendly. Eaton's feelings were only slightly veiled in writing to the U.S. attorney general, questioning the wisdom of removing the Seminoles westward, labelling the removal treaty as "not valid or binding" and, with prophetic accuracy, cautioning against force as only a "last sad alternative." He then advised against the use of the Florida militia (in which Call was a prime leader), since "they will breed mischief." The real interests in Florida, he declared, were toward the Indians' legal lands, "on which the eyes of speculators are fixed." (Call had recently secured the headship of the local land office.)

Peggy enjoyed her Florida reign to the fullest. The climate had restored her somewhat flagging health and she made the most of social occasions, casting aside social taboos and enjoying the lively political and social discussions with the male guests. She took special efforts with the tutoring of her two daughters and, breaking another taboo for the 19th-century women, took them swimming often in the lake adjoining the governor's mansion. But, the relaxed frontier spirit was a far cry from Washington's social rigidities. If the First Lady of the Territory was slightly mad to swim in the lake, well,—it was her prerogative. By accident, she discovered that a suntan enhanced her natural beauty and, thereafter, took daily sunbaths, at a time when the sun's rays were considered harmful and no lady of quality went out without her parasol. On state business visits to Pensacola, a city still strongly under its early Spanish influence, she delighted in adopting Spanish dress for carriage outings and being mistaken for one of Spanish descent. (She was not then aware that the president would soon reward Eaton for his Florida service by making him ambassador to Spain, in 1836.)

On leaving Florida for their new post, it seemed almost in character that they should depart on a note of criticism. Both Eaton and his wife had always viewed slavery with great repugnance. They had found it distasteful that all the servants of the mansion staff were slaves. Therefore, just before she left, Peggy officially freed all seven blacks who served on her personal staff. The outcry over this act was so clamorous that Peggy must have chuckled quietly to herself all the way to Washington.

Thus, a triumphant Peggy returned to her hometown where the "dowdy frumps" who had so maligned her for political purposes now lay properly chastened at her feet. At least one of Florida's first ladies would now be long remembered, for better or ill, not only in Florida but American history as well.

31.
Osceola: The Seminole Patriot

*One of the colorful figures of Florida history fought to his death
to keep his people from the Trail of Tears.*

Osceola, the colorful Creek Seminole Indian leader who defiantly resisted
the U.S. Army in the Second Seminole War (1835–1842), was certainly
Florida's most celebrated Indian resident.

His spirited daring had also captured the imagination of a country—so
much so that when General Thomas S. Jesup betrayed a flag of truce to seize
and imprison the warrior, there was such an indignant public outcry that
Congress itself demanded a full probe of the incident.

When the Army told Osceola, in effect: "Go West, young man," the
chieftain retorted, in effect: "Go to blazes!", and then plunged his knife into
the document that called for westward emigration of the Seminoles. This
dramatic gesture rallied and united the Seminole tribes as no other single act
of war could have. Yet in the end it would cost him his life—not on the bat-
tlefield but in a dark fortress prison where he succumbed to acute tonsillitis.
And, aside from the legend surrounding this complex figure, all that
remained was his severed head, preserved and passed around by several doctors for some 28 years before it was consumed by fire in a museum in 1866.

Few white men knew Osceola, but various officers and others who came
into contact with him generally described him as of medium height, with
"an elastic grace of movement" to his lean and sinewy build. His face was
large-featured with prominent high cheekbones, but finely chiseled, a European influence which prompted some to believe him to be a half-breed, off-
spring of a squaw and a white man named Powell. This may have been true,
but little evidence of record supports this view. Many historians agree that
he was what he himself declared, "a pure-blood Muskogee (Cow Creek)."

One observed of him "a cheerful and agreeable countenance, polite and
gentlemanly in manner, but a thoughtful face with eyes that, in animation,
could flash full of dark fire." Another officer observed a face of "worn linea-
ments of incessant thought and ever active passions; it is strikingly expres-
sive." A few noted painters who visited him in prison to do his portrait found
a baffling complexity in this face, an elusive blend of traits that rendered
each finished work markedly different. He was a fierce fighter, yet always

forbade the mistreatment of women or children. To his fellow redmen, he was swift, skillful, and fearless, whether as gamesman, hunter or warrior. To his foe he was an extraordinary man, brave and of keen intelligence.

Asi-yaholi (phonetically crunched in English to "Osceola") was probably born in an area northwest of Tallahassee, a Cow Creek, around 1803. In the First Seminole War, when General Andrew Jackson was raiding the north Florida tribes, the boy and his family fled southeast where Seminole tribes ranged over the lush green fields and forests, rivers, and lakes stretching from the Green Swamp, north to around Alachua County. When the war ended in 1818 and after Florida was purchased from Spain, the U.S. government attempted to make amends to the war-ravaged Seminole nation with the Treaty of Moultrie Creek, in 1823. In return for ceding title or claim to Florida, the U.S. gave them a four-million-acre reservation, cash annuities for 20 years, and other immediate aid. But through the years, as white settlers and adventurers raided Indian lands and committed other depredations, thus inciting retaliatory raids by the Seminoles, Florida whites began demanding westward removal of all Indians.

This clamor set in motion a series of sordid maneuvers: In 1830, Congress passed the Indian Removal Act (grossly violating the Moultrie Treaty), and then in 1832 and 1834, Indian chiefs were deceived into signing treaties, at Payne's Landing and at Fort Gibson, Arkansas, respectively, that purportedly gave their (the Seminoles') consent to emigration. Thus, when the new Indian agent, Wiley Thompson arrived at Fort King (near Ocala), he was furious when the chiefs claimed they had signed no such consent and insisted that the Moultrie Treaty still had nine years to run. The agent hotly warned of wrath to come if the Indians did not agree to go west, but then ended the talks on a conciliatory note and had the chiefs agree to a full meeting in April 1835. But he had not failed to note a "bold and dashing" young brave among them who, though not a chief himself, appeared to be counseling all the chiefs together—Micanopy, Jumper, King Philip, Arpeika (Sam Jones), Abraham (a Negro), Holata Mico, and the brothers Holata and Charlie Emathla. The brave was Osceola.

Thompson had summoned the imposing presence of General Duncan Clinch but the principal chiefs were conspicuously absent at the April meeting. The agent simply struck their names and induced an alleged 16 minor councilors to sign a document agreeing to documentation. But when Osceola approached the table, he brushed aside the pen and drew his knife, plunging it into the document and exclaiming: "The only treaty I will execute is with this!"

Then the following May, another fateful incident occurred. Thompson wrote: "Osceola, one of the most bold, daring, and intrepid chiefs in this nation . . . more hostile to emigration and who has thrown more embarrassments in my way than any other, came to my office and insulted me by some insolent remarks." Whatever Osceola's grievance, Thompson overreacted by clamping the Indian in irons and placing him in prison. The chieftain would not forget this humiliation. But meanwhile, Osceola feigned contriteness and even publicly signed the removal document. A grateful Thompson released the prisoner and presented him the gift of a custom-made rifle. The gift would prove grimly ironic.

Although some Indians moved into Fort Brooke in Tampa that year to await removal, the major chiefs voted to resist. Of the two chiefs resigned to emigration, Holata and Charlie Emathla, only Holata escaped; Charlie was ambushed and slain by Osceola. The war had already begun.

In December 1835, Fort Brooke sent a detachment of 108 men, under Major Francis L. Dade, to reinforce the undermanned Fort King. But on December 28, 280 Indians, led by Micanopy, ambushed the column near present-day Bushnell, killing all but three men. That same day, Osceola and a small band crept up to Fort King. Catching agent Thompson and an army officer taking a stroll, Osceola fired from his brand new rifle the first of a flurry of shots that felled both men. That night, the tribes gathered for a revel of celebration and then retired to their stronghold in the Cove of the Withlacoochee River.

The war dragged on for months. The elusive Indians struck only with hit-and-run skirmishes, wearing and discouraging their foe as one General after another—Scott, Gaines, Clinch—were relieved of, or left, command. But the tribes too, were being taxed heavily, especially in critical shortages of food and ammunition. They expressed willingness to meet the white man and discuss terms of peace, any terms—except emigration. In this, their resolve was expressed in Osceola's own declaration: "When I make up my mind, I act. If I speak, what I say, I will do. If the hail rattles, let the flowers be crushed. The oak of the forest will lift up its head to the sky and storm, towering and unscathed."

Osceola continued to be the army's nemesis, his daring raids skillfully planned and executed, his casualties minimal. Yet even as the Army futilely pursued him, they had come to admire his courage, ingenuousness, and logistic skills. Thus, they would later feel a tinge of collective shame for the manner of his capture.

In October 1837, a new commander, General Thomas Jesup, after talks with the dispirited leader, Micanopy, and several other chiefs, persuaded them to surrender their bands into Fort Brooke. But before this could occur, Osceola kidnapped the old chief and his aides and fled to camp near Fort Peyton, south of St. Augustine. He then informed Jesup he would meet him for talks, but only under an official flag of truce. The frustrated Jesup consented, but then he secretly ordered his peace delegate to surreptitiously have his troop escort surround the party as they talked, and seize the Indians. And this they did; the unwary Osceola and his group had no chance to resist. They were then marched to the prison at Fort San Marcos, St. Augustine. Then, on January 1, 1838, Osceola with his two wives and two small daughters, Micanopy, Coahadjo, King Philip, Little Cloud, 116 warriors, and 82 women and children, were transferred to the island prison of Fort Moultrie, at Charleston, South Carolina.

This betrayal of Osceola elicited such strong condemnation from the public and press that Congress launched a full probe of the matter. But Jesup insisted that he had to make exceptions to the unbroken traditions of honoring the flag of truce with the Seminoles. And the Secretary of War, reluctantly, had to accept this contorted explanation. (Nevertheless, even 20 years later, Jesup would still be explaining this dubious act to his critics.)

At the prison, Osceola, although worn and ailing from fever, maintained a peaceful serenity. He was cordial to curious visitors and, when strength permitted, even consented to pose for noted painters, such as George Catlin and Robert John Curtis.

The chieftain was being personally attended by Dr. Frederick Weedon, of St. Augustine. The doctor admired the warrior and had partially won his confidence. But when Osceola learned that Mrs. Weedon was none other than the sister of agent Wiley Thompson, whom he had slain, he refused to let the doctor treat him when he developed violent quinsy, causing a fatal inflammation of his tonsils. On January 30, 1838, sensible of his approaching death, Osceola had himself dressed in full warrior splendor. He then summoned the chiefs, his wives and daughters, and the doctor; wordlessly, he shook hands with each. Finally, he placed his knife on his breast, folded his hands across it, smiled, and expired soundlessly.

But only Osceola's body was buried at Fort Moultrie, for Dr. Weedon had taken a curious, even somewhat ghoulish, memento of the great warrior; he had severed the Indian's head, prior to burial, and then took it back to his St. Augustine office where he preserved it with a special embalming method. Several years later, he gave the head to the physician son-in-law who, in turn, presented it to the renowned surgeon, Dr. Valentine Mott, who placed it in his private medical museum in New York. But the museum caught fire in 1866 and the head was destroyed.

Throughout history, legend and folklore have enshrined Osceola. Among the Seminoles who have remained peacefully in Florida up to this day, hardly a family existed that did not have at least one son bearing his name. History has ranked him with the great American Indian leaders, from Tecumseh to Sitting Bull.

Floridians, some of whose ancestors fought Osceola, perhaps regard him with more mixed sentiments—a die-hard militant, an intelligent but dangerous savage, a brave and daring defender of what he considered to be native homeland—but without exception they probably agree that he was one of the most singular and colorful figures of all Florida history.

32.
Jackie Cochran: Born to Fly

Jacqueline Cochran rose from the extreme poverty of the North Florida mill town of her birth to become one of the nation's most famous woman pilots.

Jacqueline Cochran: filled with determination, grit, and a love of flight.

She was a "refugee from Sawdust Road," (not too distant from famed Tobacco Road), except that existence in the sawmill towns of North Florida in the late teens and twenties was a bit more bleak, bitter, and harsh.

She never knew her real parents; as an infant, she was taken in by a poor white family who eked a marginal existence from the infamous company milltown circuit in Florida's panhandle—Sampson, Panama City, Bagdad, Millville, and others.

"Usually a shack on stilts, down near the swamp, served as home," she recalls. She had no shoes until she was eight; her bed was usually a floor pallet; her diet, at best, was mullet, sowbelly, and beans; at worst, she foraged the woods and fields for "pine mass" (pine cone nuts), fished for perch or crab, or trapped some neighbor's "unbranded" chicken. Her "Ma" and "Pa" and two "brothers" were paid by the sawmill company in wood "chips," redeemable only at the company commissary, and they never had enough "chips" on payday to meet the week's deductions. The company doctor charged extra for delivering babies so she became a midwife at an early age. "I delivered babies before I even knew that the stork was a bird," she says.

Her schooling? "I learned my ABC's by watching the [railroad] boxcars and began to figure out words. This was my first adventure into the literary world and it intrigued me."

You could have never convinced nine-year-old Jacqueline Cochran that she would one day be among America's most famous woman flyers and test pilots; that she would be the first woman to break the sonic barrier; that she would head the woman's WASP service in World War II; that she would dine with presidents, kings, sultans, shahs, prime ministers, and assorted dictators. If you would have told her what was to be she might have thought you were mocking her in the flour-sack dress she often had to wear.

As with many children in such environments, she aged tough and prematurely; at 10, she was supervising 15 other children in a Georgia "sweatshop" cotton mill where "human beings did not count." After a long employees' strike that was broken, she decided to strike out on her own and was "taken in" again by a beauty shop operator who taught her the trade.

By the time she was 15, she had earned enough to buy a Model T Ford and go to nursing school for three years, after which she returned home and worked for a while as a nurse in Bonifay, Florida. But she soon returned to her first vocation and shortly earned enough to buy half interest in a Pensacola beauty shop.

She then sold this and headed for "the big pasture"—New York City—and talked her way into a job with Antoine's well-known Saks Fifth Avenue Salon. She did so well that he sent her to take charge of his beauty salon in Miami Beach each winter season. Here she met her future husband, financier Floyd Odlum, who encouraged her in another new love—flying.

In the summer of 1932, Jackie began her first flying lessons. Applying her usual gritty determination, she soloed within three days and had her pilot's license within three weeks. She at once bought an old Travelair for $1,200 and flew to Montreal for her first air meet. Next she bought a new Waco for $3,200 and took it to London for the London-Australia race, but had to drop out when her supercharger failed over Europe. In those years, jobs as airline or test pilots went to men, not women, and only a few thousand people in the country had pilot's licenses.

Flying was still experimental and dangerous. Once Jackie took a fabric-covered biplane to an unheard of 33,000 feet, without heat, pressure or oxygen mask. She ruptured a sinus blood vessel from pressure, almost froze to death and became so dizzy from lack of oxygen that it took her an hour to regain her orientation enough to land. But such pioneering led to mandatory pressurized cabins and oxygen masks. Other pilots, such as Howard Hughes and Wiley Post (before his ill-fated flight with Will Rogers), gave her valuable help with instruction.

But in those risky days, nearly all pilots had a few crashes under their belt, including Jackie. Once her engine caught fire at 10,000 feet and she crashed landed at the runway's end, leaped from the fire and suffered only a fractured toe. Another time her engine failed just after take-off with some passengers. She raised her wheels and belly landed in a pasture; no one was injured but the plane was totaled. When her propellor governor broke on a long distance record run, she ignored radio tower pleas from General Ralph Cousins at March Field near Los Angeles to bail out and instead tried a tricky "dead-stick" landing. She made it.

Exerting a "great effort," she persuaded Bendix Air Race authorities in 1935 to open the race to women for the first time. In her first try, she lost her radio antenna which caught on a runway fence after a low takeoff. But she finally won the Bendix race in a Seversky pursuit plane in 1938, having to fly the plane all the way with the wing tank tilted to feed the engine because of the manufacturer's tissue paper left in the tank.

During the period of barnstorm racing and record-setting, she also found time to marry Floyd Odlum and they made a 1,000-acre ranch in Southern California their home. Jackie was also building up a cosmetic business which, within 20 years, would become a nationally known industry, Jacqueline Cochran Cosmetics.

Jackie brought her close friend, Amelia Earhart, out to stay at the Odlum ranch to rest and prepare for what would be Amelia's last, fatal round-the-world flight in 1937. The young aviatrix reported that she had such a strong, ominous premonition about the flight that she went out and bought Amelia a bright-colored kite that could be spotted by rescuers, a set of fish-hooks and lines and an all-purpose knife. She was still stunned, however, when news came that Amelia failed to arrive at Howland Island in the Pacific; a vast search by planes and ships failed to locate the missing flyer, and no trace has been heard of her since.

Jackie had already earned preeminence as a woman flyer by the time World War II had erupted in Europe, but was still excited when General H. "Hap" Arnold made her part of the British Ferry Command, shuttling badly needed bombers to England. Her contacts with Lord Beaverbrook and Winston Churchill, plus her meetings with personal friends in England, prompted President Franklin D. Roosevelt to invite her to lunch to discuss the British situation.

This honor was extended a few days later when Mrs. Roosevelt invited her to discuss the recruitment of women pilots for England and the formation of a similar service for the U.S. in case it might be needed. Therefore, when the U.S. entered the war, Jackie was called home from the ferry command and made Director of WASP (Women's Air Force Service Pilots). This service performed a vital emergency function in both the training of pilots and the release of pilots for active duty in the war theaters, and the waif from Sawdust Road, still in her thirties, garnered official commendation for it.

It also led to an exciting venture at the war's end when she was given both official Army as well as a magazine's foreign correspondent credentials to cover the immediate post-war scene. After witnessing the execution of the

infamous General Yamashita, Japanese occupier of the Phillipines, she
became the first American woman to enter Japan with the occupying forces.

From this base, she flew to interviews in China with Madame Chiang
Kai-shek, wife of the Generalissimo, and the Communist leader Mao Tse-
tung. She then went to Iran, to interview the Shah, Greece, for a talk with
Queen Frederica, and on to the Nuremburg War Crimes trial of top Nazis.
After touring Hitler's tomb in Berlin's Reichschancellery bunkers, she went
to, first Russia, then Spain, to interview officials in those countries. After a
final interview with the Sultan of Morocco, she returned home, anxious to
enter politics herself. But here she found herself out of milieu, knowledge or
experience and she later removed herself from the activity. Still, she stayed
long enough to lead a campaign to get General Eisenhower named the Republican nomination over Robert Taft in 1951. Eisenhower saw to it that she was
on the platform when he gave his acceptance speech and he and wife,
Mamie, stayed as guests at the Odlum Ranch after he became president.

Her cosmetic business was now thriving, but Jackie was still restless
over her overriding interest, especially the new jet-propulsion. She wanted
to test one badly. At that time, all jets were owned by the U.S. Air Force.
But the enterprising Jackie wangled permission from General Van Vanden-
berg first, and then went through a tangle of channels to get the Canadian
manufacturers of the Sabre-jet to send her one for testing. She was soon setting three speed records for both men and women over the California desert.
But this was not enough. Her chase plane companion, Charles "Chuck"
Yeager, was the first person to dive through the tremendous shock waves of
the sonic barrier and live to tell about it. Many crack test pilots had tried and
failed. Jackie was determined to be the first woman to do so.

It was a clear, sunny day when she crawled into her jet and gradually
climbed it to 45,000 feet. Then, with fullpower thrust, she tipped the nose
over and headed straight down for the tiny airport hangar below. By the time
she had passed Mach I (the speed of sound) the shock waves were so violent
that the plane's nose tried to pull completely under and awry. It was a tight
moment, but a very gentle touch at the controls enabled her to level out just
in time before passing below an altitude of 18,000 feet. Pulling out of a dive
below this altitude, where the heavier air is met, can literally pull a plane to
pieces.

A jubilant Jackie then later topped this achievement off with a new altitude record for women of 48,000 feet. For this and for other test records
made, Jackie received in 1954 her highest flying honor, the International
Flying Organization's gold medal for the outstanding accomplishment by
any pilot—man or woman—during 1953.

If she had been around and in her prime, Miss Cochran would doubtless
have been the first woman astronaut, for she once advised earthbound souls

to "go up higher—above the dust and water vapor—and the sky turns dark until one can see the stars at noon. I have." But it was tenacity, courage, and faith that enabled her to swap her sawdust road for stardust, and a packed life of unequalled achievement.

33.
Sister Bedell Woos the Indians

Deaconess Harriet Bedell had the determination necessary to win the hearts of the Everglades' most reluctant Indians.

The slight, elderly lady's dark blue habit and high button shoes contrasted sharply with the vibrant colors worn by those with whom she was feasting, but the distinction marked something more than a festive holiday; it was almost an historic occasion.

Because the animated lady in blue was white, and her friends were the proud Miccosukee Seminoles who, for almost a century, would not deign to acknowledge even the existence of a white person, much less feast with one at Christmas dinner. But this "In-co-shopie" (white sister) was different. Or, rather, she herself had made the difference.

When Episcopal Deaconess Harriet M. Bedell arrived in Everglades City in 1933 to revive the defunct Glade Cross Mission, she was cautioned about her "impossible task." Over the years, some Seminole tribes had consented to live on reservations. But the Miccosukees, whom the Deaconess sought to reach, remained deep in the vast Everglades. They had fought the westward removal of 3,000 Seminoles after the last war in 1842—and they had remained unconquered. They wished nothing from the white man, least of all his company, after so many years of betrayal and defrauding at his hands. They would buy necessities at his stores and, occasionally, work on his farms in harvest time but—in total silence. "They neither like nor hate us," a townsman told the missionary. "They act as if we just aren't here." The tribes often made and sold dresses, jackets, dolls, canoes, and other handmade items to tourists from little stands along the Tamiami Trail. Mainly they hunted and fished over the jungles and prairies of the huge sea of slow-moving water called the Everglades. They could do without "the fork-tongued one."

The deaconess secured a small mission home in Everglades City with the aid of Barron Collier, who had taken a benevolent interest in her work (and who all but owned Collier County). She also came by a second-hand Model A Ford sedan and, within a week's time, learned how to drive it. Now, at the zestful age of 58, this ruggedly independent woman was determined to begin a formidable new work—bringing Jesus Christ to the Miccosukees. But, after all, Harriet Bedell was no stranger to Indians.

It was in 1905 that a slim, attractive young school teacher with a strong but "pleasing sense of natural self-possession" became overwhelmed one Sunday with a surge of unfamiliar emotions that made her tremble as she sat in her hometown church in Buffalo, New York. She had just been hearing of the desperate need for missionary teachers in China and, by the time that this strange but exalting feeling had passed, she was as certain of her life's work as if she had been planning it for years.

But she did not get to China after finishing mission school two years later; instead she was sent to work with the Cheyenne Indians at the Chief Whirlwind Mission in Fay, Oklahoma. Many of the braves were veterans of the Indian wars with the U.S. Army, but a few of them had already turned to Christianity. By the time she left this reservation eight years later, she had won their love and confidence to such degree that she was formally initiated as a full Cheyenne Indian princess—"Vicsehia." She had even converted the medicine man, a major feat for an Indian missionary.

In 1915, Miss Bedell became critically ill with a terminal stage of tuberculosis. She went to Denver for the climate and rest and, she was convinced, to die. While there, she attended a healing service at a local church. A week later, every symptom of the disease had disappeared. Her doctor refused to believed it and administered repeated tests over the next weeks— all negative. She never claimed a "miracle" recovery and refused to inform even her family of it, but she never doubted afterwards that God had deliberately healed her so that she might continue to serve Him.

Her next assignment in 1916 took her to an area more remote than even China—an isolated Alaskan Indian village in a wilderness far up the Yukon River. Here she struggled to teach, heal, and in hard times, grub food for the near-destitute villagers. She stopped the swindling of white trappers who gave Indians whiskey for the valuable furs. Once she so surprised a band of Indians secretly revelling at a wild drunk party, that they meekly slinked back to their cabins under her furious commands. Another time she astounded grizzled old Alaska veterans with the unheard of feat of driving a dog sled over untracked mid-winter wilderness 160 miles to get an Indian girl a doctor. She was so remote from "Outside," that she had not even heard of the Great Depression that would force the mission to cut back in 1932 and bring her home—and to Florida.

Her first encounter with the Seminoles was hardly encouraging. She entered a village near Ochopee, extended her hand to the first man near, and he, without regarding the hand or her, turned and walked away. She then approached a woman, smiled and placed a hand lightly on her shoulder, saying "Friend." The woman shrugged disdainfully and walked away. "Why, I feel like a whipped puppy," she recalled murmuring. The cold indifference was more painful to her than if it had been hostile anger. But the scene repeated itself in village after village.

At this time, the Depression was hurting the Indian as much as the white man, if not more. And so the lady put the bad times to a good end with an ingenuous plan. She arranged to sell the Indian's handiwork articles wholesale to retailers, as well as to tourists. She would act as middleman for the tribes, but without taking the middleman's percentage. She accomplished this by winning the confidence of an older Indian called Frank Charlie who spoke fair English and often came into town driving an ancient car. He finally agreed to take her to the Indian Council (the tribes' governors) and they drove to the camp of one Cufney Tiger—a rough and muddy ride 62 miles deep into the 'glades. This was her first real contact with the wild mystery and beauty of the great swamp. She would get to know it like an Indian in the years ahead.

At the village, she was assigned a "chickee," or hut, for the night. Next day, the Council and families politely heard her describe—with all the Cheyenne symbolism she could muster—how their "Great Spirit" and the white man's "Holy Spirit" were one and the same. They were impressed. And they also approved the plan for selling their craftwork. Three years of prayer had been answered.

By the end of the following year, the Indians were beginning to appear regularly with their dolls, baskets, shirts, skirts, canoes, and other items at the Glade Cross Mission. And the mail orders and tourist purchases were keeping pace with the supply. In fact, so pleased were the tribes with this munificent arrangement that the Council finally consented to let her perform religious education work in the villages.

The deaconess now spent most of her time visiting villages, sometimes driving, sometimes hiking or, in inaccessible areas, taking off her high-button shoes and wading. Florida historian Marjory Stoneman Douglas then described her: "The deaconess, like a small steam engine in petticoats walks fast in and out the trail camps, speaking to everybody by name, asking about the sick babies, bringing some old man a mattress for his aching bones, trying to get them to use and scald individual drinking cups, scolding a man after a long drunk, taking somebody to the hospital, or getting work for the boys." She was often seen along the trail "firmly driving her small car which was often full of Indians."

She also taught them in less spiritual matters such as hygiene—burying garbage and waste, etc.—and larger problems which she took up with government officials such as new game laws which restricted tribal hunting. On the proposed new Everglades National Park, that would eliminate 1,200,000 acres of hunting ground, she wrote one official that she approved the park but wanted assurance that the Indians "have the same chance for survival that we're offering animals." She successfully persuaded Collier to permit construction of a village compound near the town depot, where Indians could stay while awaiting treatment at the local hospital.

In 1936, she began the first of her annual Christmas feasts which soon became as popular to the tribes and their families as their own Green Corn Dance. They would pour in from all over the 'glades, exchanging gifts, offering prayers, and singing carols (in whatever pidgen English), and gorging down huge sides of roast beef, pork, and turkey, with all the trimmings.

Many individual Indians had been converted to Christianity but the Council still refused to allow the baptism and other church rites. Their reasons in summary were: "We believe what you say. We believe in your Holy Spirit and the message of Jesus. He spoke truly. But don't ask us to accept your (white man's) rites. Why are they so necessary?" The deaconess was not entirely sure of an answer there, although many individuals would later receive personal baptism.

In 1943, Miss Bedell was obliged to retire, at age 68, but was permitted to continue her work on a parochial status. In December 1947, she enjoyed having lunch with President Harry Truman at the Rod and Gun Club; a nice enough man, she thought, even though he was a Baptist. He invited her to give the invocation before thousands at the dedication of the Everglades National Park. But her real interest was the huge crowd of potential customers for Indian goods, and she made a profitable time of it.

Nothing could irritate Deaconess Bedell more than to overhear some bubbly tourist exclaim: "Poor, frail dear! She's actually driven Alaskan dog teams for scads of miles through snowstorms and now she kicks alligators aside as she wades waist-deep through the dreadful Everglades mud. A saint!" Saint indeed, she would quietly fume. What shocking rubbish. She was just a woman, sometimes much too blunt, and occasionally cross-tempered, but simply doing whatever her work required her to do.

The missionary continued her dawn-to-dusk ministry well into her seventies and eighties, mainly with Indians but also with area white and black families and with tourists who visited her by the hundreds. She had in fact become a woman of national and international reputation, although she was hardly conscious of such attraction. But two events—major and minor—would soon occur that would hasten the end of her missionary career.

In 1960, Hurricane Donna smashed across the Keys and nearly wiped out the town of Everglades City, including the Glade Cross Mission. The cottage was a shambles and the flooding destroyed all her books, papers, records, and personal effects. She could now only work haphazardly from temporary quarters. Then, two years later, at 86, she lost her driver's license due to age. This she accepted equally: "I knew I was pushing my luck get-

ting licenses as long after 80 as I did. But I have always been alert and phys-
ically fit." Remarkably, this was true enough, but it forced her final
retirement to the Bishop Gray Inn in Davenport, Polk County. Even here she
continued making speaking engagements and caring for the ill among the
Inn's retirees with a seeming renewed energy and spirit, affirming by example her oft-spoken assertion: "There is no retirement in the service of the
Master."

And so there was none, until the Master took her home, peacefully, at
the age of 93, on January 9, 1969.

34.
Jonathan Walker: Freedom Symbol

Imprisoned, tortured and convicted of helping slaves escape in Pensacola, Jonathan Walker later settled in Michigan.

He was an unassuming, modest man without formal education, a shipwright by trade, often hard put to care for a wife and eight children—altogether an obscure person who hardly seemed destined for any singular achievement.

But he was also a man of strong but simple religious faith, matched only by his belief in what he termed "certain inalienable rights" endowed to all men. Thus, in June 1844, in the little seaport town of Pensacola, where he lived, he considered it simply a moral duty to aid the escape of seven runaway slaves.

Caught, imprisoned, and sentenced, he could not even realize that the red-hot branding iron that sizzled the letters "SS" into his hand (for slave stealer) would also sear a nation's conscience and make the case of "the branded hand"—immortalized by the poet John Greenleaf Whittier—a touchstone for the expanding anti-slavery movement in America, one that would culminate in the crucible of the Civil War.

Jonathan Walker had left his family's small Massachusetts farm at 17 and gone to sea in 1816. He would leave this then-hazardous calling in 1835, but not before marrying, learning the shipwright's trade, and becoming an abolitionist in 1831. Though not formally educated, he was an intelligent, observant person and no doubt strongly influenced by the abolitionist writings of William Lloyd Garrison whom he quoted more often than any source except the scripture. In Walker's words, slavery was "the most heinous, God-provoking system that ever cursed mankind, poisoning, corrupting, and debasing . . . the life streams of" the Union.

Yet Walker viewed the South—geographically at least—as an ideal place to work and live, and in 1837, he moved his family to Pensacola where he worked as a boat-builder and railroad construction contractor for which work he hired a number of slaves from their local owners. These blacks boarded at Walker's home on terms of equality, whether at the dining table or in family prayers and services held in the home. But this treatment also prompted warnings from friends about hostile resentment from white neighbors. Nevertheless, Walker expounded his abolitionist views freely, and in the community generally, he was regarded, as one editor put it, as "a very devout Christian . . . of uprightness, integrity, and humility." Thus the years passed for him without any untoward incidents.

Nevertheless, after six years, Walker became convinced that he did not want to raise his eight children around the "degrading" influences of slavery. His wife, Jane, agreed with him and so, in 1844, he moved the family back to Massachusetts but returned himself to Mobile to secure a small sloop he had purchased. While stopping off a few days in Pensacola to say goodbye to his friends, seven of the blacks who had once boarded with him sought him out to ask if he would aid them to escape north—to freedom. Realizing his small boat could not make such a long coastal voyage undetected, Walker agreed instead to take them to Nassau from which they would be free to move anywhere. Accordingly, the men set sail on the night of June 22, 1844 and, despite Walker's suffering fever and sunstroke, freedom seemed assured when they reached within 50 miles of Cape Florida.

But they were spotted by a Key West wrecking schooner, overtaken, arrested at gunpoint, and returned to Key West. Here Walker was charged by a magistrate and, with hands and feet in irons, returned aboard a U.S. naval vessel to Pensacola, while the seven blacks and his boat were returned by another vessel.

A threatening and noisy crowd was on hand to meet the prisoner but he was escorted to the jail without incident. While he was shackled to a heavy chain in his cell, Walker's fever worsened. Within weeks, the poor, meager food and lack of exercise had reduced his robust six-foot frame "very near to a skeleton." But a sympathetic local grocer arranged to get adequate food to him, his chain was removed, and slowly he regained his health.

Accepting his fate with a stoic faith and grace, Walker continued to expound his anti-slavery views, with no apologies for his "crime;" in fact, his honesty and sincerity soon began to evoke sympathy from many townspeople. Meanwhile, Northern abolitionists like Garrison, Wendell Phillips, and Frederick Douglass made appeals as far as Great Britain for funds to aid Walker's legal costs and also his now destitute family. The governor of Massachusetts even wrote Florida Governor John Branch, asking Branch to prevent "needless severities" against the prisoner, but Branch reacted hotly, even suggesting the death penalty for any "intermeddling with our . . . institutions."

Finally, in November, Walker was brought to trial and convicted on four "slave-stealing" counts. He was sentenced to stand in a pillory for one hour (where one of the fugitive slave-owners pelted him with garbage), jailed 15 days more, fined $150, and branded. Few in the crowd watched the branding, which took place in the courthouse prisoner's box. Walker's hand was tied to the rail while a marshall placed the red-hot iron on the ball of hand for 20 seconds. It made a "splattering noise" but the prisoner remained firmly calm.

Yet hours later, he recalled he was "somewhat staggered" to be informed that he would be tried again for the other three slaves. With no legal funds having yet arrived and after an ominous warning that local extremists were plotting "extra-legal punishment" for him, Walker succumbed to a moment of desperation by prying his cell door open one night. But the jailer, living above, heard the noise and quickly apprehended the would-be escapee.

The following May he was tried again. But although the judge directed the jurors to find him guilty, the latter, noting the "revulsion of public feeling in his favor," assessed a penalty of only a $15 fine on each of the remaining three counts. Walker was elated with what he believed to be a "magnanimous and humane" verdict, and even more so, soon after, when some $2,000 arrived from the North for his fines, fees, and court costs. On June 16, 1845, he walked out of jail a free man.

Returning North to a hero's welcome, Walker would spend the next several years on the anti-slavery speaking circuit where, across New England and the Midwest, his branded hand became a powerful abolitionist symbol, the infamous letters, to many, signifying "slave saviour." He later wrote a book fully explaining his ordeal. But, unlike much abolitionist literature, it held no rancor toward his tormentors, noting the kind acts accorded him by many Southerners at the time, and suggesting that many were simply themselves victims of a degrading institution.

After the Civil War, he and his wife lived quietly on a small fruit farm in Muskegon County, Michigan; yet he remained active in most of the reform issues of the day. He died there at age 79. But even in quiet obscurity he was not forgotten. More than 6,000 people attended the unveiling of a simple monument subscribed for him and heard a eulogy read by Frederick Douglass to "a brave but noiseless lover of liberty" who was not "less entitled to grateful memory than the most honored of them all."

35.
He Replaced Another on the Gallows

A Seminole warrior agreed to take the chains of a condemned man to die in his place. They were not even friends.

Among men or deeds, there were few examples of man's more noteworthy or nobler traits displayed in that long, costly, and tragic conflict called the Second Seminole War, waged by the United States against the Seminole Indians from 1835 to 1842.

And yet there was an incident occurring toward the close of that war—between a U.S. Army officer and two Seminole warriors—that easily might have rivaled any tragic morality play from ancient Greece. In fact, some elements of this true story, faithfully recorded and later published anonymously by an officer present at the scene, strikingly parallel the classic Greek tale of Damon and Pythias.

It is recalled that Damon, a Pythagorean philosopher of ancient Syracuse, and Phintias (known today as Pythias), shared the strongest bonds of personal friendship. When the hard-spirited ruler, Dionysius, condemned Pythias to death for allegedly conspiring against his throne, Pythias pleaded for a brief time to permit him to journey to his neighboring hometown to settle family affairs before his death, and Damon offered to replace Pythias before the executioner if his friend did not return before the appointed time. Dionysius, skeptical that such a friendship could exist, was nevertheless curious, and so consented. As the appointed day drew to a close and there was still no sign of Pythias, Damon was led to execution. Then, at the last minute and after overcoming many obstacles of delay, Pythias arrived. The king was so struck by such a rare display of loyal friendship that he pardoned Pythias.

Yet—there was a difference or two in the later, modern version which occurred in 1842, the last year of the Seminole War. Indians who had been captured, or surrendered, were being transported by the hundreds from Tampa to reservations out West. One day an army patrol out of Fort Brooke (Tampa), discovered a party of 20 Indians, comprising men, women, and children. Most of the party fled, but the soldiers captured three of the warriors and brought them to the fort.

Colonel W. J. Worth, the commandant, soon learned that two of the prisoners were responsible for the slaying of an army mail rider the previous March. He thereupon informed the prisoners that they would be hanged within 15 days unless, within that period, the rest of their kinsmen should surrender themselves. He then released the third prisoner to go out and locate the remaining Seminoles. This prisoner returned within five days, bringing with him a warrior named Holate Fixico, along with several women and children, including the sister and mother of one of the condemned prisoners, Talof Hadjo.

In an open outdoor court in front of Worth's headquarters, Holate Fixico and the other Indians were seated on the ground before the Colonel and several other officers. Talof Hadjo sat in chains on a bench, his head leaning back against a tree, starring skyward with a passive, resigned expression. His sister and mother, the latter weeping silently over the fate awaiting her son, sat at his feet.

The recording officer then relates the following exchange, as Colonel Worth addresses Holate, asking: "Where are the rest of your people?"

Holate: "They are separated and cannot be found. Your troops have scattered them and they have taken different paths."

Colonel: "Don't you know that unless they are brought in these men (pointing to the prisoners) will be hung?" The colonel pauses. "If I send you out for the people, will you bring them in in time to save their lives?"

Holate: "I know not where to look for them. Like the frightened deer they have fled at the presence of your troops."

Colonel, impatiently: "Indians can find Indians. If they're not here, these men will surely die."

Holate: "The track of the Indian is covered; his path is hidden and cannot be found under ten suns."

The colonel then turns to address Talof Hadjo, asking: "Have you a wife?"

Talof: "My wife and child are with the people. I wish them here that I might take leave of them before I die."

Colonel: "Do you love your wife and child?"

Talof, indignant contempt in his voice: "The dog is fond of his kind. I love my wife and child."

Colonel: "Could you find the people who are out?"

Talof: "They are scattered and may not be found."

Colonel: "Do you desire your freedom?"

Talof: "I see the people going to and fro, and would be with them. I am tired of my chains."

Colonel: "If I release you, will you bring in the people within the time fixed?"

Talof, with an incredulous look: "You would not trust me—yet I would try."

Colonel: "If Holate Fixico would consent to take your chains, and be hung in your place if you should not return, you may go."

A long silence then ensued. Talof leans his head back again and stares skyward. His mother and sister regard Holate with diffident but imploring glances. Holate, on hearing the last statement by the colonel, has struggled to maintain his bearing, as evidenced by the "heaving of his chest and gaspings," as if the rope were already around his neck. His condition is not eased with all eyes resting upon him. Finally, recovering himself and with much composure and firmness, he states: "I have no wife or child or mother; it is more fit that he (Talof) should live than I. I consent to take his chains and abide his fate. Let him go."

Colonel: "Be it so. But do not deceive yourselves. So sure as Talof Hadjo does not bring in the people within ten days, Holate dies the death of a dog."

Then, with a sort of grim solemnity, the two Indians are marched to the armory where the chains are transferred. Fifteen minutes later, Talof is on his journey.

In a few days, a messenger arrives at the fort bearing news that Talof is on his way in with the people and should arrive within a day or two.

Comparatively, up to this point, this incident seems more remarkable than the Damon and Pythias story inasmuch as here there were no strong personal bonds of friendship; the sacrifice by Holate apparently has risen from an instinctive selfless, disinterested motive, simply a desire to save the life of one whom he considers of more consequence than himself. Pythias placed perfect faith in the promise of his friend to return. Holate had no such assurance; on the contrary, he believed it highly unlikely that Talof would find the Seminoles and return in time to save his life.

This foreboding was confirmed when, in spite of the messenger's news, Talof failed to appear by the deadline day. The cause of this failure was not known until some months later. It was learned that, on the night that Talof was expected to arrive, some Indian captives near Fort Brooke had escaped and chanced to meet Talof a few miles from Tampa. To dissuade him from returning with his people, they contrived the story that Colonel Worth was determined to hang the two Indians who had been involved in the mail rider's death and that the execution was postponed only in order to first catch Talof's people. The tale was urged upon Talof with such guile and intense feeling that the latter finally accepted it as truth. Moreover, Talof was not aware of Worth's general reputation as a man who, in spite of his stern official mien, held a generous and humane disposition toward the hapless redmen and who was, unlike some of his peers, a man of his word. Thus Talof was not heard from again for several months when he and his people were later captured.

Meanwhile, the fate of the hapless Holate was to be sealed. But the inexorable event was causing the colonel no little concern. His strongly humane instinct churned in conflict with the strict military code by which he lived, plus his sense of the need to set an example under the circumstances. His doubts so disturbed him that, on execution day, he removed himself from the scene completely, riding off with several aides on a "routine reconnaissance."

The gallows and platform had been erected, with the troops parading briefly as the prisoner was brought forth. Holate appeared deeply depressed as he ascended the platform, his eyes rolling upward momentarily to regard the dangling rope that would take him away from the woods, rivers, fields, and wildlife that he had known for so many sunrises.

An historian once observed: "Of all deaths, that which results from hanging is perhaps the most shocking to an Indian. He may face danger in every other form with fearless courage and stoical indifference, but this death by choking completely unnerves him. In his contracted view, the tightening of the cord chokes down the spirit within him, and prevents it from descending to the Great Spirit of his race, and this, as he considers, destroys the hope of partaking in the pleasures and enjoyments of the spirit land."

Among the crowd surrounding the platform, there was scarcely a person who did not have more than a usual interest in Holate's fate, considering the circumstances leading to it. Therefore, with the rope snugly fitted around the man's neck and only the signal awaiting, a buzz of excitement spread quickly as a uniformed rider galloped toward the scene, furiously waving a piece of paper in the hand he held over his head. He almost threw himself off his mount before the astonished gazers as he shouted toward the platform: "Pardon for Holate Fixico!"

Loud shouts of approval arose from the crowd, and then a hushed silence fell as the executioner read the pardon aloud and explained to Holate that he was now a free man. This news was apparently too much for the noble brave and he collapsed to the platform, unconscious. But he was soon revived and taken to more comfortable quarters.

The just colonel, removed from the scene, had wrestled up until the final hour with an anguished conscience—and then acted accordingly, and swiftly. In one stark decisive moment, he had determined that he could not let so worthy a man perish, especially on behalf of one whom he now deemed (however unwittingly), so unworthy.

Holate, in turn, proved himself so grateful for the pardon that, ignoring his strongest contrary desires, he set about during the following weeks hunting out and urging roving Seminole parties to voluntarily surrender. But during one of these sojourns, he contracted yellow fever and died soon afterward. In an unusual tribute, both officers and troops of Worth's command officially mourned Holate's death. They apparently agreed with the officer-narrator's appraisal of the Seminole's virtues—"gentle, unobtrusive, generous, brave, and high-souled." And—perhaps—even a bit more than the Damon he played to Talof's Pythias.

36.
Lake Okeechobee's "She-Doctor"

Doctor Anna Darrow was the Okeechobee area's complete health-service agency.

The attractive, young Indiana farm girl, an honors graduate in medicine, could easily have remained in thriving urban Chicago to enjoy a posh and lucrative medical practice.

Instead, Dr. Anna Albertina Darrow came in 1912 to the wild frontier settlement of Okeechobee City on Lake Okeechobee. And there, in the land of "custard apple trees and moonvine, catfish and moonshine," she became the redoubtable "Doc Anner," a matriarchal symbol of balm and healing to the rough-hewn Crackers, blacks, catfishermen, cowboys, and Indians who comprised this turbulent section of early Florida.

Earlier, her ailing husband, Dr. Charles Roy Darrow, was compelled to go south for his health, and he accepted a post as surgeon for Henry Flagler's Florida East Coast Railway. With two small children, the Darrows moved from Chicago, having been assured by Flagler promoter J. E. Ingraham that Okeechobee City was destined to be another Miami or Palm Beach once the FEC railroad reached it. But on arrival, they found only a few ramshackle wood buildings surrounding Taylor Creek, set against a barren prairie speckled with cabbage palms.

The town boasted shootings, fights, and drunken vandalism between rival catfishermen and cowboys as a Saturday night ritual. It was the era of William (Pogey Bill) Collins, the lawless catfisher king who, in a change of heart, later became the area's dauntless Sheriff Pogey Bill. There were the desperadoes, too; the Ashley gang, the Rice brothers, the Mobleys, the Upthegroves, (Doc Anner would once be led blindfolded to a deep-woods hideout to treat wounded gang leader John Ashley).

The Darrows adjusted. They built a modest brick building for a drugstore and office; he tended the office while Anna rode the circuit on housecalls, from northern Fort Drum and Bassinger to southeastern Indiantown. It was a rugged circuit, and Doc Anner traveled alone, day or night, often as long as five days at a time through swamps, woods or sawgrass to reach a remote cabin or shanty and treat the ailing patient by kerosene light. When the terrain permitted, she drove her old Model-T. But more often she traveled by horseback, oxen, canoe or foot. Her fees were modest; a dollar a call, a dollar a mile, ten dollars for babies. But for the cash-poor, she often settled for a side of venison or a slab of wild hog.

Thirtyish, with flaxen hair and blue eyes, Anna Darrow was regarded as a handsome woman, even-tempered, firm, boundlessly energetic, and "unafraid of the devil himself." She also had an eye sensitive to the region's wild natural beauty, and she developed an amateur skill in oil and watercolor landscape painting.

Anna quickly learned the taciturn ways and Cracker talk of her backwoods clients, and they, in turn, came to trust and respect this "she-doctor with the pink Yankee complexion." To them she was always Doc Anner. As for her lesser known husband, he was simply called Mr. Doc Anner.

Her work conditions were often in horrendous contrast to the sleek, antiseptic surgery rooms of the day. Not untypical was a journey with two Cracker guides over a pitch-dark lake and a half-mile wade through knee-deep swamp to reach a lonely, corrugated-iron cabin to treat a young malaria-ridden expectant mother. The baby was still-born, and Anna laid it aside while she fought to save the mother. Glancing back later, she saw rats gnawing the tiny corpse. She wrapped it in a towel and placed it on the bed before her as she worked. Only after dawn, when the mother's fever broke and the danger had passed, did Doc Anner notice a crawling, burning sensation on her legs. She hastily stripped down and spent the next half hour picking fleas, hog lice and redbugs from her underclothing.

Doc Anner treated the Seminoles camped around Indiantown without charge, but they invariably paid the "squaw doctor" with foodstuffs, such as a turkey or a big batch of huckleberries. Occasionally, a sly Cracker would hand her a $50 bill; if she couldn't make the change the fee was considered cancelled. She finally solved this problem by carrying $100 in change on every call. Her calls were always varied: men in cold sweat and nausea from black widow or tarantula bites; a successful curettage performed on a tossing houseboat for a woman who was bleeding to death; a critical stomach-pumping on a man who, mistaking it for whiskey, drank a glassful of "high life" (carbon disulfide); an earful of swaggering outlaw Leland Rice crying "Mama" as the doctor and her husband worked all night tying off arteries, after the gangman got shot in the face trying to raid a Negro dwelling; losing only four patients (the only ones she ever lost) out of scores saved in the nationwide flu epidemic of 1918.

By 1915, when the FEC rail line reached it, Okeechobee was a thriving town of 1,200, with brick commercial buildings, wide streets, a decent hotel, and a weekly newspaper. Its timber, truck-farming, and $1,500,000-a-year catfish industries were prompting FEC promoters to hail the town as a coming metropolis. But the post-World War I recession brought industrial slumps, and the town seemed to drift in a torpid status quo.

By 1922, the Darrows were so discouraged over the lack of local progress that they decided to move, first to Stuart and then, in 1924, to Fort Lauderdale. Anna Darrow remained in practice there until 1949. That year, she retired to her daughter's home in Coral Gables, where she died in 1959.

But for years afterward, in every pioneer shack, fish camp, and homestead around the great lake, the angel of mercy who brought a healing hand to a dark and wild frontier would be long remembered—Doc Anner.

37.
Lakeland's Female Lindbergh: Ruth Elder

A 23-year-old dental assistant captured the world's attention when she became the first woman pilot rescued from the Atlantic.

Charles Lindbergh had hardly made the first solo transatlantic flight from New York to Paris in 1927 when, in Lakeland, Florida, an obscure, pretty young dental assistant was already dreaming of becoming the 'female Lindbergh'—or at least the first woman to fly the Atlantic.

It was, of course, a risky dream in those days of pioneer aviation. Both before and after Lindbergh, more than a score of men and women had lost their lives in the Atlantic attempt, the latest female being 63-year-old British Princess Lowenstein-Wertheim, who had been lost with three male pilots in an England–New York flight.

But 23-year-old Ruth Elder, who had just completed flying lessons, had enough determination, confidence, and charm to persuade her flight instructor, George Haldeman, another Lakelander, that it would be a first. Her proposal: She would fly with him as passenger/co-pilot. Haldeman, at 29, was already considered one of the country's best pilots. He had also begun Florida's first airline, "Inter-City," and he already had on order a Stinson-Detroiter monoplane. Earlier that year, like so many other pilots, he was making plans for his own Atlantic hop when his old mail-barnstorming buddy, "Slim" Lindbergh, beat all of them to it. Ruth had already interested local real estate agent T. H. McArdle and citrus grower Edward Cornell who, in turn, interested some banker and businessmen in Wheeling, West Virginia. Together the promoters raised $35,000—enough to buy the Stinson and pay the two flyers' expenses. Finally, to the cheers of area dignitaries and well-wishers, the pair took off from old Drew Air Base in Tampa and arrived at Roosevelt Field, New York, on September 14, 1927.

The hyperzany mood of the Roaring '20s was almost made to order for the daring young female. She immediately infused an aura of sex and glamour into aeronautical public interest, and the national press sensationalized her by doting on her with reams of copy and pictures. One typical effusion: "A stunning young woman with a diminutive, curvaceous figure, hazel eyes, and a husky contralto voice . . . not only very pretty but (she) can actually fly a plane." As Lindbergh was the All-American Boy, she was dubbed the All-American girl; the plane itself was named "American Girl." Even the colorful bandeau she wore around her bobbed brown hair became a popular fad, with women wearing "Ruth ribbons" that quickly became the rage. The modest Haldeman gladly deferred the limelight to his "star" partner.

But the limelight could prove embarrassing, too. The press discovered that Ruth had been married for two years to Lyle Womack, a young businessman working temporarily with his father in Balboa, Panama, even as she affirmed her unmarried status and planned the trip with Haldeman. Ruth admitted she was married, calling the denial a press "misunderstanding," and then, with what one scribe called "an enchanting pout," asked "Why does everybody butt into my affairs?" The press quickly forgave and forgot—except *The New York World,* which had suggested editorially that "Miss Elder be officially restrained from attempting such a dangerous feat."

Finally, after days of overcast skies, the weather cleared and at 5:05 p.m. on October 11, with an excited crowd watching, the "American Girl" took off, barely clearing some telephone lines with its record fuel-load of 520 gallons. Within a short time, however, the plane ran into a severe storm and, for the next eight hours, all of Haldeman's skills were put to test as he guided the craft through a merciless buffeting. After the plane finally emerged into sunlight, Ruth relieved her exhausted partner at the controls. Haldeman (wisely, it developed) had chosen the much longer southern route over the shorter northward Great Circle course used by Lindbergh and others. This avoided the danger of icing and also put him and Ruth Elder along the busier shipping lanes. But although the flight went smoothly that day and night, they had not spotted a single ship and so, for 28 hours, their course remained unreported to an anxious world on shore.

Then, early on October 13, Haldeman was dismayed to see the oil pressure drop as the plane's speed slacked to 70 miles per hour. He quickly throttled back but discovered that an oil line had ruptured. For the next five hours he nursed the engine along but the oil pressure steadily dropped to five pounds. Finally, the pair spotted their first ship, the Dutch oil tanker *Barendrecht*. As they circled the vessel, Ruth leaned out and dropped a message to the deck, asking directions. Sailors painted the deck to tell them they were 350 miles north of the Azores. They had 130 gallons of fuel, enough to reach land, but Haldeman knew the severely knocking engine could not last much longer and they would have to ditch the plane.

With expert skill, Haldeman stalled the plane and gently set it down on the crest of a long swell rolling in front of the tanker; the craft floated without mishap and a tanker lifeboat reached them within minutes. As the crew attempted to hoist the plane aboard, a heavy wave smashed it against the ship's side, causing an underwater explosion that sent flames swirling to the surface. Understandably, the tanker crew cut her loose and backed off as the craft slowly sank to a watery grave.

Ruth Elder and Haldeman had been in the air 36 hours and had set an overwater record of 2,632 miles, which would have got them to Europe had they taken the northward route. Ruth had the dubious distinction of being the first woman flyer rescued from the Atlantic. (The honor of the first woman to fly the Atlantic would go to Amelia Earhart in 1932).

Excited crowds greeted the two at Horta, the Azores, where they were dropped off. Messages flew out to America and Europe and once more the daring couple were back in the headlines. At home, a banner headline in *The Tampa Tribune* shouted: "ELDER SAFE ON SHIP," while a news story reported:"Lakeland's joy . . . literally blew up tonight in the huge public celebration that resounded throughout the city."

Taken first to Lisbon, then Madrid, Elder and Haldeman were dined and feted by government officials. The French government provided them a plane at Bayonne, and Haldeman gunned it to Paris in record time. After rounds of more parties and appearances, the couple sailed for New York on the *Aquitania,* to be greeted by Mayor Jimmy Walker and official host Grover Whalen for a ticker tape ride up Broadway. Happy husband Lyle Womack, also on hand to greet his wife, was surprised to see her sudden coolness to him. (He would later file a divorce complaint against her, claiming she treated him with indifference, scorn, and a superior attitude. The divorce was uncontested.)

Haldeman went on to become a distinguished U.S. test pilot, setting many records, and more recently was a consultant on the controversial B-1 Bomber. His lifetime residence remained in Lakeland. Ruth was flooded with offers but decided to sign on for a $100,000 speaking tour. Later, she contracted with Paramount Pictures to star in Florence Ziegfield's film *"Glorifying the American Girl."* She would fly one more time, in the first women's cross-country derby in 1929, placing a creditable fifth. She reportedly married several more times.

But, in spite of marital misfortunes and a screen career that would reach something less than stardom, Ruth Elder could always look back on that glorious time when her youthful skill and daring captivated a worldwide audience and, more significantly, blazed a trail for a generation of women pilots.

38.
Father Luis' Cross Conquers the Sword

Father Luis tried to settle Florida with nonviolence in 1547 for Spain's King Charles V, but the murderous Indians martyred him. The state remained unsettled another 200 years.

The record of brutality suffered by hapless Indians in Florida and elsewhere under the early Spanish conquistadors is a marked and ignoble one.

But it would be a distorted record if it failed to include a remarkable individual who, for a time, turned upside down the repressive policies of the empire.

The 16th-century Dominican friar, Father Luis Cancer de Barbastro, did in fact convince Spain's King Charles V that Christianity and ruthless soldiery made for an unconscionable and volatile mix for those seeking to colonize the Land of Flowers. Not muskets and dogs, he contended, but only a loving kindness born of "the true faith" could win the Indians.

Only too aware of the years of disastrous expeditions to Florida, from Ponce de Leon, its discoverer, to Hernando de Soto, and the vital strategic position it held for protecting Spanish New World commerce, the king also had been disturbed much earlier when Father Luis' superior, Father Bartolome de Las Casas, protested to him personally of Dominican outrage over Spanish treatment of the Indians. And, finally, he heard of Father Luis' "astonishing" work with Indians elsewhere.

And so, in 1547, a medieval version of "try a little tenderness" was royally decreed; Father Luis was given carte blanche to undertake the Christian conquest of Florida.

No one seemed more ably equipped to undertake this challenge. In earlier mission days in San Domingo and Puerto Rico, Father Luis had earned a reputation for holiness and zeal and an evangelizing boldness. Yet his demeanor was tempered with a quietly practical wisdom and a kindly nature. Then, in 1535, on a journey with Father de las Casas to Peru to instruct— and protect—the Indians recently conquered by Francisco Pizarro, the team was shipwrecked and forced to return to Guatemala. And here lay the scene for Father Luis' most triumphant achievement.

Guatemala's mountain region of Tuzulutlan was called Tierra de la Guerra (Land of War) because the fierce warrior tribes had successfully turned back three invading Spanish armies. Having mastered the native Quiche language, Father Luis proposed a bold plan to local civil heads to convert these Indians. But he exacted one condition: that no white man be permitted to enter Tuzulutlan territory for five years or otherwise molest the Indians. Cynically dubious, the civil heads nevertheless agreed to the plan.

Father Luis organized a team of native Christian peddlers to sing, in native style, a story outline of Christian doctrine as they traded among these people. So impressed were the tribes with this simple story of man's redemption and destiny that they sent a deputation to Father Luis to learn more of it. Traveling alone, the friar returned with the group to the Land of War and, before long, converted the chief of the tribes. The chief's son soon became an enthusiastic assistant to Father Luis as he and his peddler-musicians journeyed from mountain village to village singing and teaching the gospel. So completely did he win the hearts and minds of the Tuzulutlans that, by 1538, the whole region had exchanged idols and weaponry for the cross. In subsequent years, aided by Father de las Casas and others, he evangelized the neighboring Coban nation and soon united the two peoples. As one historian recounted, Father Luis established these tribes "in stable towns and villages, cultivating the soil, and gradually acquiring the arts and benefits of a happy, prosperous, and civilized life."

As civil authorities shook amazed heads at this "miracle," a royal edict changed the region's name from la Guerra to Tierra de la Vera Paz (Land of True Peace), the name it remains today. And the friar won royal approval for his proposed Florida effort, but with the stipulation that he go to the upper east coast and avoid the Gulf coast, which was "running with the blood of the Indians."

Taking with him Fathers Gregorio de Beteta, Diego de Tolosa, Juan Garcia, and a Brother Fuentes, Father Luis sailed from Vera Cruz to Havana in 1549. Here he acquired a "highly recommended" converted Indian woman, Magdalena, as interpreter, and the team set sail for Florida.

But the ship's captain Juan de Arena, proved a fateful choice. Whether by ignorance or design, Arena brought the caravel to the forbidden Gulf coast and the mission made its first landing a distance south of Tampa Bay. Encountering some 20 Indians on shore, Father Luis, Tolosa, Brother Fuentes, and Magdalena knelt in prayer beside them and then presented them small gifts. Learning of many villages in a "great harbor" northward, a day and a half's journey by land, and observing the eager friendliness of these Indians, Father Luis permitted Tolosa, Fuentes, Magdalena, and a sailor to accompany them there, enlisting natives along the way. But when the caravel entered Tampa Bay on June 23, only Magdalena and a number of Indians were there to meet them. Father Luis saw that the woman was "much changed," and even attired in only the brief native moss skirt. She explained that the others were guests of a local chief and that she had convinced the Indians that the fathers had only peaceful intentions. But, on returning to the caravel that evening, they found on board a Spanish sailor, Juan Munos, who had been a captive slave of the Indians since the de Soto expedition and had just escaped. Munos told them that Tolosa and Fuentes had been killed and the sailor kept as a slave.

Alarmed, Fathers Beteta and Garcia urged that they leave at once and go to their original destination, the east coast. But the impassioned leader now felt the place to be "hallowed by the life-blood" of his aides. He had met similar dangers before and, moreover, he had "promised God" he would undertake this task, whatever the cost. Releasing the two men from any constraints to remain, he set about writing letters, completing his diary, and gathering small gifts. Then, on June 26, he, Beteta, Garcia, and Munos rowed toward shore, observing there a large number of Indians armed with clubs and bows. The natives were shouting for the release of their slave, Munos, and as Father Luis slipped over the boat side to wade ashore, Beteta pleaded once more for him to remain. But the friar only smiled and wished

The Indians were adept at using special clubs to kill wrongdoers of their own. These were the same weapons used to kill Father Luis.

them well. As he walked ashore, the Indians receded to a small hillock, watching him fixedly as Father Luis knelt in prayer for a while. As he arose, an Indian came forth and embraced him, urging him forward. Then, as the two drew within a few feet of the group, the Indians suddenly rushed on the Father and clubbed him to death.

"And thus perished," as historian Woodbury Lowery noted, "a noble, brave, and gifted man," due to be duly recorded as a church martyr, and in whose honor the Church of St. Louis in Tampa would be erected.

Thus perished, too, hopes for the earliest peaceful development of the state, most of it remaining thereafter unsettled for more than two centuries. A noble experiment to transplant the cross over the sword, tragically aborted by placing the right man on the wrong shore, might also have totally altered the historic destiny of an entire state.

39.
Florida's Heroines for Suffrage

It took 60 years for Florida to ratify the amendment that allowed women to vote, but the suffragettes never gave up. There were some notable warriors along the way.

If the lightly patronizing billboard jingle, "You've come a long way, baby," is a correct assessment of women's social progress to date, it is a quick and easy gloss-over of the facts. Women have come a long way in two generations because of their overall struggle for equality and their specific fight for the right to vote. Much of that was still being fought right here in Florida as recently as two decades ago.

The American women's suffrage movement, born in the mid-19th century, arose from acute dissatisfaction with a host of social inequities. Women were barred from professions and from enrollment in most institutions of higher learning. They were disenfranchised and had few if any rights concerning property, buying and selling, and even retaining their own salaries. Yet led by such diverse crusaders as Elizabeth Cady Stanton, Lucy Stone, Sojourner Truth, Susan B. Anthony, and others, they steadily progressed. By century's end, many were attending universities, engaging in businesses and professions and, in a few states, they even were permitted to vote.

But through most of the South, including Florida, the subject of women's suffrage was anathema— especially to politicians. The latter often viewed the movement as everything from an attempt to "soil . . . women's purity . . . with the filth of masculine politics" to a "socialist-Negro-radical element" out to overthrow the government.

In Florida, the suffrage movement began in Tampa, in 1893, after Mrs. Ella C. Chamberlain, of that city, returned from a suffrage conference in Des Moines, Iowa. Inspired to carry the crusade to her state, she first obtained permission from a local newspaper to write a column.

But when it suggested that she write on topics of interest to women and children, she replied that "the world was not suffering for another cake recipe, and the children, seemed to be getting along better than the women." She was then allowed to write on women's rights, but there was little public sympathy with her ideals. Later she began to speak to social groups, using the theme "taxation without representation" and asserting, "I deny that my brother American can properly represent me." A gradually favorable audience response soon enabled her to organize the Florida Woman Suffrage Association with 20 members, eight of them men. The group spoke, wrote, and distributed literature on the movement and also affiliated itself with the National American Woman Suffrage Association, headed by Susan Anthony. Membership steadily increased. But after Mrs. Chamberlain left the state in 1897, the group's activities dwindled virtually to dormancy.

They were reactivated in 1912 when, in Jacksonville, Mrs. Roselle Cooley and 30 other women organized the Florida Equal Franchise League. This league began to branch out and, by 1916, would have 21 groups in cities from Pensacola to Miami, with 800 members. Several men's leagues also were formed. In the 1913 session of the Legislature, they began lobbying the lawmakers for a referendum bill for a state constitutional amendment grant-

When these suffragists met in Fort Myers in 1913, they may have looked like an ineffective group, but their long fight finally paid off.

ing women the vote. H. L. Bussey, of Palm Beach County, was persuaded to introduce a bill, but the House rejected it 39-26, one opponent charging that women "would be lowered from the exalted position which they now hold" and their "purity would suffer at the polls."

But the suffrage groups continued a flurry of efforts. They sponsored teas, banquets, musicales, and booths at fairs, mailed literature statewide and enlisted the aid of such notable Florida residents as Mr. and Mrs. William Jennings Bryan and Mrs. Frank Stranahan. They soon won endorsements from such diverse groups as the Florida Federation of Women's Clubs, the state's school principals, and the State Federation of Labor. They invited well-known suffragist lecturers like Jeannette Rankin (later a U.S.Congresswoman) and Anna Howard Shaw. The *Miami Herald* acclaimed a speech by the latter as "one of the wittiest, wisest, and sanest expressions of the suffrage arguments." However, views of the state press in general were mixed, some supporting suffrage, some opposing and a few offering lukewarm tolerance of "the inevitable."

After suffering a setback in the 1915 legislative session, when the amendment bill was promptly killed in committee, the suffragists found an eloquent ally in the 1917 session. Here they had a champion in Representative A. C. Hamblin, of Hillsborough, who argued that he did not believe male voters were any better qualified to govern than female, adding that, in the realm of moral fitness, women might be superior. "Go to the saloons and see which sex will be found there," he observed. But opponent George Brooks, of Monroe, perhaps unwittingly confirming Hamblin, declared that he for one "would not lower women from their traditional pinnacle. Politics is a dirty game . . . and women can not mix with filth without some of it sticking." A majority of both houses carried the bill, but it still failed for lack of the required three-fifths vote. Still, the suffragists were more successful with the local bills permitting them to vote in local elections in 23 different cities.

By 1919, the movement's strong national drive had thrust before the U.S. Congress the 19th (Susan B. Anthony) amendment, granting nationwide suffrage, and President Woodrow Wilson eloquently urged its passage. In emotional debate, there surfaced from the Florida delegations a blatant racism, so long veiled beneath the catch-all shibboleth "state rights." Noting that "two million black women" would have the vote, Senator Duncan Fletcher declared the amendment would also authorize federal intervention to protect their voting rights, a violation of state rights, he warned, under which "the Republic cannot long endure." Senator Park Trammel agreed, reminding his colleagues that "in our state at present, elections are exclusively in the hands of white men." In the house, Frank Clark, of Gainesville, angrily denounced the suffrage movement as dominated by a "socialist-

Negro-radical element," out to overthrow the government. "Let us leave woman where she is," he pleaded, "and not soil her noble character with the filth of masculine politics . . . the loveliest of all creation . . . undisputed dictator of the destiny of man."

But apparently the fair "dictators" decided to dictate their own destiny. On June 4, 1919, the amendment passed, 66-30 in the Senate and 304-89 in the House. Jubilant Florida suffragists pleaded with the Legislature, which was about to adjourn, to secure the honor of being the first state to ratify. The lawmakers declined, and Governor Sidney Catts refused to call a special session because, he said, he was sure the solons would vote against it. By August 1920, Tennessee became the required 36th state to ratify, in time for the general elections, and the rolls took on 25 million new voters. Florida, incidentally, won the dubious honor of being the last state to ratify—in 1969!

As Florida women flocked to register that first year, only a slight difference was noted—many women refused to give their age. But the election supervisors, with diplomatic tact, permitted them to register as "twenty-one plus."

War and Peace

40.
Fast Cars, Rich Men at Ormond-Daytona

The hard sand of Ormond Beach was the world's first major race track, decades before Daytona's popularity.

When Floridians think of speed and auto racing today, they think "Daytona" without a pause.

But few realize that the Daytona Beach races trace their celebrity and origin a little further up the silvery beach track, to Ormond Beach, where over 70 years ago the "Golden Age of Racing" was born—on a bicycle.

It was in that plush era of ostentatious wealth of the 1900s, when the fabulously affluent fled the chilly North annually to gather at the huge luxury Ormond Hotel—"Millionaire's Colony"—for fun, games, and sniffish camaraderie. Here sported the Whitneys, the Wintons, and the Vanderbilts, and here John D. Rockefeller Sr. passed out shiny dimes, and homilies on thrift, to little children after church, as if to say, "It's those dimes, kids, not old dirty greasy oil, that cuts the Golden Pie." (And here the rich remained until railroader Henry Flagler, the hotel owner, grew bored and dragged most of them in tow to another playground farther south, Palm Beach, years later.)

In the meantime, pioneer auto makers and racers were about to make Ormond Beach the original speed capital of the world, and names like Olds, Marriott, Chevrolet, Mercedes, Ford, and Lancia, to name a few, were among the christeners.

The aforementioned bicycle belonged to one J. F. Hathaway, a hotel guest, who noticed one day in 1902 that its tires barely left an imprint on the hard-packed sandy beach. He then drove his small Stanley Steamer over it and made a similar observation. It's a natural race track, he mused, and, with the aid of some selective publicity and the hotel's promoter, "Senator" W. J. Morgan, the first speed trial with two racers was set up the same year.

First car to hit the sands was Ransom E. Olds' "Pirate." The year before, Olds had made history with his Curved Dash Oldsmobile, America's first mass-produced car, and by the next year, he was selling a third of all cars sold in the country. The "Pirate," a spidery-looking hulk with a water-cooled, one-cylinder engine was joined by Alexander Winton's "Bullet No. 1," an oblong vehicle, resembling a half-open casket, mounted on wooden

165

wheels and cooled by a bulky front-end radiator. Both clocked the mile at a sensational 57 miles per hour.

In March 1903, the first official races were held and the course was stretched five miles south to Daytona. It was Olds and Winton again, joined by Oscar Hedstrom on an Indian motorcycle. This time, Winton pushed his "Bullet" to a winning 68.198 mph. His car was the star of the Madison Square Garden Auto Show that year. The country-wide publicity had packed the hotel, and by the time of next year's race, 1904, an exclusive new club, the Florida East Coast Auto Association, was formed. Meanwhile, Senator Morgan had toured Europe to entice noted continental racers to Ormond, and they were soon to come.

The 1904 beach track drew names of both nobility and notoriety—the Count D'Armande, actress Irene Bentley, the Duke of Manchester, Sir Walter DeWar, and others. A fatal cloud hung over the near future of two of these clubmen. Stanford White, the millionaire architect, would be casually shot to death in a Manhattan supper club by coal heir Harry Thaw over the affections of teenage beauty Evelyn Nesbit, prompting the country's most salacious murder trial. Later, the club received the dues of John Jacob Astor, sent just prior to his fatal voyage on the "unsinkable" *Titanic*.

Ransom Olds' "Pirate" was the first auto onto the Ormond Beach sands in the 1902 race which earned the beach the title, "Birthplace of Speed."

That year saw both auto and motorcycle dueling at Ormond Beach. William K. Vanderbilt won the auto race with his 90-horsepower, four cylinder Mercedes, cracking the world's record at 92.30 mph. On the cycles, the airplane whiz, G. H. Curtiss, topped both Hedstrom and automaker W. W. Austin.

A tall, slim, dejected-looking young man stood on the sand among the dapper millionaire spectators. The previous year, his hand-built "999" racer had set an unofficial world record of 91.37 mph on frozen Lake St. Clair in Michigan. He had borrowed the money to bring his car from that state to Ormond but it cracked an axle in transit and he was too broke to repair it. His quarters were a tent pitched on nearby sand dunes where he took his frugal meals of cheese and crackers. His auto peers treated him with cool politeness—and no more—as befitted some "rustic mechanic" trying to crash the upper leagues. Such icy hauteur must only have honed more sharply young Henry Ford's ambition. He never won a race but, ten years later, he would be selling 248,307 of his famous Ford "Tourers" at the unheard of low price of $490, to revolutionize mass production in the U.S.

By January 1905, the racing fever was at high pitch, and Flagler ordered a special train to haul in spectators to Ormond from a pickup point at St. Augustine.

By now the "foreigners" were crowding onto the oceanside track, and a Scot, Arthur McDonald, won with a record 104.6 mph in his 90 horsepower Napier, while Vanderbilt slid three seconds behind his 1904 record. H. L. Bowden in a racer with four-cylinder Mercedes engines coupled in tandem hit 108.58 mph but was disqualified on a technicality.

A singular year was 1906 with an impressive crop of drivers arriving at Ormond—Fred Marriott, in his "Rocket," a Stanley Steamer; Louis Chevrolet, Victor Demogeot, and Vaughn, in Darracqs; and Lancia and Cedrino, in Fiats. Marriott's "Rocket," a fragile-looking upside down canoe with four bicycle wheels, had a body of wood and canvas and was steered by a tiller. But it set the first world's record of two miles per minute; the Ormond Beach sands allowed its driver to earn the title, "Fastest Man on Earth." But, later that same month, the famous French racer Demogeot raced along the ocean to top the 120 mph by seconds and was, in turn, dubbed "Auto Speed King of the·World."

As the years passed, other famous drivers found Ormond Beach the place to make their mark as a new record beckoned to be—and was—broken each successive year by such famous speedsters as the colorful Barney Oldfield, both Charles and Frank Duryea, Ralph DePalma, and Tommy Milton.

But the speed trials were to take a long lapse—up to and through World War I—with the last record set by Oldfield, his perennial teeth-clenched cigar stub profile and his unique Blitzen Benz burning the sands at 131 mph.

The trials resumed again in 1919 when DePalma drove his Packard over 149 mph, only to be topped by Tommy Milton, in 1920, with 156 mph in a Dusenberg. Then came another long six-year lapse. Meanwhile the speedway had moved farther south each year until it was now south of Daytona. Then, in 1927, some powerful streamlined monsters moved onto the scene. Britain's Sir Henry Segrave drew huge crowds to see his big red "mystery" two-engine Golden Arrow attempt the unheard of speed of 200 mph. The record was then held by another Briton, Sir Malcolm Campbell, who had blazed his Bluebird 174 mph in Wales the year before.

Segrave's first failure was baffling until his mechanics discovered that closed air shutters had almost suffocated his rear engine. The shutters were opened and he made his mark, 203 mph. Campbell brought his Bluebird over in 1928 and out-ran Segrave with 206.95 mph, but a month later, Ray Keech topped Campbell in the Triplex, a monster racer decked with three 500-horsepower Liberty Aero engines, to hit 207.55.

Tragedy stalked one of the entrants that year, the popular Frank Lockhart, an Indianapolis 500 winner, who struck a tiny dip in the beach and flipped his Stutz Blackhawk end over end into the surf, where it leaped and flipped high in the air for another 200 yards. Lockhart barely escaped drowning. This was a warning of things to come, for later that year, in April, the gritty sand burned his tires to fringes, causing him to lose control. His racer flipped forward at full speed, catapulting him like a bullet against the hard beach; he was killed instantly.

In 1929, Britain's Segrave set the record again with 231.36 mph. That year saw a double tragedy when Lee Bible, a veteran racer, took a turn at the monster Triplex, after Keech had taken leave of the racer. Some racers considered its size and triple engines as too much for its frame, making its speed inadequate to control in deceleration. One man, a Pathe News photographer, Charles Traub, was so sure of this "jinx" that he set his tripod camera down at the far end of the speedway to snap a shot of the wreck he was sure would come if Bible "lifts his foot too quick (from the accelerator)." Traub was right. Bible apparently did lift his foot "too quick" and the huge machine skidded awry and crumpled up against the dunes, killing Bible instantly. Traub's predicting did not go far enough. As he focused his camera the wreck careened toward him, killing him and mutilating his body as it smashed into and over him in its fatal path.

Afterwards, the races became intermittent, with few spectator events or records. The powerful speeds were becoming too great for even the hard-packed sands of Daytona and race drivers were increasingly flocking to a newly discovered speedway out in Utah—the vast Bonneville Salt Flats where the speed limits had, literally, "no limit."

But the Ormond-Daytona track was to see one last great record set on its sands, as if in a fitting finale to a golden era, in 1935, its last year. Thousands of spectators were on hand, but all they could see was a blue-streaked blur as Sir Malcolm Campbell roared his new Bluebird, with a 2,500-horsepower Rolls-Royce engine, to a record-shattering 276.816 mph.

And an era ended. The stockcars and other events were to come later to the Daytona International Speedway, but the colorful, pioneer years of the birthplace of speed would come again only in the memories of those awkward, comical, ingenious machines that first coughed and sputtered out onto the silver sands of Ormond Beach at the turn of the century.

41.
Pristine Lake Worth is Discovered

Lake Worth, near Palm Beach, was late to develop. But, when it came, the change was rapid.

In the near-modern era of late 19th-century America, the area of Lake Worth and its eastern sandbar called Palm Beach remained the most primitive, if idyllic, wildland on the U.S. Atlantic coast.

Long after most early Florida settlements had blossomed into townships on either coast, this primitive paradise on a large fresh-water lake had been curiously overlooked by everyone, and for a quarter-century its handful of pioneers would live an almost Robinson Crusoe existence. The Spanish, who ran the state for three centuries, barely gave Lake Worth a glance; the British ignored it altogether. Later, almost overnight, it would gestate from frontier wilderness into an American Riviera.

But as far as its first inhabitants were concerned, it was a strange, beautiful, unexplored territory—one in which few would have been surprised to see some Columbus step ashore one day and claim it for Isabella.

The Rockefellers, Flaglers, Kennedys, Vanderbilts, Wanamakers, and Posts were still a world away when the first settler on the lake squatted alone in a palmetto shanty on the west side of Palm Beach. Ironically, like the rich and royal dwellers to come later, August Lang, a German immigrant, was trying to get away from it all, too, but for another reason. He was dodging the Confederate army draft during the Civil War. After the war, he returned to his Fort Pierce home, only to be fatally shot, presumably by some irate local patriot.

The nearest postwar settlement to Lake Worth was a handful of people at the Jupiter lighthouse, some 12 miles northward. The lighthouse keeper, James A. Armour, held the lonely vigil from 1868 to 1908, supplementing his modest income by buying exotic bird plumes from the Seminole Indians and reselling them to a Northern maker of ladies' hats.

However, a singular glimpse of the rugged but free-ranging day-to-day life in this unique Shangri-la setting was best recorded by Charles W. Pierce, son of the first family to settle on Lake Worth.

The plans of Hannibal Dillingham Pierce, of Chicago, to take his schoolteacher wife, Margretta, son Charles, and brother-in-law, William

Moore, to settle in Florida were greatly hastened by the Chicago fire of 1871. They escaped injury in this calamity only to have the deserted cabin they had occupied south of Fort Pierce on their arrival burn down, destroying most of their possessions. After temporary aid from a job as assistant lighthouse keeper at Jupiter, Pierce, lured by the placid long lake he could view from the tower southward, decided to move his family there and, in 1872, they arrived on Hypoluxo Island, in the middle of the lake.

Before moving, however, the destitute family was unexpectedly blessed with a shipwreck—a periodic event off Florida's coast in those days, offering up surprising varieties of gifts to any nearby shore-dweller. The steamer Victor, breaking apart off Jupiter Inlet, washed ashore to the Pierces a Saratoga trunk, boxes of cloth, fifty men's suits, perfume extract, ten 100-pound kegs of butter, a sewing machine, and many cases of Plantation Bitters, a potent water that enabled the Indians present to indulge in a noisy week-long beach dance. A huge castoff lifeboat, sloop-rigged by Pierce, served to transport them to Hypoluxo Island on the lake.

Lumber for their new home was secured in the only way possible then— beachcombing for pieces of it washed ashore from wrecks or lost cargoes. The numerous shipwrecks would also leave large chunks of brass and copper, in bolts, nails, or sheets. "This junk metal was the bank on which the first settlers drew for their food, clothes, and ammunition," Pierce recalls. They were traded at Sand Point (Titusville), the nearest general store almost 150 miles away. Thus a trip to the store by the only means of getting there— boat—could mean several weeks, weather permitting.

A small, crude, but sturdy and solid home was constructed by the Pierces from heavy ship timbers, while palmetto fronds served as shingles temporarily. A damaged boat was also salvaged on the beach and, after repairs, proved to be durable ocean transport for the whole family. Within a year, the Pierces had several new neighbors—Charlie Moore, H. F. Hammon and Will Lanehart, and Mrs. and Mrs. W. M. Butler and young daughter, Mary.

The primeval beauty of this isolated wilderness settlement on the three-mile island—blanketing acres of purple and red morning glory fields and gleaming moonflower vines, the tropical white and blue heron, white ibis, pink curlew and, in winter, thousands of bluebill ducks—was still a sharp contrast to the hard business of sustaining existence.

But, aside from fish, there was much game to be hunted, on both island and mainland. Their first Christmas dinner was a large possum that Moore had fattened on sweet potatoes and, to the Pierces, it tasted like a young suckling pig. Turtle season from May to July was also a critical time. A major food supply to the lake dwellers was the eggs of the green turtle, loggerhead, and trunkback, which were boiled, scrambled, fried, or used in pancakes, cake, and bread. Turtle meat, which the young Pierce described as "poor beef but good," was another staple. The eggs brought another tasty meat—bears that would swim over to the island just for this delicacy. Pierce spent more than a few nights on the grass at the edge of the beach, "sitting for bear;" as the lumbering animals pawed the beach for eggs, they were sitting ducks for Pierce's double-barreled shotgun. Deer were also plentiful—if you could get close enough to one—and fresh venison soon became a regular staple.

Two of the meanest nuisances in this Crusoe-like living were the mosquitoes and sandflies. At night, all light was extinguished and the Pierce family would sit around a fumy smoke pot in the middle of the room, until they retired to their floor-mat beds ringed with mosquito netting.

A few more individual or family settlers came to Lake Worth in these early years but the rugged living forced most of them soon to return to the more "civilized" areas of Sand Point or Jacksonville. Because of the numerous shipwrecks along this wilderness coast, due to storms and hurricanes, the U.S. Government in 1876 set up a series of five Houses of Refuge, stocked with food staples, at points along the 60-mile stretch from Lake Worth to Miami. The elder Pierce was offered the job of keeper of the nearest House, just south of Lake Worth, and the Pierces now had two homes. The new temporary dwelling, with its greater comfort and convenience, proved a healthful boon to Mrs. Pierce, ailing and pregnant with Charles' sister, Lillie Elder, who was born in the Refuge that same year. But the isolation of the Refuge, the small pay, and the long idle hours that could be spent on the development of his lake island homestead, prompted Pierce to resign and return to Hypoluxo in January 1878.

Meanwhile, three new families—the David Browns, E. N. "Cap" Dimicks and Frank Dimicks—began homesteads on the lake on Palm Beach. Cap Dimick would be the first to see the value of the area as a tourist attraction and would build Palm Beach's first hotel, Coconut Grove Hotel, in 1880.

Schools were nonexistent but Mrs. Pierce, a school teacher, provided her son and daughter with the basic "three-R" skills, supplemented with books that occasionally washed ashore in boxes from shipwrecks.

Into the 1880s, subsistence remained primitive, dependent on gun, fishline or net. Occasionally, the Pierce family was forced to live on palmetto cabbage, fish, Indian pumpkin, and wild game when they had the powder and shot and could locate it. Ingenious substitutes were often contrived; some dried leaves of wild hammock plant made passable tea, and sweet potatoes, baked to a crisp, dark, brown and ground in a small coffee grinder tasted almost as good as Postum, Pierce recalled. The great single benefactor, however, was the beach. When supplies ran short, "it was not hard to

gather four or five hundred pounds of old metal in a week of beachcombing."
The brass and copper would net them up to 15 cents a pound in trade at the
Sand Point store. A hardy soap was produced by boiling alligator fat,
leached in a barrelful of mastic tree ashes.

Shipwrecks, seen or unseen, often washed up some small or large
bounty of varying value. The "great wine wreck" of 1886 strewed thousands of kegs of wine along the beach from Indian River to Biscayne Bay. At
Palm Beach, the 100-gallon casks of Spanish claret blanketed the beach for
a mile. The Pierces kept one 100-gallon cask, plus four 15-gallon kegs of
Malaga and another keg branded "Double Superior." Charles Pierce later
regretted that they did not bury a number of 100-gallon casks in the sand
"where I am sure they would have kept in good condition for years." Federal
jurors called to Miami to serve at this time were unduly delayed and the
Judge was forced to grant them a week to sober up.

Palm Beach might never have had its beautiful palms and hence, might
never have been picked by Henry Morrison Flagler as a resort site had not
the Spanish brig Providentia been broken and beached, strewing thousands
of coconuts along the shore in 1878. Those not used for food were planted
up and down the shoreline and inward and took root immediately.

Mail service was erratic at best until the advent of the famous "barefoot
mailman," in the mid-eighties. The carrier walked barefoot in order to travel
at the water's edge where the sand was firmer. His six-day route, from Palm
Beach to Miami and return, was a lonely and often hazardous one; at least
one carrier lost his life trying to swim the dangerous inlet currents. Charlie
Pierce took the route for a while but few ever stayed long at this wearying
task.

A few of the thousands of tourists who were flocking into Florida in the
late 1880s dribbled down to the Lake Worth area and Cap Dimick's hotel
began to enjoy a brisk seasonal visitor business. During the rest of the year,
the lake settlers gathered at the Coconut Grove for picnics, dances, and a
variety of social occasions, finding some respite from the still hard, pioneering days. And then—almost overnight—this lonely wilderness setting would
drastically change, never to be the same again.

When Henry Flagler passed Lake Worth in the early 1890s, he spotted
the beautiful long line of coconut palm trees on the long ocean key and made
up his mind at once. He sent his agents out to buy up tracts of the property—
including Dimick's hotel—and then pushed his railroad line all the way to
what is now West Palm Beach. People poured in; money and goods poured
in; the lake bustled with steamers, barges, and sailboats, and a small city of
tents sprang up around the largest hotel in the world, Flagler's 2,000-room
Royal Poinciana, which opened in 1894. As people had gradually flocked to
the area, the game had correspondingly disappeared and although settlers

were now excited over the lower east coast's first land boom, they were never so pointedly reminded that the adventurous old days had gone forever as when they had to swap their bear, venison, and turtle eggs for cans of Armour's corned and roast beef.

Charles Pierce would swap his romantic life as sailor, hunter, explorer, and student of flora and fauna in this often idyllic semitropic wilderness to become postmaster of West Palm Beach where he remained until his death in 1939. But he left behind a minor history classic of memories *Pioneer Life in Southeast Florida,* to recall one of the most unique areas and eras of Florida history.

42.
When Nazi U-boats Stalked Florida

While tourists frolicked on the beaches, German subs were attacking ships not far off the shore.

Americans, fortunately, saw neither the shell nor fire of World War II on their own soil.

But in the early months of that war, east coast Florida citizens shared a gruesome, almost front-porch witness to it, as the night skies flared periodically with flame and explosion, and the fine beach sands stood awash by morning with great heavy sheets of oil, mixed flotsam, and more than a few charred corpses.

The world conflagration had been declared barely weeks before, but it was to come with destructive swiftness—and disturbing proximity—as Florida's coast became the scene of a deadly submarine warfare that marked one of the worst chapters in the Allied cause.

It all seemed a little unreal that winter of 1942. True, the press blared its bold headlines of faraway battle places and the first dread War Department telegrams had begun to trickle into shaken homes. But it was, after all, just that—faraway.

The tourist business still bustled in the coastal resort cities. Winter visitors still sipped their Scotch or daiquiris in opulent resort lounges or frolicked at surfside. Residents still scurried about with their home or job affairs. And, as one walked past rich greenery on tree-lined quiet streets in the splendid sunny weather, the big faraway war did seem a little unreal.

But in those same moments, in one of those faraway places, a wily Nazi sea lord was cooking up some bad news for the local chambers of commerce. And it came like what it was—a torpedo blast.

German Admiral Karl Doenitz wasted little time getting his menacing subs to the lush shipping lanes in the Florida straits and along its coast; he had figured this congested area to be the soft underbelly of American shipping. He was right. And before the U-boat blitz was over, it took one of the most devastating—and humiliating—tolls of ships, supplies, and men in the war's history.

This lethal undersea silence was broken without warning on the night of February 19, 1942, just southeast of Cape Canaveral. The captain of the first

German sub, *U-128,* to enter Florida waters, raised his periscope to an invitingly large, dark silhouette on the horizon. He moved in swiftly and fired two torpedoes point blank. Within seconds, the tanker *Pan Massachusetts,* riding low with 100,000 barrels of oil, became an exploding inferno. This Nazi calling card was illuminated with an ocean aflame for a mile around; 38 men jumped into it and the Coast Guard managed to save 18 of them. Two days later in the same area, the sub *U-504* joined her sister and sent two more tankers down, the *Republic* and *Cities Service Empire,* but most crewmen were saved. Next day, off Palm Beach, the huge tanker *W. D. Anderson* was hit in a vast explosion; only one man survived. And the blitz had only just begun.

As the days wore on, the toll of ships mounted alarmingly. From Fernandina Beach to Key West, often over one a day would hit bottom as the seawolves moved almost leisurely, picking off the virtually unarmed, defenseless merchantmen and tankers. Defenses were so inadequate that

A tanker buckles amidship under a torpedo hit from a Nazi U-boat and sinks in a black smoking inferno.

U-boats could save their torpedoes for selective shots, letting ships in ballast pass unscathed in favor of a heavily-laden vessel.

Coastal residents could clearly hear the ominous gun roar when sub captains chose to save torpedoes and finish off their prey with shellfire. Vacationers in Miami area hotels watched as the night sky lit up from the tanker *Portrero del Llano* as it became a roaring fireball from which only nine of her crew escaped. Farther up the coast, according to U.S. Coast Guard reports, on a clear June day, two large American freighters were torpedoed within full view of thousands of bathers.

The U-boats didn't help the tourist business much. But in one of those curious inversions of justice, the tourist business certainly helped the U-boats. Hotel owners for months refused to black out or even dim their bright and glittering lights which, like Miami and its suburbs, threw out six miles of glow. Against this glow the southbound ships that hugged the reefs to avoid the Gulf Stream were silhouetted like sitting ducks. The resort people claimed that turning the lights out would ruin the tourist business. Leaving them on certainly ruined a lot of ships, vital supplies, and human lives.

Recalling this episode with some bitterness, U.S. historian Samuel Eliot Morison termed it "one of the most reprehensible failures" of the war effort for those communities not to dim their lights and for authorities not to force them to do so. Not until May 18, 1942 was a stringent dim-out ordered.

Lifeboats were sometimes not even allowed to escape the U-boats riddling them with machine-gun fire. Men from attacked tankers were forced to swim through heavy, syrupy layers of fuel oil, ducking to avoid flames or accidently igniting the oil scum with the signal flares on their life preservers.

Authorities estimated that if a sub sank only two 6,000-ton ships and one 3,000-ton tanker, the total loss would be equal to: 42 tanks, 8 six-inch Howitzers, 88 25-pound guns, 40 two-pound guns, 24 armored cars, 50 Bren carriers, 5,210 tons of ammunition, 600 rifles, 428 tons of tank supplies, 2,000 tons of stores, and 1,000 tanks of gas. If those three ships had made port and their cargoes dispersed, the enemy would have had to fly 3,000 successful air bombing sorties to knock out the same supplies.

The initial defenses against sub warfare were woefully negligibile. For the Gulf sea frontier (which included the Florida coast, the Gulf part of the Bahamas and Cuba), there were only three Coast Guard cutters, a converted yacht, 19 unarmed Coast Guard airplanes, 14 army airplanes with machine guns and two battered army medium B-18 bombers. Nearly all other vessels had been ordered to the crucial Japanese Pacific war or for North Atlantic convoys.

It was a harried game of hide and seek as the little cutters scurried fruitlessly around the vast sea from one "sighting" to another. Effective radar and sonar devices had not yet been developed. Adequate air coverage was unavailable and the strict requirement of ship convoys had not been adopted. Few could catch up to the fast, sleek 500-ton raiders at surface speeds and the subs could crash dive within seconds. They each carried enough fuel for a 42-day cruise. Aside from 14 torpedoes, all carried guns of sufficient calibre to sink most merchant vessels by shellfire alone.

Against such scanty defenses, U-boat captains became bolder: attacking in broad daylight, even surfacing. Lifeboat survivors often observed "young, healthy, sunburned" Germans on sub decks, taking snapshots or moving pictures of a sinking, like so many happy tourists.

For lack of ships and equipment, although shipyards worked around the clock, the entire Atlantic warfare sank only six subs in the first six months of war; the Nazis were launching one a day. The situation became so critical that General George C. Marshall wrote in June 1942, that losses by subs off the coast "threaten our entire war effort." He warned that it could tip the balance of war to the Axis and called for emergency means to bear on it.

In the highest loss month, May 1942, 86 vessels were sunk in or near the Gulf sea frontier. Worse yet, only six U-boats were known to be operating in this area. The next month, however, a "killer-pack" of six cutters sank one sub, *U-157*, near Key West.

A valiant Coast Guard, with unarmed spotter planes, plodded desperately in a hopeless sea game. But the Coast Guard's rescue of crews from flaming or sinking vessels was a distinctive chapter in this one-sided sea duel.

Later, as more planes and vessels were coordinated into highly efficient "killer" groups, the U-boats began to smart heavily. The development of huff-duff (a new high-frequency direction finder) came as a deadly surprise to U-boat commanders. It could pinpoint the exact location of a sub, even at great distance. Ironically, Admiral Doenitz aided huff-duff greatly by insisting, over their protests, that U-boat captains keep daily radio contact with Berlin.

By the summer of 1943, new, more, and better equipment and methods turned the tide against the U-boat. Doenitz was soon moaning to Hitler the "impossible losses" his crack fleets were suffering.

But for six long, devastating months Floridians were a grisly eye-witness to it all.

43.
The War Over a Rogue's Ear

In the days when England and Spain were extremely hostile to each other and Florida was their battleground, a war could start over nothing.

Throughout history, powerful nations have employed every manner of deception, intrigue, and "incident by which to veil predatory designs, clothing the most naked mercenary aggressions with professions of the most righteous motives.

But England's invasion of Spanish-held Florida in 1740, called "The War of Jenkins' Ear," probably took the all-time prize for a dubious "incident" invoked by a nation to justify war and plunder.

Poor Robert Jenkins, a humble and honest smuggler, had grieved mightily before the House of Parliament in 1739 as he related how the "savage and brutal" Spaniards had perfunctorily separated his ear from his head for no good cause after boarding his privateer brig off the Florida coast in search of contraband. The poor man's ear was indeed conspicuously absent, and a sympathetic House of Commons roared its indignation over this outrage against a British subject. Those "barbaric" Spaniards had gone too far this time, they choroused. And, soon enough, the sharp tattoo of war drums reverberated throughout the kingdom.

There were, of course, combined elements of intrigue, deception, and hoax enmeshed in the affair, but such trivial elements were surely irrelevant to the ennobling march of retribution. Besides, General James Oglethorpe, Britain's colonial governor of Georgia, had long shared with his British peers a covetous appetite for the gold and rich trade enjoyed by the Spanish with their colonies in the West Indies, Mexico, and the southern Americas. Florida was the guardian fortress protecting this bountiful commerce flowing through the Caribbean. Seizure of St. Augustine and the St. Johns River country, the main redoubt of Florida's hegemony, would leave this rich commerce undefended, ripe for British exploitation.

An earlier treaty with Spain had legalized a limited trade by England with the former's colonies, but the main trade, the most lucrative, was a semi-underground smuggling business carried on by British merchants. Violent conflicts arose from this trafficking, however, prompting mercantile Britain to clamor all but openly for outright war on Florida.

Of course, English gentlemen—even then—were ever conscious of what was and what was not "cricket," and to so basely lust after another nation's sovereign booty was definitely "un-cricket." Unless . . . unless there were good cause.

Enter "good cause" Jenkins and his lonesome ear. The unfortunate member, Jenkins admitted, had been severed from his head some seven years earlier but he vividly recreated the scene of violent Spanish malignity as they boarded his ship and became furious at finding no contraband in the cargo of the innocent smuggler. The captain then solemnly begged leave to submit to the right honorable House his lamentable Exhibit A, whereupon, he withdrew from his pocket, carefully wrapped in cotton, the ear itself. And with careful pause for effect, concluded: "I commend my conscience to God and my cause to my countrymen."

Gasps, followed by applause, followed by cries of patriotic outrage, led to an open declaration of war against Spain within hours. As for Jenkins and his now famous amputation (so remarkably preserved over seven years), Westminster immediately named him supervisor of the East India Company's office at St. Helena.

Meanwhile, over in Savannah, a jubilant General Oglethorpe plunged into some warm-up exercises before preparing a major onslaught against St. Augustine. He seized river forts and blockaded the St. Johns River to Spanish patrol boats. He seized and burned Picolata and then captured San Francisco de Pupo and Fort Diego. By the end of May 1740, he was ready for the big prize itself and, with an army of 2,000 men and six ships laden with heavy artillery, he prepared to enter that city's harbor.

But ill fortune was to plague the general from this moment. Spies had forewarned the Spanish of Oglethorpe's approach and they quickly placed a circle of small fighting vessels in the harbor. This prevented the general from setting up the vital shore batteries he would need against the massive coquina-shell fort, Castillo de San Marcos. Nevertheless, he kept the fort under steady siege while he awaited the heavy reinforcements which he had been promised earlier. He was confident that the siege itself would greatly cripple, if not capitulate the enemy, since his warships blocked any Spanish supply ships from entering the harbor. But his geographical ignorance of that coastline proved costly. Spanish ships loaded with both provisions and reinforcements slipped quietly into the long waterway through Mosquito Inlet 60 miles south of St. Augustine. In the meantime, balls fired from the cannon of his distant warship, bounced off the massive walls of the great fort like so many BB's.

The long-awaited reinforcements never arrived and, as summer's unbearable heat moved upon them, with a scourge of sickness, mosquitoes, and flies, Oglethorpe and his troops were plunged into a state of gloom and demoralization. Finally, on July 17, an embittered General lifted his siege. After burying a few cannon and destroying their stores, the defeated army drank the remainder of their liquor rations and blearily departed the scene.

The governor's dreams of preempting the vast colonial riches of the Caribbean empire were not only shattered but both his competence and his conduct of the war were inpugned by his English peers, even though England bickered over and delayed aid to him until it was too late.

But, two years later, Oglethorpe would secure a satisfying consolation prize for his efforts. Spain, seeking revenge for the General's previous attack, with some 3,000 men and over 50 ships, attacked the Georgia colony and seized the inland passage to Frederica. But Oglethorpe met the outnumbering forces in the coastal swampland and completely routed them, slaying more than 200 Spaniards on one spot in what he would later dub "The Battle of Bloody Marsh." Now it was the Spanish turn to beat a hasty retreat. However, the general still seethed over his aborted dreams of conquest and in a somewhat feeble "Last Hurrah," he took a force of friendly Creek Indians and raided St. Augustine, pushing right up to the city's gates, but through dissension, fever, and treachery in his mixed command, the force was routed and driven back at the city's walls. Once again, Oglethorpe marched the hard road back to Georgia, spending his fury by burning plantations along the way and slaughtering small pockets of hostile whites, blacks, and Indians. But it was all over now for the ambitious governor. Soon he packed his bags and sailed for England, never to return to his colony.

Thus, the glorious "War of Jenkins' ear" came to its decidedly inglorious conclusion. The struggle between Spain and England for the north bank of the St. Johns River had ended. As one historian summed it: "After the official close of war between the two nations, in 1748, the enmity between Georgia and Florida degenerated into casual border raids, wherein theft, murder, and arson all figured with an equal frequency and a shared inconsequence; both sides maltreated, where they did not abolish, the perplexed Indian; and the St. Johns River began to lose the only permanent population which it had ever possessed, the aboriginal." Earlier, by example, the poor Indian came to admire, emulate, and covet the white man's civilized ways, i.e., murder, rapine, and pillage. Little did he realize how gradually he would come to be the victim of the civilized embrace.

But for at least one comfortable soul, this tragic and bloody little war had paid off quite handsomely. Basking in the balmy, isolated tropic paradise of the island of St. Helena, far down in the South Atlantic and away from worldly power struggles and cares, Captain Jenkins thoroughly enjoyed the sinecure so graciously awarded him for his regrettable loss. The large salary he annually drew from the wealthy East India Company was more than adequate to meet his needs and pleasures in the role of company supervisor.

Besides, the smuggling business had been suffering periodic fits of recession and depression and, furthermore, was becoming increasingly risky to life and limb itself. Moreover, he had convinced himself that his noble contribution to the mother country's march of progress had certainly entitled him to his lifetime emolument.

Of course, some unsettling facts had since surfaced regarding the Captain's dislodged auditory member. It seems that the mummified relic the man proffered to the view of Parliament was simply a dried bit of rabbit skin. Lest this appear as mere quibbling, the man's indisputably missing ear, it was also learned, had been taken from him while he was in a pillory stock. The pillory in those days was a common means of punishment meted out to common thieves and criminals. But, by that time, with Britain's heroic crusade against Spanish infamy in full swing, it might have proved dangerously subversive for any citizen to indulge hair-splitting objections over these facts. Later, the captain himself would repel any such detractions with a hurt and dignified silence. After all, it was bad enough to have to lose the bloody war. But to have its very tenuous justification exposed would have amounted to the rankest heresy, one that any self-respecting English gentleman would have termed as shamelessly "un-cricket."

44.
Bartram Remembers
Florida's Eden

William Bartram was a naturalist who traveled Florida's wilderness recording in poetic phrases its beauty and its beasts.

Historians have taken much care in recording Florida's early past—its wars and strife and civil progress—but only a few have given glimpses of the once splendorous beauty of its Eden-like natural state long before the dragline and bulldozer ushered civilization into the land.

It took a Quaker natural scientist of the late 18th century, William Bartram, to celebrate the wild garden paradise that once was Florida, and preserve a picture of it for our own day. Like his famous naturalist father, John Bartram, who years earlier had published a brief description of this unexplored wilderness, William traversed the great St. Johns River and traveled deep into north central Florida to study and collect specimens of the flora and fauna of a primeval wonderland.

He was no doubt the country's first conservationist and ecologist, for when most men were out to exploit, despoil, and lay waste a virgin continent, Bartram and other noted botanists such as Linnaeus, wanted to investigate, cherish, and preserve these great assets. Sympathetic friends like Ben Franklin and Thomas Jefferson aided and encouraged the young naturalist. But today there are only a scientific record and a colorful portrait in word and sketches of the plants, fish, flowers, birds, animals, and forests that once flourished but no longer exist.

Bartram was also the state's first natural tourist-camper when he set forth on his expedition along the vast, wild expanse of the St. Johns in April 1773. But without motels, campers or air-conditioning, living outdoors then could occasionally be as primitive and dangerous as it was idyllic and awesome in beauty.

Yet his poetic impressions of this natural grandeur were such that writers like William Wordsworth and Samuel Taylor Coleridge would borrow its imagery for some of their famous writings, and Thomas Carlyle once praised Bartram's book to Ralph Waldo Emerson, noting that "it has a wonderful kind of floundering eloquence."

With a small sailboat and simple provisions, Bartram sailed alone from Cowford (Jacksonville) that spring, heading for first destination of a British trading post for Indians 100 miles up river. He would stop at many points along the way to camp, explore, and collect. But at the end of his first day out, he could only exclaim with ebullience: "What an elysium it is!"

Compared to whatever spindly species survive today, what Bartram enjoyed and studied was literally a king-size universal garden. The great forests of the mammoth live oak—trees of "astonishing magnitude," up to 20 feet in girth, "evergreen . . . and incorruptible," he wrote. Its sweet acorns were roasted by Indians like chestnuts, or mashed for cooking oil. He wrote of the huge laurel magnolia tree, often 100 feet tall, with the pervasive fragrance of its huge roselike flowers, and the majestic, lofty cypress stands, in swampy, clustering forests, thick enough to cast the tropic floor into darkness. These trees were often 12 feet in diameter. Eagles nested in their flat tops and Indians used their trunks for sturdy sea-going canoes. Great flowering vegetable vines would thrust up from the river banks and entwine these huge trees, some vines a foot in thickness. At every river bend, one might find a sudden wall of impenetrable forest or a panoramic level sweep of "vast enchanting savannas."

Meanwhile, overhead, thousands of birds (many now extinct), beat the air with a roll like muffled drums—loons, herons, wood pelicans, Spanish curlews, ibises, glossy black snakebirds, joined by squadrons of the "loud, sonorous great savanna cranes," as, nearby, one heard the "social prattling coot robed in blue, and the squealing water-hen," or the tower bird, butcher bird, and cuckoo.

In the water beneath swam thick schools of catfish, stingrays, skate, spotted bass, flounder, sheepshead, jumbo trout (up to 30 pounds, Bartram's favorite seafood), and the famous golden yellow bream of which only the naturalist's delicate color sketches remain today. Also now extinct, the great brown speckled garfish, a voracious hunter coated with a thick alligatorlike mail, and measuring six feet in length, swam these waters.

Bartram would often pitch his sail as a lean-to tent against a spreading live oak on a promontory of the river bank. Keeping a fire through the night, he would then fish for his supper—usually broiled trout and boiled rice with oil, salt, and pepper. He even invented his own gourmet delight, fish heads boiled in the juice of the abundant sour oranges.

Lure fishing is no modern invention. Trout were taken by pole, line, and three large hooks covered with the white hair of a deer's tail, shreds of red garter, and feathers tied in a multicolored tassle. This was called a "bob." One skimmed it back and forth across the water until the "delicious repast" leaped for it.

But the forest storehouse contained an abundance of other fresh food— the "stately, beautiful" great wild turkey, weighing up to 40 pounds, the tender venison steak of the rosebuck deer, along with bear, opossum, quail, squirrels over two feet long, and in season, wild geese and duck and other game.

Rising each dawn to explore, Bartram impressed in his daily notes his elation with each new discovery of some species of flora or fauna. The echoing mingled chorus of cries from bird and animal throughout the wilderness were to the scientist "a universal anthem of the worship of nature for its Creator . . . the peaceable and happy state of nature which existed before the fall."

But it was not all balm in Elysium. The mosquitoes and sultry heat could at times give the lonely sojourner great discomfort. The hungry wolf or bear might creep up at night while he slept and snatch his breakfast of barbecued or salted trout hanging from a bush snag. However, it was the hordes of alligators that gave him his scariest moments. He had to shoot a few, and fend off others with an oar on the snout. The great beasts could measure up to 20 feet in length. Once when he prepared to pitch camp, he found his way blocked by "incredible numbers" of the reptiles, log-jammed in a narrow neck of the river. As he attempted to make a hasty detour down a side creek, two large monsters came after him. They leaped at the gunwale of his boat and "struck their jaws together so close to my ears as almost to stun me and I expected every moment to be dragged out of the boat and instantly devoured." But he managed to club them off and reach his campsite. As the "tumultuous roar" of the mass increased, Bartram peered over the bank and saw a fantastic sight: from shore to shore a solid bank of thousands of fish were trying to force through the narrow pass, while the thrashing "gators waited with yawning jaws. The floods of water and blood rushing out of their mouths, and the clouds of vapor issuing from their wide nostrils were truly frightening." The gory affair continued through the night and Bartram slept little. By morning, the satiated beasts had mostly dispersed and Bartram edgily set sail again.

Along his route, Bartram visited a few of the isolated plantation settlements along the river and was received with "great hospitality" by his hosts who often freely supplied him with staples and ammo, so great was their interest in the scientific purposes of his lonely expedition.

When he reached Spalding's trading post he joined several traders making another journey inland to an Alachua post (Gainesville), and then over to the Little St. Juan River (the Suwannee). Bartram found inland Florida as fascinating as the river. He made studies of the huge land gopher (that could walk with a man on its back), the unusual painted vulture that ate only animals roasted in the fires set by Indians to flush game, the fields of pistia, the elegant Carica papaya flower-fruit, the coachwhip and other snakes, along with dark groves of cedar, zanthoxylum and myrtle, the "perfectly black, rich, soapy earth'' like clay or marl, along the Suwannee and, above all, the hundreds of sinks and grottos, bubbling springs of cool, pellucid water.

The Seminole Indians, whose villages he visited, dubbed him "Puc-Puggy" (flower hunter). He kept his fish hooks and sewing needles in a packet to swap with them for a fawn-skin of honey or a side of venison. When he and traders visited Chief Cowkeeper at Cuscowilla, they were regaled with a great banquet of barbecued bear ribs, venison, fish, roast turkey, corn cakes, and conte jelly, a mix of conte roots ground into powder and set in honeyed water. Bartram observed that the Siminoles (Seminoles), "appear as blithe and free as the birds of the air. The visage, action, and deportment of the [Seminole] form the most striking picture of happiness in this life; joy, contentment, love and friendship, without guile or affectation, seem inherent in them." Even in age, he found "a gladdening, cheering blush . . . of serenity." In war, they do not slay women or children and their captives are allowed considerable freedom in the villages. Their morality is the strictest, he observed, cropped ears for adulterers and disgrace for the fornicators through shunning. Yet, once at an Indian festive occasion, he noted how quickly this morality dissolved under "civilized" influences. After consuming 25-gallon kegs of trader's rum over a ten-day period, the "most ludicrous bacchanalian scene" took place, "both sexes taking such liberties with each other . . . as they would abhor when sober or in their senses."

Puc-Puggy became a hero in one village when he slew with pine knot a giant rattlesnake that had been terrorizing the huts. (Killing serpents was taboo to the Indians, for fear other snakes would seek revenge.) Bartram actually wanted "nothing to do with the reptile" but their insistence, plus the lucky throw of his weapon, saved the day.

Bartram would first discover and classify America's great scientific range of plants and wildlife, along with a list of 215 birds, mostly now extinct. Thomas Jefferson invited him to be the official naturalist with the Lewis and Clark expedition years later, but the ailing naturalist was forced to decline. His book of *Travels* influenced scientists, naturalists, and even statesmen on both sides of the Atlantic and his original wildlife paintings now hang in the British Museum.

But he is especially revered by Floridians for combining "the mind of a scientist with the soul of a poet" to bring them a movable visual feast of the wild and beautiful king-size Garden of Eden that once was their native state.

45.
Tampa's 'Splendid Little War'

The city was not prepared for the international attention it got as the point of embarkation for U.S. troops during the Spanish-American War.

When the City of Tampa (population 12,000) suddenly found itself "the cannon's mouth" for the Spanish-American War of 1898, the little town was plunged into the national spotlight, the effects of which would make it boom over the next 10 years.

Yet there were moments when the "cannon's mouth" was not quite sure on which end of the cannon it was perched; the wild, freewheeling excesses of an army town would soon lend the village all the features of an "occupied" territory.

Selected by the War Department as a point of embarkation because of its deep port and rail facilities, the town's capacities were strained to bursting as population doubled, then tripled virtually overnight. Packed railroad cars daily disgorged thousands of soldiers, arms, supplies, workers, sightseers, plus a horde of camp-following vice lords and ladies. Many soldiers did their only fighting in the hot dusty streets and saloons, and vandalism made some areas look like battle zones. Worse yet, the torrid heat, the foul sanitary conditions and the often putrid canned meat rations would cause disease outbreaks—mainly typhoid fever—that would kill more soldiers (4,784) than all war casualties combined (379). "Horrible!" exclaimed Red Cross founder Clara Barton.

And, certainly, it was all enough to make one look askance at Secretary of State John Hay's glib sobriquet about "that splendid little war."

Still, the country was psyched up with jingoistic war fever, largely due to the sensational efforts of powerful New York publishers like Joseph Pulitzer and William Randolph Hearst. Their inflammatory—sometimes fabricated—stories of Spanish atrocities against Cuban insurgents and their florid editorials about America's "Manifest Destiny" gave coinage to a new phrase, "yellow journalism." Once, when Frederic Remington (not yet the Western painter, but still a war correspondent) wired Hearst from Havana, "There will be no war. I wish to return," Hearst promptly replied: "Please remain. You furnish the pictures, and I will furnish the war."

187

The conflict was virtually ignited with the explosion of the U.S. battle-ship "Maine" in Havana harbor on February 15, 1898, killing 266 men. The cause was never known, but most historians doubt that Spain, whose shaky royal court was frantically seeking a peace effort with the United States, was the culprit. Anyway, all peace talks withered before the thunderous cry, "Remember the *Maine.*" Congress declared war, effective April 21, 1898.

Tampa itself, with nearly a third of its residents Cuban cigar workers, had been a hotbed of activities for Cuban independence even before the Insurgent Revolt in 1895. Jose Marti, renowned Cuban patriot, orator, and martyr in the war, visited Tampa often, giving impassioned speeches and collecting funds for the rebels. The doors of Cuban homes opened wide to fete the soldiers with dinners, picnics, and dances. Tampa's establishment, like the state in general, saw an independent Cuba as an economic threat, since it was a rival marketer of fruits, vegetables, sugar, tobacco, cigars, and tourism. But when the Spanish threatened to embargo tobacco in the city's 90-plus cigar factories, which virtually supported Tampa's main families, that establishment would hardly outdo its Ybor City brethren in shouting, "Cuba libre."

At peak, some 50,000 troops would "occupy" Tampa that spring and summer, accompanied, in one weekend alone, by another 20,000 visitors and tourists. On the first army-civilian payday, May 4, $325,000 gushed into the city. Merchants were giddy with the windfall (it would leap to $1 million in June), and most stores could not keep shelves stocked. Private firms like Armour and Swift jubilantly waved fat government contracts, but the troops were somewhat less jubilant when they found most of their food rations rotten. Mud oozed into already rancid stacks of pork and bacon, and hardtack had softened to a paste. A *London Times* correspondent reported the canned beef "execrable—simply the offal of a beef factory," and troops found the beans soaked in pork fat "nauseating."

The most colorful troops to arrive were Colonel Theodore "Teddy" Roosevelt's Rough Riders, a motley crew of frontier types with names like Cherokee Bill and Rattlesnake Pete, oddly mixed with Eastern bluebloods like tobacco heir P. Lorillard Ronalds and William Tiffany. Their first "action" was dubbed "the charge of the Yellow Rice brigade" when a squad of them galloped right into a new restaurant run by Manuel Menendez, the man who had recently created a tasty new dish called chicken and yellow rice. But owner Menendez, founder of "Las Novedades," which remained a landmark until it closed in the late 1970s, ignored the damage and cheerfully treated the "liberators" to free rounds of drinks.

The town's adopted theme song was "There'll be a Hot Time in the Old Town Tonight," but it sometimes got a little too hot as the troops chafed rest-lessly in the heat and sand, waiting for D-Day. They drilled by day and brawled by night in the streets and bawdy gambling houses. Often they would "commandeer" street cars and take wild joy rides, ending in sprees of vandalism, or they would invade the local brewery and distribute free beer to one and all. Authorities were finally driven to inflict strict measures, including jail sentences for the worst offenders.

Officers and war correspondents like Remington, Richard Harding Davis, or writer Stephen Crane, headquartered in the luxurious Tampa Bay Hotel, also fumed impatiently as they sat on the hotel's broad veranda, munching steak and eggs, and sipping a fashionable new drink called "Scotch Whisky." Perhaps, to counter their own foul food, the troops came up with a new drink called "Cuba Libre," Cuban rum mixed with a certain cola laced with cocaine. (The government, in 1906, made the cola makers remove the drug, but its heady effects in Tampa were already obvious.)

Finally, on June 9, there arrived the long-awaited "message from Garcia," the insurgent general, informing U.S. General William R. Shafter that 9,000 Cubans had occupied the beachheads around Santiago. This was it. At 3:30 a.m. on June 14, 35 transports carrying 16,000 soldiers and 2,300

In 1893 cigar workers like these raised $1 million to help free Cuba from Spanish rule.

horses and mules, plus four tenders, a hospital ship, and 14 naval escorts, slipped away from Port Tampa, soon to hit Santiago and pour over the Cuban mainland. The Spanish navy was trapped and destroyed in Santiago Harbor; "Teddy" would make his famous charge up San Juan Hill (and later, consequently, into the White House); and Admiral George Dewey would blast another Spanish fleet out of Manila Bay. The brief war, ending August 12, forced Spain to give up Cuba, the Philippines, and Puerto Rico, and an exhilarated country celebrated its new role as an imperial world power.

Meanwhile, Tampa would wax prosperous from the war's tremendous economic transfusion; the worldwide publicity would also cause its population to more than triple over the next decade.

But, despite the economic and physical growth, most Tampans were thankful their city had survived the "splendid little war" since, in the role as "cannon's mouth," much of its splendor was completely lost on them.

46.
The 'Dogs of War' Who Were Puppies

The Cuban bloodhounds imported to beat the Seminoles proved unable to follow a scent.

When the U.S. Army found itself bogged down in the torrid Florida swamps and jungles after four bloody dead-end years of the Second Seminole War (1835-42), it turned in desperation to a dubious tactic—but one that, ultimately, would provide one of the few amusing interludes in an otherwise tragic conflict.

In 1840, after a succession of generals either resigned or were relieved of command in their fruitless efforts to capture the elusive Indians, the War Department decided it would "unleash the dogs of war"—literally.

The dogs, imported Cuban blood hounds, were reputedly expertly trained and ferocious trackers whose sophisticated nostrils would quickly sniff out the foe and thus shorten the war dramatically.

However, in a nation already disgusted with the war and still indignant over the betrayal and death two years earlier of the imaginative and daring Seminole leader, Osceola, the move provoked a critical storm. U.S. congressmen labeled it "an atrocious and barbarous policy" and "a stain upon our national honor." One solon accused Florida politicians (who had purchased the dogs without U.S. authorization) of wanting them to track runaway slaves who had joined the Seminoles as much as for "tearing the red devils to pieces." U.S. Representative John Quincy Adams, the former president, questioned the hounds' "nice discrimination of scent" between Indian and Anglo-Saxon. A point well taken, it turned out.

The dogs themselves seemed, at times, to more resemble pampered poodles than predatory stalkers. They were expensive to begin with, at $151.72 a dog. They understood no English; their Cuban trainers had to be hired also. They had expensive tastes. For them, no beef jerky, hardtack, or beans but only tender young calves' meat in large bloody chunks. The calves had to accompany each search mission. And, in order not to fatigue their pure-bred sensibilities, the hounds were often mounted on the horses while the men walked. They may have been the Army's first truly "elite corps;" no foot-slogger ever had it so good. In most respects, they certainly appeared to be the sleekest and finest of thoroughbreds. But—they had one glaring defect: they couldn't seem to find any Indians, although they did sniff out a lot of General Zachary Taylor's troops.

The use of dogs to track the fast-moving, hit-and-run Seminoles had been discussed by Florida Militia leaders and General Thomas Jesup as early as July 1837, but—sensitive to public opinion—privately. Jesup thought the hounds would be "worth an army" and seemed determined to procure some. (This was before his removal from the Florida command for betraying and capturing Osceola under a flag of truce.) In fact, Jesup wrote Colonel William Harney at the time: "When you see Osceola, tell him that I intend to search [throughout the state] and take all the Negroes who belong to the white people and that he [Osceola] had better not let Indian or Indian Negroes mix with them. Tell him I am sending to Cuba for blood-hounds to trail them and I intend to hang every one of them who does not come in." Harney, who was perhaps the ablest Indian fighter in Florida but who nevertheless was sympathetic to the Seminoles' grievances and made efforts for a peace accord with them, made no response to the letter.

Later, in 1838, U.S. Secretary of War Joel Poinsett wrote to General Taylor (Jesup's successor) suggesting the use of hounds. Taylor approved, since the Seminoles' "swamp and jungle warfare in small parties makes it impossible to follow or overtake them." But, he added, "I wish it distinctly understood that my object in employing dogs is only to ascertain where the Indians can be found and not to [destroy] them."

Still, the politically sensitive issue lay dormant until December 1839, when Florida Territorial Governor Robert Reid, remarking about "four long years" of the white Floridian's "magnanimity and forebearance" in contrast to the red man's "ferocity and bad faith," asked the Legislature to purchase the dogs. "We are waging a war with beasts of prey," he declared, "and we must fight fire with fire." As for public sentiment, he added: "It is high time that sickly sentimentality . . . by fanatic pseudophilanthropists, should cease." The Legislature agreed and, in January 1840, Militia Colonel Richard Fitzpatrick returned from Havana with a kennel of 33 hounds. Soon after, they were offered to General Taylor, who after seeking Poinsett's approval, agreed to try them out. But, already sensing the Congressional reaction, the secretary directed that the dogs track "Indians only," not slaves, and that they be "muzzled and held with a leash."

But the news leaked out quickly, eliciting a barrage of public criticism. Senator James Buchanan (later president) was joined by colleagues in a memorial against "inhuman warfare." Representative Joshua Giddings (later author of the history classic, *The Exiles of Florida*) called the policy "barbarous," claiming the Floridians wanted the dogs mainly to track slaves "since the Florida militia is far more efficient in capturing Negroes and claiming those captured by U.S. troops than in facing them on the field of battle." Representative Adams demanded to know the hounds' "martial history" and fitness to serve in the army, and their "nice discrimination of scent" between "savage Seminoles and Anglo-Saxon pious Christians." He wryly queried whether the hounds might next be used to resolve a current Canadian border dispute and might not the Canadians employ dogs also, and should the U.S. secure this auxiliary force "exclusively"? Concluding, he asked if Poinsett "dreams it expedient to extend to the said blood-hounds and their posterity the benefit of the pension laws."

In the end, however, the dogs proved neither inhumane nor useful. Indeed, they sniffed out everything in sight—horses, mules, soldiers, even a disgusted General Taylor himself. With some glee, Representative Giddings later recounted an incident where the troops and dogs on patrol discovered Indian footprints and became excited. "When all hearts were palpitating with stern resolve," Giddings related, "ready to bear aloft the stars and stripes as they engaged in deadly conflict with the wily foe, lo, just at that moment as they turned to the dogs to lead them on," the pooches were otherwise engaged in frisky play. "They were blithe and froliksome but paid no more attention to the tracks of the Indians than those of the ponies on which they [the dogs] sometimes rode."

Later, when the Legislature tried to bill Taylor for $2,429.52 for the dogs, old "Rough-and-Ready," noting that the hounds had failed their tests miserably, curtly informed the lawmakers of what they could do with their bill. It was never paid.

Needless to say, the dogs were unceremoniously—and permanently—retired thereafter, having been apparently the only parties involved who thoroughly enjoyed their brief but luxurious hitch as the U.S. Army's dubious "dogs of war."

47.
A Surgeon Assesses the Seminole War

U.S. troops in the Seminole War found the enemy elusive.

Jacob Motte told the truth about the Second Seminole War, which put both a soldier's bravery—and endurance—to the ultimate test.

To young army surgeon Jacob Rhett Motte, Florida was "the poorest country two people ever quarreled over . . . it is a most hideous region to live in, a perfect paradise for Indians, alligators, frogs and every other kind of loathsome reptile."

Therefore, the physician later wondered, "why not in the name of common sense let the Indians keep it? Every day served but to convince us of their inflexible determination to fight or die in the land of their fathers."

There has been much history dealing with the highlights of Florida's Second Seminole War (1835-1842)—the generals, the Indian leaders, the issues in contention—but seldom was heard the individual voice of the "soldier in the field," the one who bore the daily brunt of the longest, costliest war of its kind in American history. Nor was there (before the Vietnam War) so unpopular a conflict.

Motte shared the frontline danger and hardships of the infantryman and articulated that soldier's frustrations and grievances over fighting a thankless war under devastating physical conditions, a war in which fever, disease, and sweltering heat would exact a toll of lives almost matching those lost in combat. Later, in a book based on his experiences, *Journey Into Wilderness,* he sought to correct a historical malignity perpetrated for so long on the memory of that soldier.

Motte was a self-styled Southern gentleman from an old Charleston Huguenot family. Harvard educated, he was steeped in the classical arts and sciences and possessed a distinct literary flair. (One of the "greatest privations" was the absence of books on the desolate war frontier. "Oh! how I longed for even the sight of an old almanac," he lamented.)

Initially Motte shared the strong ill-feeling arising among U.S. Army regulars, the Florida Militia, and "Crackers" in general. At his first post at Newnansville in Alachua County—largely a refugee camp for Cracker families that had fled their threatened homesteads—Motte humorously revealed this attitude. Fed and sheltered by the Army, the Crackers had found a very agreeable way of living, he surmised. "Imagining it much easier to be fed by Uncle Sam, they provoked the Indians by various aggressions to a retaliation, and then complained to their venerable Uncle of the mischievous disposition of his red nephews." Thereupon, concluding that the Indian "could not live in brotherly affection with his white nephews and nieces, Uncle [decided] their health must be in a bad state, and a change of air . . . west of the Mississippi . . . would be very beneficial." Disagreeing on the subject of their health, "Sam's red relatives undertook to revenge themselves upon their white cousins" who Motte observed, immediately congregated in stockades, drew army rations, and designated themselves "suffering inhabitants."

When President Andrew Jackson labeled the Florida men as "cowards" and advised the wives to swap them for new husbands who could "breed up" men of courage to protect them, Motte overheard the "fair Alachua dames" outpour some undamsel-like language "which would have withered Old Hickory into a nonentity had he been present."

Yet even Florida Governor Richard Keith Call conceded the militia was "a feeble dependency." They would not turn out if they had to walk, nor even ride horseback if it took them from home. They would perform no physical labor (a jungle necessity), so accustomed were they to slave labor. And few, if any, would respond to a government draft call.

Motte's anger was aroused by the "abusive comments . . . and condemnations of some civilians reclining on cushioned chairs in their comfortable homes," criticizing the war's prolonged duration. This prolongation, he asserted, lay in "the character of the country, not the want of valor or persevering energy" of the troops. The widespread morasses, plus the Everglades, dense hammocks, jungle and swamp, "in which no troops in the world could operate effectively," afforded the Indians safe shelter from pursuit. Meanwhile, the troops prosecuting "this inglorious war" were also constantly engaged in building roads and bridges, erecting defenses, transporting supplies and guarding the sick, all done under scorching heat or drenching rains and with "every species of privation and disease." Men marched in water, from hip- to chest-deep with no chance to dry out, and slept in their boots and clothing for four months at a time, tormented constantly by mosquitoes, fleas, horseflies, and the deadlier menace of rattlesnakes and moccasins. Their clothes, boots, and flesh were lacerated incessantly by sawgrass or saw palmettos, while dysentery, fever, and heat stroke disabled many. Inadequate or delayed food rations only weakened them further.

Yet, despite these "incredible hardships," Motte declared, the federal troops have never been "exceeded in energy, courage, or patriotism. The public was disappointed . . . because no brilliant and decisive victories were achieved; they were not aware that such victories were out of the question; that the enemy had an espionage [system] over the whole country and, knowing all our movements, was met or not, at his own convenience. The Indians never took a position from which they could not secure a safe retreat. Thus every engagement . . . was nothing but a succession of running fights from hammock to hammock, and swamp to swamp." (One modern Florida historian, John Mahon, agrees, commenting that "it is indeed doubtful if United States ground forces endured harsher field conditions anywhere," before or since.)

The lanky, 29-year-old pipe-smoking doctor himself suffered fever and often "dropped from sheer exhaustion" while tending the wounded and dying under the fiercest battle conditions.

Yet he kept a measured objectivity toward the antagonists; he could admire equally "the courage and daring enterprise" of both Osceola and an officer like Colonel William Harney.

He could record the lighter moments of relief, as well, such as a St. Augustine ball where he danced with "Minorcan girls . . . the fairest specimens of creations, with lustrous eyes and chaste bewitching smiles," or the gourmet delight of gopher soup, "a rare dish . . . no epicure in the world" could resist, or the comic relief provided by a haughty captain boasting of his horsemanship to a sergeant and mounting the latter's "unmanageable" horse, digging his spurs deep. "The next moment the Captain was seen describing a parabolic curve similar to the trajectory of a 10-inch shell . . . and alighting on his seat of honor at the feet of the unskillful sergeant."

In 1845, Motte resigned from the army, returned to private practice in Charleston and married a doctor's daughter, Mary Haig, by whom he had eight children. In that same year he published his *Journey* book.

The book was an invaluable historical memoir in its own right. But beyond that—and Motte's prime motivation—it rendered a belated but eloquent homage to a much-maligned soldier, while seeking to correct a distorted historical image that evolved even up to the time of that tragic conflict in Indo-china.

48.
Governor Milton: A Civil War Tragedy

Florida was ill prepared to fight against the Union and the strain may have caused the suicide of the state's leader.

Whether men sometimes conspire together to destroy an entire nation or merely an individual, whether in form of war or in the singular act of terrorism or assassination, there seems to be a peculiar law deriving from such ill-begotten quests, namely: whenever that bent of violence or fanaticism is frustrated to its outward end, it will often turn fatefully inward upon the perpetrators themselves.

Examples of this bizarre psychic inversion abound—the defeated Prussian Junker with pistol at head; the Japanese warlord's hari-kari; Hitler and company in the bunkers; the modern-day terrorist whose desire to kill is often perversely matched by his desire to be killed.

Occasionally, this phenomenon can be observed at more familiar range, such as in Florida at the end of the Civil War, in the tragic case of John Milton, Florida's governor during the Civil War (1861-1865).

Milton, who took his own life just eight days before Robert E. Lee surrendered at Appomattox, had been a successful, prosperous North Florida plantation owner and a political leader before the war. Born in Louisville, Georgia, April 30, 1807, Milton read for law and practiced in Georgia, Alabama, and New Orleans before coming to North Florida where he bought a plantation, "Sylvania," near Marianna. Married twice, he had a son and two daughters by his first wife and two sons and seven daughters by his second wife, Caroline Howze. With enough slaves to cultivate his 7,000-acre farm, Milton was afforded much leisure time for other pursuits. He served briefly as captain of volunteers in the Third Seminole War and then entered Florida politics as a Conservative at a time when the Democratic party was fiercely split between Conservatives and Whigs, or radicals.

Milton was a skilful orator and soon became a leading figure in the Conservative camp. He had long been an extremist in advocacy of John Calhoun's doctrine of nullification; he fervently believed that states had a special right to withdraw from the Union if the state felt its interests were being infringed upon.

He was named a presidential elector in 1848 and the following year he was elected a state senator. As he watched the national storm of discord over the slavery issue, Milton saw a clear opportunity to plant and nurture the seeds of secessionist thinking, and he seized on every chance to do so. His appeals were zealous, sometimes emotional, but he delivered them with an obsessive singlemindedness.

By 1860, leaders in every Southern state were making fiery speeches on behalf of secession and they openly debated plans to form a separate Confederacy of states.

In the elections that year in Florida, opinion seemed almost equally divided on secession. But Milton's fiery advocacy had won him the Conservative nomination for governor and in his race against Edward Hopkins, of the pro-Union Constitutional Union wing, Milton won the governorship 6,994 to 5,248. Lincoln was elected president that same month and this prompted the secessionists to galvanize their preparations for war. The Florida legislature authorized then governor Perry to purchase $100,000 in arms and munitions. By January 10, 1861, Milton successfully pushed through an ordinance of secession which declared Florida to be a "sovereign and independent nation." The vote was 62 to 7; the minority seven had tried, unsuccessfully, to submit the ordinance to public vote.

But not every state leader succumbed to the frenzied and often irrational war fervor of that period. Ellen Call Long, daughter of former governor Richard Keith Call, recalls in her memoirs how her father stood almost alone in his loyalty to the Union. Mrs. Long related how, on the day the ordinance passed, some jubilant seceders accosted Call with: "Well, governor, alright; we have done it." The elder statesman, waving his big walking cane over his head, replied: "And what have you done? You have opened the gates of hell, from which shall flow the curses of the damned." His words would prove prophetic enough.

In April 1861, Florida became the third state to withdraw from the Union. The state was ill-prepared for this drastic move. Her treasury was almost depleted and when a sale of $500,000 in bonds became snagged among legal thorns, the treasury plunged into a financial mire, barely relieved by the issuance of Confederate notes that had already begun to depreciate in value.

In Milton's extreme view of state's rights, he wanted to keep Florida separate even from the Confederate government, although he vaguely came to realize the need for a central authority to direct the war's effort. For example, when the Confederate Secretary of War called up Florida's militia units and volunteers to fight on other critical fronts, Milton, who wanted to keep them in the state solely for Florida's defense, assailed the secretary for exercising "a power inconsistent with the rights of a free, sovereign and independent state."

His reaction was even strong when, after General U.S. Grant's successes in Tennessee and Kentucky in February 1862, the Confederacy pulled up all major Florida units out of state, abandoning the naval yard and Fort McRee at Pensacola, and rushing them northwesterly for the bloody battle at Shiloh. "The effect of this order," Milton wrote, "is to abandon Middle, East, and Southern Florida to the mercy and abuse of the Lincoln government."

True enough. Federal troops moved in to occupy not only Pensacola and the Gulf port of Cedar Key but Fernandina, Jacksonville, and St. Augustine on the east coast.

The order would also create a greater problem for the burdened governor. Among citizens as well as the token bands of troops remaining in Florida, disaffection and outright desertion were becoming endemic. By December 1863, Milton reported conscripts, Union men, and deserters had formed into armed bands. They hid in the woods and swamps, he asserted, were supplied food and arms by Federal forces, raided isolated plantations and even armed runaway slaves. "A large proportion if not a majority of the citizens of West Florida," he estimated, "are represented to be disloyal . . . [they] have threatened to raise the United States flag, even in Marianna [Milton's home]."

Plaguing the governor on another critical front were the war profiteers. Seacoast manufacturers of the vital preservative salt were waxing rich from the scarce commodity, often demanding exorbitant prices from the impoverished government. Blockade runners were selling cotton for gold in the flourishing Bahamas, and in South Florida the cattle kings had all but choked off to the ragged Rebel armies this critical food supply in favor of Spanish Gold in Havana, Cuba. "The floodgates of all species of villainy seemed to be unhinged," Milton fumed.

Perhaps one of Milton's most phobic fears was the slave himself. In 1860, Florida's census showed a white population of 77,747, plus a black head-count of 62,676, mostly slaves. It was not merely, as historian William W. Davis observed, that "the material well-being—if not the existence—of the state depended on the labor of the slave." It was, to Milton, also the looming threat of their liberation. Confiding these fears to a friend, he wrote that when slaves learn that blacks "are in actual warfare for their liberation . . . is there not much reason to apprehend that insurrections and massacres would occur." By now he was certain that the Federals wanted to make Florida "a waste, a howling wilderness, or to colonize it with Negroes." And, toward the war's final months, he felt the state was almost "a waste," but he still affirmed there was "not a man, woman or child" who would not sacrifice the entire state for "the cause." In his last message to the legislature, Milton expressed the belief (perhaps with some prescience), "Death would be preferable to reunion."

Nevertheless, his broad, fleshy face began to assume a somber, brooding aspect as he struggled to manage an almost unmanageable wartime government. Cut off from telegraphy, rumors reached him of Sherman's march through Atlanta, Sheridan's victory at Shenandoah, and Lee's difficulties at Richmond. The home front presented a scene hardly less desolate—destitution, bankruptcy, casualty lists and, with meat, corn, and salt a rarity, even starvation. The words of Confederate president Jefferson Davis at this time: "There remains for us no choice but to continue to contest to a final issue," may just have struck a grimly hollow chord in Milton's ears.

Regardless, on April 1, eight days before Lee's surrender, the governor rigged his carriage and drove his wife and a son to their home at "Sylvania." There were no servants to greet him this time. And so, as one of his daughters busily prepared his "homecoming dinner," Milton quietly went to his room, took a pistol, and shot himself in the head; he died instantly.

Not a few historians are inclined to treat sparsely the administration of Governor Milton, as if the entire four years were just some brief, dark, and terrible episode in the state's history, best touched on in highlight and then forgotten. In fact, some journals not only omit mention of Milton's suicide; they even go to mendacious stretches to explain his death, such as the reputable National Cyclopedia of American Biography which staidfacedly reports: "This constant care [of Governor Milton's], aggravated by mental work, produced softening of the brain and caused his death eight days before the surrender [of Lee]." True, a lead ball traveling at close range and high velocity can indeed produce a softening—if not a pulverizing—effect on anyone's brain. But the man himself might doubtless consider himself dishonored with such a tainted historical delicacy.

Contrarily, it is just possible that the history of Milton's administration (and Milton himself), could impart some valuable lessons to a contemporary world where the dogmas of anarchy, rebellion, and Number One-ism are flourishing more than ever—and with effects at least equally devastating.

49.
The Healing Beauty of Ed Bok's Tower

Edward Bok made a fortune with his Ladies Home Journal. *What he needed was a place to escape. A garden. A tower.*

When friends woefully informed Edward Bok that he would get " out of touch" if he moved from the busy, big city to faraway Florida, he simply queried: "Out of touch with what?"

"There are minds that cannot conceive that to get 'out of touch' may sometimes mean to get into touch," surmised the Dutch-American editor of the most successful mass-circulation magazine of his day, *The Ladies Home Journal.* Those who are afraid to be alone, "to drop the lead and sound the bottoms of life," to invite their inner selves into a refreshment of quiet repose and apartness from the world's traffic, such people cannot grow, or enrich their natures, he believed. Without such a sanctuary, he claimed, the true self shrivels up like a dried-out stream bed.

So convinced was Bok of this truth that he decided to build a sanctuary, available to everyone: an artful blend of beauty, color, song, and tranquility, all set atop the highest knoll of land in peninsular Florida, Iron Mountain at Lake Wales. Thus was created the renowned Bok's Singing Tower and Sanctuary. Today its world-famous carillon drenches the surrounding scenery with some of the purest sounds of music, a symphonic paean to the deeper harmonies between man and nature.

Just a rich man's eccentric indulgence? Not exactly, because Edward William Bok was an unusual individual. In 1870, at age seven, he immigrated with his parents to New York from his native Helder, the Netherlands. By the time he was 18, he had enjoyed associations with such luminaries as Ulysses S. Grant, Jefferson Davis, Henry W. Longfellow, Oliver Wendell Holmes, and President Rutherford B. Hayes. At 26, he became editor of the *Journal,* which featured literary comers like Mark Twain and Rudyard Kipling. His autobiography, "The Americanization of Edward Bok," won the Pulitzer Prize in 1920, and his busy career was otherwise studded with a myriad of social endeavors.

Nevertheless, when he semi-retired in his fifties to a home beside Iron Mountain, the restful beauty of the region recalled to him how his grandfather had once driven pirates from a small, barren island off the Dutch coast and had then transformed the island, with plantings of trees and shrubs, into a sanctuary for both birds and man.

Beyond this, Bok had a deep desire to express his gratitude to his adopted country for the full and prosperous life it had afforded him. He would acquire the mountain and build upon it a beautiful sanctuary, open to every soul who sought repose and release from world cares. The owner, "a poor but honest" old Cracker who had refused huge offers from developers for the mountain site, consented to sell when he learned of Bok's desire to share this natural beauty with all Americans.

But the project was mammoth. To transform the sandy soil amid pines and live oaks—some 93 of 138 acres—Bok chose the celebrated landscape architect Frederick Law Olmstead. Wisely, he left the artist completely alone. Five years later, Bok surveyed a lush, sylvan setting more wondrous than he had imagined: thousands of varieties of flowers and plants and hundreds of young dogwood and magnolia trees, all enveloped by broad lawnscapes, footpaths, and panoramic viewsites over the rolling countryside below. The dean of American landscapers, William Lyman Phillips, summed up the work tersely: "A more striking example of beauty could hardly be found."

And yet, to Bok, something was missing, some essential complement to fulfill the pastoral scene. Then he thought of the great bell towers of his native Low Countries. He summoned the noted architect Milton B. Medary and told him, "I want the most beautiful tower in the world." Medary then asked, "Do you know the tower at Malines, Belgium?" Bok nodded. "Do you expect me to beat that?" Bok nodded again. The architect then answered, "That's not a commission, it's a challenge."

But Medary was up to the challenge. After months of European sketches and studies, the work began. A 30-inch concrete mat, poured over 160 concrete pilings, supports the 205-foot, steel-frame tower; the building itself is of solid Georgia pink marble and Florida coquina rock. The square base is 51 feet wide; the 55-foot-high tower is octagonal and 37 feet wide with eight arched windows 35 feet high. Colored tile panels and sculptured birds, trees, flowers, and human figures flow downward in tiers, reaching the tower's only entrance, where the heavy, brass door bears 30 molded panels telling the story of Creation. (Bok, who died January 9, 1930, is buried before this door.) A lengthy pool stretches before the tower, framing the edifice in perfect reflection.

It took 15 months to cast the great carillon bells at England's renowned Taylor foundry. Each of the 71 bells was tested for tone and quality by three famous musicians and pronounced perfect. With a range of 53 notes and four-and-a-half chromatic octaves, the bells weigh from 11 pounds to 11 tons. After the bells arrived in Jacksonville, specially constructed flat railroad cars with double flooring were used to transport them to Lake Wales. The bells never need tuning; they remain stationary and the bell clappers are swung instead.

Bok persuaded Anton Brees of Belgium's Royal Conservatory to be bellmaster; the distinguished musician remained there until retiring in 1966. The noted carilloneur, Milford Myhre, is current bellmaster. Since the sanctuary was dedicated to the American people on February 1, 1929, millions have enjoyed its "healing beauty." The Singing Tower is so named because, as the bells play, the whole structure seems to burst into song.

Bok was often mindful of a verse from Ezekiel 37:26:

I will make a covenant of peace with them . . .

And will set my sanctuary in the midst of them forevermore.

And thus did this Dutch-American set his sanctuary in the midst of them. And the generations have been grateful ever since.

50.
The Rise and Fall of Carl Fisher's Miami Beach

Carl Fisher built a strip of land into the fun and sun capital of the world. Then came the land bust of '26, and his kingdom toppled.

Carl Fisher drew attention to Miami Beach as the nation's sun and fun capital for bringing beauties, business tycoons, and baby elephants.

All the king's beauties and celebrities and all the king's flack men couldn't put Miami Beach back together again after the Florida land bust of the 1920.

But, in 1928, they tried.

The king was Carl Fisher, the colorful, dynamic developer who had scooped up several million tons of real estate from the bottom of Biscayne Bay and dumped it on a strip of swampy mangrove jungle, thereby creating America's fun, flamboyant Riviera. Or, as Will Rogers wryly observed, "Fisher was the first man to discover that there was sand under the water . . . (sand) that could hold up a real estate sign. He made the dredge the national emblem of Florida."

But the big bust of 1926 struck the billion-dollar sandbar with much of the same force as the hurricane that roared up the Gold Coast that same year, smashing the last gimcrack traces of what had been a giddy and manic era. Luxury hotels and apartments on the beach stood vacant, and property was abandoned by owners who balked at paying taxes keyed to boom-time valuations in a bottomed-out market. This left banks clutching frantically to a teetering stack of millions in worthless paper which would soon topple.

Fisher's fabulous beach was dying but he himself diagnosed it as a temporary ailment only, nothing terminal. "We built it out of nothing and we'll build it again," he declared. And he set out to do that, using the same for-

204

mula he used the first time—gala sports events, ballyhoo and beauties, big names, florid stuff. People believed him for, after all, the spectacular was his forte and his track record was formidable.

Carl Graham Fisher, who dropped out of school early in his hometown of Indianapolis, took up racing bicycles at county fairs and opened his own bicycle shop at 17. The auto was a novel contraption and Fisher and friend Barney Oldfield began racing them. He opened a garage and began selling cars, using publicity stunts like riding over the city in a car suspended from a balloon. Then, in 1904, fortune smiled. Carl met Fred Avery who had the patent on compressing carbide gas into tanks. Seeing the potential for providing auto headlights, Carl and James Allison went into partnership with Avery, and Prest-O-Lite was born. When they sold out to Union Carbide six year later, Carl was a multi-millionaire.

Fisher and his wife, Jane, bought a winter home in Miami in 1910 and, soon after, they met John Collins, a Quaker horticulturist who owned most of Miami Beach—a jungly barrier reef on which Collins was growing tropical produce. Collins had run short of funds while trying to build a wooden bridge from the reef to the mainland. Fisher, who began to envision a gleaming resort city, lent him $50,000 to finish the job. He took some choice chunks of island acreage stretching from the Atlantic beach to the bay in exchange. By 1913 when the bridge opened, Fisher was already plunging a small fortune into the mud and water. Slowly he made the Herculean effort of hacking out the tenacious mangroves, dredging the bay, smoothing the land over and quickly planting grass, Australian pines, oleanders, and other shrubbery to keep it firm. But during these years he was active elsewhere, too. He had organized his famed Indianapolis "500" Speedway in 1911 and he led the drive to build the first cross-country road, Lincoln Highway, in 1915. (By the 1920s he would do the same for the first north-south road, the Dixie Highway running from the Midwest to Miami.)

By the time Fisher was selling his first lots on Miami Beach in 1919 ($66,000 worth in a three-day auction), the land boom was gathering momentum. Fisher began his colorful publicity extravaganzas for Miami Beach with carnival displays, name bands, speedboat regattas, lavish parties, a fleet of yachts to entertain customers, bathing beauties, and celebrities as diverse as Will Rogers and Irving Berlin. He invited wealthy cronies like Gar Wood, the speedboat king, Harvey Firestone (tires), and other tycoons who bought estates on the beach. Lavish hotels such as the Flamingo went up, along with clubhouses, golf courses, polo fields, Roman pools, pavilions. His two baby elephants, Carl and Rosie, pulled carts of excited children or served as golf caddies for VIPs like President Warren Harding. And his efforts paid off. At the boom's height, assessed valuation of beach property had been boosted 200 times and Fisher was richer than he had ever been before—with an estimated worth of some $50 million. True, most of this was on paper, but paper was the currency of the boom. Unfortunately, the paper—a whirling blur of options, binders, mortgages, tax certifications, and warranty deeds—was also the basis of the boom's crash in 1926. Suddenly there was lots of property—but no takers. Big developers elsewhere were being strangled by taxes on boomtime profits, having depended on future profits to pay for their grandiose projects.

Carl surveyed the desolate scene on Miami Beach and set to work to save his dream. In 1928 he hired well-known publicist Steve Hannagan to launch a nationwide publicity blitz, featuring major sports events and bathing beauties. Hannagan recruited flocks of pretty Miami Beach high school girls to pose frolicking on the beach, then sent the pictures over the country as newspaper fillers. Thus was born the sun-sea-sex image of Florida that soon graced millions of postcards and travel folders. Press releases were ground out describing a major mid-winter speedboat regatta, followed by the Miami Beach LaGorce Open Golf Tournament, which featured major U.S. golfers like Tommy Armours, Gene Sarazen, and Johnny Farrell. Another gimmick was naming each of the golf course's 18 holes after a diverse mix of celebrity guests, including Grantland Rice, Eddie Rickenbacker, and Ring Lardner. Sports figures such as Gene Tunney and Jack Dempsey were also drawn in.

With the draw of parties, beauty contests, general hoopla, and the sporting events themselves, huge crowds flocked in and the Beach was getting national publicity. But, aside from a small brief flurry of lot sales and new building in 1929, the depression lingered. Fisher discovered that people were no longer buying real estate; the current get-rich-quick craze was focused on the stock market, a national phenomenon soon to have consequences far more drastic than the land boom's bust.

When the stock market crashed in 1929, Fisher was already over his head with due loans and an ill-fated summer resort project at Montauk, Long Island, in New York. His beach holdings were in hock for millions, and when Montauk collapsed, almost everything he had ever owned was soon in the hands of creditors. Far from saving his beach, he could barely save himself. He watched helplessly as his ailing resort queen was delivered up to the Mafia dons and gangsters—Capone, Costello, Adonis, Accardo, Guzik, Lansky—with casino gambling, bookie joints, gaudy night clubs, and the endemic corruption of government.

Fisher himself lived in a small cottage on Miami Beach in virtually penniless obscurity during the 1930s. After a long illness compounded by alcoholism, he died in 1939 at age 65, a decade too soon to see his "greatest creation" rescued by grim-eyed grand juries and Senator Kefauver's Crime Committee.

51.
Florida's Great Train Race of 1901

With a rich mail contract going to the winner, two rival railroads sped from Savannah to Jacksonville. A record was broken in the process.

Henry Bradley Plant, late 19th-century Florida promoter, might have done a little jig in the ballroom of his fancy Tampa Bay Hotel had he been around for the great train race of 1901.

And no wonder. In a thriller of a duel between the Plant System and the Seaboard Air Line railroads—a race to Jacksonville for a coveted U.S. Mail contract—his train had set a new world speed record of 120 miles per hour.

In Jacksonville itself, though the spectators were fewer and the interested parties more select, there hadn't been as much excitement since 1894, when the Corbett-Mitchell world heavyweight prize fight almost provoked a city riot.

But Plant, the railroader who laced up Southwest Florida's future development with miles of shiny steel ribbons, died in June 1899. He had taken much pride in his "highballing" trains, even setting a few more modest records. In April 1898, a special train carrying Cuban Consul General, General Fitzhugh Lee to report his talks with Spanish officials just before the outbreak of the Spanish-American War, made it from Tampa to Washington in 27 hours, despite numerous speech stops. This led to Tampa's selection as the major port of embarkation during the war.

U.S. Postal contracts were lucrative prizes in those days and often were settled with a speed trial, winner take all. This contract was for a new mail service to Cuba and the West Indies. Jacksonville was the destination and the government sent eight cars of mail to Savannah, Georgia, the starting mark. The cars were divided evenly between the two lines and, in the early morning hours of March 1, 1901, the two rivals slowly built up steam and chugged out of the terminal.

Plant's train began with a handicap. The triangular line went roundabout inland to Waycross, Georgia, then southeast to Jacksonville, 149 miles, or 31.8 miles farther than Seaboard Air Line's straighter coastal run. Ned Leake was engineer on Plant engine No. 107, one of six such engines built for the Plant System the previous summer by the Rhode Island Locomotive

Works. The engine was a big coal-burning 10-wheeler—four small front cylinder wheels and six big driving wheels, six feet in diameter. The "4-6-0" had been regarded as a mechanical wonder of strength, speed, and power even before an engineer from Cayce, Kentucky—John Luther Jones (nicknamed "Casey" for his hometown)—smashed one of them and himself into ballad and legend on the Illinois Central a year earlier.

The rival tracks ran parallel for some 12 miles south of Savannah before Plant's line veered southwesterly. No. 107 took an early lead but, apparently, set too fast a pace; it developed a hot driving box and slowed to a stall just before the turn. As the Seaboard train sped by and spotted the disabled 107, her crew let out a chorus of hoots and jeers; the contract, they were convinced, was sewn up already.

The 107 limped into Fleming, eight miles away, and a dejected crew huddled with station officials to find some way at least to stay in the race. Then, after a glance at his train sheet, the Fleming dispatcher noted that Plant engineer Albert Lodge, on a regular northbound freight run out of Tampa, was due in Fleming at the moment. Even as he said it, Lodge's single engine No. 111 pulled in for a water stop. Here was their one last chance. Informed of the crisis, Lodge eagerly agreed to switch destinations. The freight cars were side-tracked, 111 was turned and watered, and the engine, 4-6-0 sister engine to 107, was coupled to the mail train. Almost an hour had elapsed since the breakdown and every minute counted now. Orders were telegraphed down the line for a clear track, with switches set and securely locked. Guest riders in the cab with Lodge were railroader S. S. McClellan, and another engineer, James "Uncle Jimmy" Ambrose, plus the fireman, Charlie Johnson.

The small, wiry Lodge was a veteran engineer and had the reputation of getting everything from an engine it could give. Now he was determined to get what he had never tried to get from his No. 111. With an expert hand he coaxed the throttle gently. Soon the big driving wheels were only a roaring blur of motion as the speed leaped . . . 60 . . . 70 . . . 80 miles an hour, still rising after passing Jessup, Georgia. As the wheels screamed and vibrations shook the cab, Ambrose, a man of few words, turned to McClellan and remarked dryly: "This train is going awfully fast." As they whizzed past the Screven station, McClellan realized they were running at an unusual speed and, just before the 69 milepost, he and Ambrose took out their timing watches. Timing it from the 69 milepost to the 74 milepost at Satilla, both men looked up from their watches gaping. Each had the same time exactly, two minutes, 30 seconds for the five-mile stretch, or 120 miles per hour. Plant officials at line stations and some crew members had clocked the same speed. They had just surpassed the record set in May 1893 at 112.5 miles per hour by the famous New York Central Engine at No. 999, an occasion commemorated by a U.S. Mail stamp.

Seeing a curve looming ahead beyond Satilla, McClellan found himself sweating profusely, wondering if the engine was going to "take that curve . . . or take to the woods." The big wheel flanges shrieked and the engine lurched sharply, but steel held to steel as they straightened out for Waycross. At Waycross, fastworking service crews had the engine on its way in three minutes.

Lodge knew that he was fast closing the "catch-up" schedule gap but he was going for more than "catch-up" now. The wheels once more became a blur as they neared the 120 milepost at Race Pond and the arching convex of curve. Spotting the curve ahead, an apprehensive young coal passer up on the tender shouted to fireman Johnson, "Charlie, don't you s'pose he's going to shut off?" Johnson's answer did not reassure the youth. "Naw, he jus' going good now." Moving into the curve, McClellan recalled, "Lodge closed up the throttle about three notches and immediately changed his mind and pulled it out again five notches. We hit the curve. "Uncle Jimmy" grabbed me and I grabbed the hot iron pipes on the front of the boiler head, which now felt rather cool." Again the wheel flanges screamed, and again they held. The coal passer had flatted himself face down on the tender. McClellan and Ambrose were mopping their heads with relief. Fireman Johnson was laughing with exhilaration.

As they zoomed over the St. Mary's River trestle into Florida, Lodge pulled the throttle wide for the straightway ahead. At Callahan, 20 miles northwest of Jacksonville, McClellan, Ambrose, and crew members checked their watches again and, once more for several miles, Lodge hit 120 mph. As they pulled into the Jacksonville terminal, a crowd of railroad officials and well-wishers sent up a roar of cheering. Lodge and his passengers looked at each other, somewhat nonplussed at this jubilance, until they learned the occasion for it—the Seaboard train had not arrived yet. In a "tortoise and the hare" twist to the race, the Seaboard, after passing the disabled 107, had simply taken its time.

According to railroad historian George Pettengill, no other Southern railroad steam engine would ever again match the 111's speed record. After the Atlantic Coast Line took over the Plant System in 1902, the 111 remained in service until 1942.

The Seaboard train finally pulled in, on the far side of the terminal yard, out of sight of the Plant train. The Plant crew was just finishing up breakfast in the station restaurant when the Seaboard conductor walked in and inquired randomly: "Has that broken down Plant engine been heard from yet?" He looked genuinely puzzled at the roars of laughter that greeted his inquiry.

52.
Kissimmee's World-Famed Airplane Law

A far-seeing plan to regulate aircraft over town limits looked like folly at first, but it made international news. Somehow, in the ensuing hoopla, City Council failed to pass it.

Folks in the little frontier cattle town of Kissimmee were puzzled at first when they heard of a new ordinance regulating "aircraft" over the city. Then they began to titter and finally they burst into loud guffaws.

The year was 1908 and most of Kissimmee's denizens had never seen an airplane, much less envisaged one roaring down the main street, stampeding cows and wreaking assorted havoc. But there it was in the *Kissimmee Valley Gazette,* in clear and precise ordinance legalese, a law regulating any "flying machine or airship (dirigible)" moving through "any street or alley of the town within 10 feet of the surface" or vertically upward to a distance of 20 miles.

The heading read, "Mayor Takes Time By Forelock," and continued: "Determined that Kissimmee shall not be caught napping when the new means of locomotion shall burst upon an astonished atmosphere," Mayor T. M. Murphy had prepared this legislation "to meet the demands of an entirely novel practical problem." The ordinance will doubtless serve as a model to cities "throughout the civilized world."

By midday after the article appeared, the whole town was laughing— except red-faced Mayor Murphy, who didn't see anything funny about it. In fact, he angrily complained to the ordinance's author, city attorney P. A. Vans Agnew, that he, Murphy, had become the laughingstock of the town and he might have to leave for California tomorrow. He also mentioned doing some bodily harm to the attorney. Vans Agnew finally mollified the mayor, pointing out long-range benefits of the law that would accrue to "generations yet unborn."

At that moment, of course, neither man was aware that the first law ever drawn in the world to regulate aircraft was about to bring the little city of Kissimmee international fame.

Vans Agnew did concede that he had drawn up the ordinance in a "whimsical spirit"—but stopped well short of suggesting it was either a joke or hoax. True, not more than a dozen men in the entire country up to then had flown in powered airplanes, and the first actual airplane flight in Florida was still more than a year and a half away. (This would occur in February 1910, in the nearby city of Orlando, by pioneer aviator Lincoln Beachy.) But Vans Agnew had recently returned from a visit to Paris, where both airplanes and dirigibles flew over the French capital, as well as other European capitals, with regularity. Some even carried passengers. Vans Agnew was concerned about the hazard these aircraft created when they flew close to city buildings. Upon his return to Florida, he discussed this concern with the mayor, and both men, strictly in a jovial spirit, spoke of drawing up an ordinance to deal with this problem. But the attorney's mood was not entirely jestful. With some care and thought, he drew up the ordinance that appeared in full in the *Gazette* of July 17, 1908. The law turned out to be, in fact, remarkably inclusive and comprehensive.

Its jurisdiction extending to the town's fire limits and 20 miles upward, the law forbade keeping any airship in a shed, barn or garage without a city permit. Annual license taxes were as follows: balloons, $20 to $30; dirigibles, $50; airplanes, $100; helicopters, $150; ornithopters, $200; other types, $300. These taxes increased by passenger loads; a 10% hike for five to 15 passengers, on up to 400% for over 1,000 riders. But to encourage air freight transportation, no tax would be imposed for up to 15 years on freight carriers.

Speed limits forbade any aircraft moving from 10 to 20 feet off the surface of any city street or alley at a speed greater than eight miles per hour; at 50 feet, 15 mph; 100 feet, 25 mph; 200 feet, 50 mph; 500 feet, 100 mph; 1,000 feet or more, 200 mph.

It would be unlawful to "drop, throw, discharge, or otherwise eject any substance, fluid or solid" from an aircraft, or strike and damage or destroy any utility poles or city property. All aircraft would need to be equipped with the proper "bells, whistles, horns, brakes, lights and other signalling" equipment, along with nets, parachutes, flying belts, artificial wings, and similar safety apparatus.

The council was also authorized to purchase a modern-type aeroplane "for use of the [town] marshall," both to enforce the ordinance and for other public duties.

Violations of any provision of the new law could net the violator a fine of up to $500 and/or jail time up to 90 days "in the town calaboose."

But the mayor's embarrassment was to be short-lived; the ordinance soon threatened to make both men not legalistic jokesters but wise and farsighted leaders.

Letters first trickled and then began to pour into the city from around the country and Europe, all asking questions about the ordinance and requesting copies of it. The inquiries were from diverse groups. There were queries from members of German and French legations whose countries would later use the ordinance as a model for legislation; the Aeronautic Society of New York, the Aircraft Manufacturers Association, the city of Chicago, and dozens of other cities. The War Department would write for a copy for its archives. It would be reproduced for the archives of other nations and became a framework for international treaties.

The media, too, from Missouri to Massachusetts, gave it full coverage. The law was printed in full in *L'Auto,* a French journal, and magazines like *Case and Comment* and *Aeronautics* devoted articles to it. Editorials from the *Jacksonville Times-Union* to the *New York World* hailed its foresight. And when the *New York Tribune* deprecatingly suggested that Kissimmee was just trying to be "cute," the *Buffalo Times* editorially rapped that journal and referred to Kissimmee as "a progressive and farsighted little city." It became the subject of poems, cartoons, lectures, and scientific discussions. Many U.S. cities, along with London, Berlin, Paris, and Amsterdam, lavished praise on the document, copying it and even adorning their own cities' aircraft ordinance with Kissimmee's attractive city seal.

None of the Kissimmee townsfolk were laughing now; instead, and for some time to come, they would bask delightedly in this spotlight of world-wide attention.

As for the citizens responsible for such celebrity, they had long since shed their images as jesters and now modestly assumed the proper mien befitting such farsighted legislative statesmen.

Indeed, the only one who seemed to be neglected toward this historic document was the Kissimmee City Council. Somehow, it just never got around to actually passing the law.

53.
A Private's Eye-View of the Olustee Battle

Letters from the front, published almost a century after the skirmish, supported charges made at the time that the Union botched the battle of Olustee.

"The great 'expedition' from Hilton Head [South Carolina] has sailed, landed, gone in, and come out; or at least part of it, all that ever will," wrote young Union Private Milton M. Woodford to his wife on February 23, 1864. " . . . Tired, dirty, ragged, sore, but still alive, thanks to a kind providence."

Little did Woodford realize his letters would be discovered and published almost a century later, providing an unusually balanced and objective account of what really happened at the Battle of Olustee near Lake City, the only major Civil War battle fought in Florida, and one which, because of "very spotty" official records, has spawned many partisan, and often erroneous, accounts. Here Confederates checked and repulsed a Union advance into the state's interior in a bloody five-hour engagement. But it was a battle that wasn't supposed to happen, and Woodford—in blunt, soldierly comments "neither glib nor eloquent," according to historian Vaughn D. Bornet—offered some incisive reasons why.

Bornet, who published the letters in 1949, also found in them "keen powers of observation and knowledge of human nature." Woodford, a mechanic, was a staunch Baptist whose "strong moral and religious train" prompted him on September 4, 1861, to enlist in the Seventh Connecticut Volunteer Infantry for a three-year term. He was a seasoned veteran by the time his unit arrived in 1864 at Hilton Head, where he became part of an expedition to Jacksonville which was supposed to try to "reconstruct a loyal state government in Florida."

Under the command of General Truman A. Seymour, the army occupied Jacksonville first and then took Baldwin, driving back small Rebel units as they went. But despite strict instructions not to advance beyond the Little St. Marys River 30 miles west of Jacksonville, the ambitious Seymour set out with some 5,000 troops, hoping to reach the Suwannee River railroad bridge. Meanwhile, Rebel General Joseph Finegan, with an equal number of men, dug in near Olustee, 13 miles east of his Lake City base.

213

Woodford's Union company, a spearhead unit, had been pushing back Rebel skirmishers along the way when they met forward positions of Finegan's line shortly after noon on February 20. In a "running battle," the Seventh drove them back several miles until they suddenly came up on the main Rebel breastwork. By then, the Federals had been marching over rough terrain some 36 exhausting miles without break. But to an officer's suggestion to Seymour that the troops pause to catch breath, he replied: "No, this is just what I want; I shall get rid of the poor trash, and get the cream of the army."

Seymour then ordered Woodford's outfit forward, and the private wryly noted later: "Our general seemed to think the Seventh ought to take the whole thing. Our men then rushed up to within good fair rifle shot, and such a rattle of riflery (Spencer carbines) is seldom heard from so few men. The 'Johnnies' couldn't stand that long and had to send out two regiments to drive off our line."

By now the Seventh New Hampshire and the Eighth (the latter all-black) regiments began coming up, with two other brigades further behind. Finegan, alarmed, brought his troops out of the breastwork and a full battle was on.

And then it happened; most of the Seventh New Hampshire broke and ran. Only later did a stunned Woodford learn why, for they were tried veterans. Two officers gave these men directly conflicting orders just as they were coming up for deployment under the "hottest of the fire." Thus, confused and formlessly exposed under withering rifle fire, Woodford observed later, "it is no wonder" they broke. Of the black unit, holding its ground under the heaviest fire, the private noted that they "fought as well as any of us and lost heavily." In spite of the later testimony of the two officers, Seymour insisted on blaming the repulse on the New Hampshire men, whom he derided as "conscripts and substitutes of a very inferior class."

But Woodford's analysis held Seymour as "the only one" responsible. "He (Seymour) showed very poor generalship in taking us into such a place in the way he did," Woodford wrote, "for although his own was the advancing army, it is plain . . . that he was *surprised*. He didn't expect a force at that place; but as commanding general he *should* have known something about it. We have lost heavily and it seems to me unnecessarily" in a battle "that should not have been fought." The day's toll was: Union, 203 killed, 1,152 wounded; Confederates, 93 killed, 847 wounded. Woodford's Seventh, the unit which was longest in battle, had only four killed.

As night fell, Seymour ordered retirement and, with Woodford's Seventh in the rear guard, an orderly withdrawal was made back to Jacksonville.

Back in camp, Woodford wrote: "I hear there is to be an investigation of the circumstances of (Olustee). I hope it will be thorough. [Seymour] has led more men to death, and accomplished less in doing so than all the generals in the department." In later hearings, Woodford's analysis was confirmed. It was concluded that General Seymour was indeed "surprised" into the battle, after disregarding previous orders not to advance further. Seymour was soon after removed from the command.

Woodford's religious faith and personal God were still ever before him, and they only enlarged his appraisal of the war generally. "I hope we may, as individuals and as a nation, recognize the hand of God leading us . . . and that in God is our only hope. I don't like the way our people have, of making a little god of a man when he is successful. I don't think anyone man is going to save this country, not even [General Grant]. We want less of man worship. I am sick of hearing and reading so much of these great and good officers. If the truth were known, these very men are guilty of practices that would disgrace a private citizen or soldier . . . . Many of them I should not consider profitable companions at home."

Woodford's letters bear little if any personal malice for his enemy. Once, while transporting some refugee "Cracker" families to safety and observing their "sickly pale" and near starved, barely clothed condition, he commented: "I do pity the poor white people of the South, for it is very little

More than 300 died in the bloody battle near Lake City in February 1864.

real sympathy they get from either party. The Rebs conscript the men, and leave their families to starve, and our folks care little for them because their husbands are in the Rebel army."

After a final battle at Petersburg, Virginia, and his promotion to corporal, Woodford's term ended and he was discharged. But it would be many years before a Connecticut Yankee at Olustee would help to set that battle record straight, where professional chroniclers had repeatedly failed to do so.

Calamities and
Social Turbulence

54.
A Killer 'Cane Hits Okeechobee Land

Without warning, the Lake Okeechobee region was hit by a monster storm in 1928 which left 2,000 dead.

They expected a little wind and rain from the big blow, but that's about all.

True, it was a "killer" hurricane. Several days earlier, it had smashed through Puerto Rico leaving hundreds dead or homeless. But even up to the last hours of that fateful Sunday, September 16, 1928, weather bureau reports said the big wind would pass far clear of the Palm Beach–Okeechobee region. Earlier, a few cautious souls had packed the family into the Model T and headed for West Palm Beach, "just in case." But now people relaxed, smiled, sighed a relief.

Yet to some oldtimers around the small towns at Lake Okeechobee, the morning seemed "different." The dull, sunless sky looked off-color, the air too clear and cool, the dead still calm unnatural. They grew uneasy. "Something's wrong," one muttered.

Something was indeed wrong (including the weather bureau), because the monster storm had long since begun to veer in a deadly arc westward, heading straight for Palm Beach. By Sunday afternoon, just before the last telephone lines went down, the first and only frantic warning calls came in from West Palm Beach to all towns around the lake—Belle Glade, Pahokee, Canal Point, South Bay, Chosen, and many smaller settlements. But they were too late, and there were no exits. The roads north and east led straight into the 'cane's path. There were no roads south and west.

As residents braced for the winds (which would gust up to 150 mph), their greatest fears focused now in only one direction—toward the big lake, 730 square miles of solid water, held back by a flimsy dike of muck and sand and already at an unnerving high level from the steady rains of August.

They recalled the big "Miami" hurricane two years before. Moving up the state, it had barely sideswiped the western edge of the lake, but this was enough to burst a section of dike that flooded and obliterated the little town of Moore Haven, killing upwards of 150 people. And now they would get the full blast of the killer's fury, dead center. They were caught, literally, between the devil storm and the huge blue inland sea.

Their fears were justified. Before this longest night was over, and the grisly days to follow, they would have passed through the greatest natural disaster in Florida's history and, aside from Galveston and Johnstown, the greatest in the country.

By late afternoon, dark squalls hovered with rain and brisk winds. Night came early and rains were swept in torrents, filling the lake to brimming. In Belle Glade, scores of families, white and black, found shelter in the town's two hotels, the Glades and the Belle Glades. Still others huddled onto sturdy canal barges. In South Bay, more than 150 survived by boarding a canal boat secured in nearby locks. Many elected to stay in their homes, but for hundreds of others on the margin of the southeast lakeshore—homesteaders in the flatlands, black and white tenant farmers and sharecroppers— shelter was minimal, comprising small frame dwellings and scores of shacks and sheds.

The first blast struck in a pitch black night; one could not see even his own raised hand, nor hear a shout or scream above the deafening roar of the fury. The rains pounded walls like water cannon, while 150 mph winds shrieked and tugged at the sturdiest dwellings, stripping roofs away like banana peels, smashing walls down, flattening smaller buildings, and sending the fleeing occupants sprawling awry. Those on canal boats were tossed in dizzying patterns as the new rushing waters sped through the opened flood gates. Floating timber poked holes in many a hull, while men frantically manned bilge-pumps to keep from sinking. As shelters were ripped to pieces, men, women, and children clutched to any support still standing— posts, chimneys, tree trunks, or just human link-chains.

And then, shortly after 10 P.M., the winds suddenly stopped, the rains became a mere drizzle. People rose up from their refuges and fumbled out into the darkness, searching for loved ones with the few oil lamps and flashlights available. They were confounded by the eerie silence. But many of them shivered at this scant comfort, for they knew what was happening: the dead calm eye of the giant 'cane was passing over. The worst was yet to come.

There was no sky, no land, no lake, not any visible form, only blackness. It seemed like the end of the world as the "second wind" of the mammoth storm smashed down once more. The shaky seven-foot dike (hardly built to withstand any storm) slowly wore down as the raging waters mounted. And then, it was if some giant hand had tipped up one end of a huge flat pan of water; the north end became empty mud flats, and the south end burst over, dissolving the sandy dikes like sugar, sweeping like tidal waves over the low-lying towns, swamps, sawgrass, and custard-apple tree jungles.

Hundreds were caught up as the raging water roared and swirled and tumbled everything in its path. People were scooped up flatfooted and carried swiftly into the torrent, struggling, choking, strangling, and going under, grasping at any solid object they could feel in the darkness.

Within a short time, Belle Glade's streets, a mile and a half away, were seven feet under. (At its highest, the flood would crest over 11 feet.) Houses were picked up, pushed along and finally set down as much as two miles away as families scrambled to rooftops and rode for their lives. A man and his pregnant wife, clinging to a log, were jarred from the refuge and spun into the torrent. An 18-year-old girl held her six-year-old brother aloft for hours as she half-swam, half-floated, only to have him swept out of her hand into the current as they approached the light of a rescue team.

Scores of people scrambled into trees to escape the rushing flood, only to face a menace just as deadly. The legions of venemous semi-aquatic water moccasins, along with other poisonous snakes, always seeking shelter above rising water, and now they swarmed into nearly every tree or outcropping; they outnumbered humans by at least 10,000 to one. Many a climber felt the sharp plunge of fangs in the darkness. Many died from the bites. Others who survived to recall it required painful treatment.

With little or no light available, those who had found secure refuge knew only an anguished helplessness as they listened to distant screams or shouts for help somewhere in the inky darkness. Finally the great 'cane passed, the waters slowly stopped rising and the siege was over, and people waited out the longest night in their memory, half anxious for, half dreading, the dawn.

Morning broke under dark, dirty-gray clouds as survivors stumbled out into the drizzling rain to survey an appalling scene of desolation. The entire countryside, from the lake eastward and south into the Everglades, was one massive tangled wreckage of uprooted trees, flattened sawgrass, homes, barns, stores, sheds, and warehouses. Some buildings had just vanished, while others had been picked up and carried far from their sites. In Belle Glade, the hotel and several other buildings remained, but South Bay, Bean City, Pahokee, and other settlements were virtually wiped away; all were near a point where over 1,000 feet of dike had crumbled. The water rose here to 11 feet 8 inches.

But even more sickening was the spectre of death that shrouded the grim dawn. Tears and anguished cries punctuated the silent pall as people identified a friend or loved one. The disaster had been no respecter of persons—a prosperous white landowner and a penniless black sharecropper shared the same muddy tomb. Many who survived but had been swept far away into the vast reaches of sawgrass, cane fields, and custard-apple thickets, died later, lost to the searchers. Hardly a family did not have at least one dead or missing.

Not until late that Monday, when a few survivors straggled into West Palm Beach, did the world learn of the great tragedy at Okeechobee. Aid and rescue workers poured in from counties near and far, but their efforts were severely stymied. Nearly every road and bridge been been washed away. The canals were choked with timber and the wreckage of houses. The first essentials—food, water, and medicine—were rushed in by Red Cross teams, while hundreds of others joined in for temporary repair of the roads and waterways.

But the grisliest task was already underway—rounding up the dead. Anyone with hammer and nails was kept busy around the clock making coffins from salvaged lumber. But as the week wore on, the coffin-makers found their task futile. On a single stretch of lake road, nearly 200 bodies were found. By the second week, the decomposing corpses were posing a serious health menace. They had to be burned. For days, the ugly black columns of smoke rose high from these funeral pyres, causing a grim shudder among those who survived.

The final death toll was estimated at over 2,000, but even this figure may have been far short. Nearly three-fourths of these fatalities were Bahamian sugar-cane and vegetable harvesters who learned too late (if at all) of the approaching catastrophe, and who, regardless, found little shelter in their flimsy shanties.

Soon after the disaster, estimated to have caused $25 million in damage to land and buildings, President Herbert Hoover approved construction of a vast stone levee 34 to 38 feet high and 85 miles around the lake's southern end. It has proved adequate since then to contain the lake's waters in any storm or turbulence, but it has yet to be tested against such torrents as the great hurricane of '28.

55.
To Burn in a Turpentine Hell

Florida's turpentine industry was "repulsively medieval" —
where men were enslaved by debts to the company store.

> *Teppentime man got a lonesome dollar,*
> *Grits is cold and the snaps is dry,*
> *Freeze in winter an' sweat in summer,*
> *Burn in the teppentime hell when he die.*

"There were, I understood from the beginning, special horrors in the history of what is properly called the naval stores industry," a modern historian laconically notes. And so it seems.

Few Floridians know that turpentine was once the state's second largest industry, but even fewer know that it once contained one of the harshest and most brutal feudal systems ever to function unmolested in the shadows of an enlightened modern state.

For nearly a half a century, it yielded fabulous profits (mostly to outside interests), but it extracted such riches from one of the most shameful forms of peonage ever foisted upon men, women, and children. This pine pitch fiefdom was a dark and alien land that few outsiders ever glimpsed, shut away deep in the vast pine forests which blanketed both the pan and the handle of North Florida.

Above all, there was no law in turpentine land—the camp boss was the law. There were no churches, no schools, no hospitals, no home or family life to speak of, and the only store was the company store, to which a man might truly owe body and soul when he found out at the end of the year that his meager supplies of grits or calico or pork back or whatever, unaccountably added up to more than his wages. The only time a sheriff or state trooper ever did come around would be to help catch some wretch trying to flee this subtle economic serfdom. Justice could be as swift as a bullet. It could also crack like a leather whip of the woodsrider (tree crop overseer) who could make blood ooze from a man's back as easily as the gum oozed from a slashed pine face. In the rare instances where children had a makeshift school to attend, they had to drop out early to help sustain the bitter existence. The only relief from this exhausting ritual and isolation was a shabby camp juke joint where oppression was lightened by a fierce, frenetic escape into wild dancing, "rotgut" moonshine, fist and razor fights, and promiscuous love. The brutalized, true to Adamic law, brutalized each other in turn.

"Don't you ever mess with no teppentime folks," one visitor was warned by black townspeople. "They savages without a God."

Turpentine workers were nearly all black, although in the early century, many immigrant Mexicans, Germans, Irish, Jews, and Poles were lured and bound by Southern firms into this virtual slave system. And they could often even be sold for debts incurred at the company commissary (where goods were almost invariably priced over 50 percent above the market). But most turpentine workers are a special breed, born into "the teppentime" over generations, their fathers before them having followed the industry down through the southeast states.

Sir John Hawkins, the famous English privateer, first discovered Florida's turpentine in 1565 and rushed back to England to tell of this miracle substance so vital to the caulking of vessels. But the English began first operations in Virginia in the 17th century. Here the virgin forests were slashed and sapped in great swaths southward. Within two centuries they had moved into the Carolinas. (Slaves trampling through the spilled pitch gave North Carolina its nickname, "Tar Heel.") By the end of the 19th century, the pines of Georgia had been laid waste. Finally, Florida was next.

By the turn of the century, camps were clustered across north Florida, pushing in deep and southerly from a line along the Old Spanish Trail (SR 90), from Crestview west to Lake City east.

A laborer might make $1.00 to $1.75 per day in the turpentine during the 1900s; by the early 1940s, he was still making the same. In the early years, many operators leased convicts from the state at $150 per year to supplement the labor. These men were harshly overworked, overexposed, often dying from scant and poor food, beatings, snakebites or malaria, controlled always by the guns, whips, bloodhounds, and manacles of the camp foreman.

The practice was stopped by the reform Governor Napoleon Broward in his campaign against the "trusts and combines" he claimed ran the industry. These were usually large out-of-state corporations. They would employ agents to work with individual camp operators to finance and market the valuable pitch and its rosin by-product. The profits were enormous, but unlike most native industries, these riches rarely benefitted the state.

As one West Florida operator conceded once: "It seems incredible that these millions of acres of pine should have been (sapped) cut, transferred through the channels of commerce to other climes, and so few people have been enriched by the process." And it took less than 40 years to deplete the huge stands of slash and long leaf pine by almost 80 percent, due to rapacious cutting, overcupping for gum, fires, and the absence of reforestation practices.

A typical camp harvests about ten crops, a "crop" comprising about 5,000 trees on 250 acres. Each camp is self-contained, from its huge copper kettle to distill the turpentine and separate the rosin, to living quarters for the camp foreman, store owner, and woodsrider (usually white) separated from the cabins and shanties of the workers (mainly black). The season runs as long as the tree gum flows, from about late February to the first cold snap.

"Repulsively medieval," historian Stetson Kennedy described these camps in 1940. The often weather-rotted shacks each had a huge black cauldron in the yard and a nearby reeking outhouse. Water came from a single camp pump.

A company store owner boasted to Kennedy: "With the commissary we make a gross profit of 60 percent and a net profit of 20 percent. You know that's pretty good—it takes a good slice offen the salaries. We don't hardly have to pay no salaries." True enough. Short of murder, the law rarely intervened in the camp life; the foreman was the law. But if a worker tried to leave the camp while in debt to the store, local authorities would set up road guards so that no one passed until the wretch was caught.

In the event of any other disruptions (such as the presence of a government worker or union organizer), the local Klan would stage an intimidating parade in the area. More than a few men attempting to escape this servitude were beaten to death and thrown into shallow pine forest graves. State foresters were often fired upon if they ventured too near a camp; "conservation" was a red-flag word to turpentiners in those days.

In the interests of "keeping order" but often mainly to cut down on housing needs, the camp foreman could arbitrarily pick a man and woman to "marry" each other and then assign them to one shack. This joining of hands was called a "commissary wedding," legitimized only by the word of the foreman. Once in a while, a rare visiting minister would protest this condition and the couples would then be transported to town for a legal courthouse wedding. But these were exceptional cases.

When the Social Security Act took effect, the operators were enraged and government people were harassed often with arrests for trespassing. This stopped, but only after the U.S. Supreme Court ruled that turpentine workers were in agriculture and therefore excluded from the act.

Over the years, there were also a few cases where operators were caught and fined for conspiracy to commit peonage. But these wrist-taps were few and far between. More often, in some strangely perverse irony, it was the operator, rather than his "peon," who garnered establishment sympathy, such as that in an unusual report by a study team at the University of Florida in the 1930s. After discovering that turpentine work was "too severe and the pay too small for white workers," the study then reported "a difficult problem" posed for the operators by workers who piled up "unpaid accounts" at the company stores, and then left for another camp. It was therefore desirable, the report concluded, that an "impartial economic dictator" be set up to watchdog these "shiftless" people.

But the report somehow failed to suggest how long rainy days (without pay), a bad market, or exorbitant commissary prices would prevent their dollar-a-day wages from being gobbled up. A worker, too, might have been puzzled at being called "shiftless" for doing work "too severe" for a white man, at "pay too small."

But, for most of these men, the word over generations might have been summed up in the Mexican phrase; "Sal Si Puedes" (Get out if you can). As one oldtimer, when asked why he went into the work, replied; "You is *born* into the teppentime. Ain't nothing you *go* into. Something you get out *of*."

In the past generation, many have done just that. New jobs, new laws, shifting population centers, and changing attitudes have changed and altered many camps. With a surging exodus of the young to larger towns and cities, a scarce labor market hiked turpentine wages to well above subsistence levels. The cruelty and lawlessness of a foreman or woodsrider is now remembered only in old stories and the supermarket has pushed out the company store. Some camps have neat, white-washed four-room cottages, with plumbing, and the children get bussed to school.

But there are yet more than a few reminders of what it must have been like for nearly half a century, when a man had all but lost his birthright if he worked "in the teppentime."

56.
The Notorious Alston-Read Duel

It was a time when life meant less. The Alston-Read duel was typical of many. Started over political differences, it ended in a chain of bloodshed.

Of all the vice and violence of olden Tallahassee's wild frontier days, when Florida was still a territory, perhaps no other tribal custom contributed more to the capital's periodic lapses into anarchy than the lethal "sport" indulged by its ruling clans—dueling.

The Code Duello—*rex pugnandi*—a somewhat pathological social virus that gestated and thrived for generations among the scions of privilege in monarchical Europe, found fertile root-soil in the posturing deference of antebellum plantation society to royal Bourbon trappings.

The practice, of course, revealed too much of man's sinful, homicidal, ignoble impulses and, hence, it was essential that these traits be somehow perversely exalted into a virtue, namely a code of "honor." Naturally, it was difficult at times to discern how much prima donna ego trips, with their base—if not barbaric—estimation of the value of human life, could in any way be construed as honorable. But it served other, less obvious, conveniences, too.

If, for example, you did not like a man's politics, or that his wife spurned your advances, or even the way he parted his hair, then you could on the most trivial pretext solemnly march him off to the dueling grounds and there ceremoniously blow his honorable head off. This was especially convenient if you were an expert marksman, as was often the case then with affluent men of leisure who had much idle time in which to practice. The custom also imbued a curious image of "machismo" which, (as we see in our own day), revealed still another effort to euphemize ill motive, i.e., making weakness appear to be strength.

At all events, these grave consequences were never so tragically illustrated as in one of Tallahassee's most notorious duels between the heads of two leading families—Leigh Read and Augustus Alston.

The Alstons were a prosperous planter family who, in the 1830s, came by some large tracts of rich farmland north of Tallahassee and decided to move their home near Miccosukee. The elder Alston had three grown sons—

Augustus, Willis, and Gideon—and two daughters. The Alston brothers had that reckless confidence that wealth endowed in frontier days; they were accustomed to coming by whatever they wanted, and sometimes by whatever means. They were all fascinated with guns and possessed a rare collection of dueling pistols.

It would early prove a foreboding hobby. One night Gideon and a family friend stepped outside to "test" two old pistols. The friend returned to the house, alone, to inform the two brothers that he had shot and killed Gideon "by accident." Although the Alstons had no choice but to believe him, it was only a few months later that the family friend was reported to have mysteriously disappeared in a storm at sea.

At their new home, the Alstons moved in Tallahassee's most respected social and political circles. Willis moved to Texas later, but his brother and two sisters remained. Augustus joined the Florida militia during the Indian wars and soon became a colonel. He also became a leader in the conservative Whig party which, at that time, was heatedly opposing new bank reforms being pushed as a result of the Panic of 1837, a panic that busted Tallahassee's Union Bank, leaving many speculator-planters in dire finances.

The opposing Democrat party just as ardently insisted on the bank reforms. Leading their ranks was Leigh Read, an attractive, likable political figure who, many agreed, had a bright future in state politics. Read was an official of the Territorial Council, a constitutional convention delegate, and a Brigadier General in the Florida militia, a promotion he earned as a wounded hero in the Battle of Withlacoochee, against the Seminoles. He was also married to Eliza Branch, daughter of John Branch, the state's last territorial governor.

The temper of those days might best be understood by the backdrop itself. Writer Malcolm Johnson reported that the capital streets "were the scene of duels, brawls, knife fights and all the violence [of the later Old West]." Reform mayor Francis Eppes, Thomas Jefferson's grandson, labeled the town's popular Marion Race Course "a hotbed of vice, intemperance, gambling and profanity." Earlier, writer Ralph Waldo Emerson took one visiting look at the town, called it "a grotesque place . . . (of) land speculators and desperados," and promptly returned to Concord. Politics, consequently, could beget inflammatory, emotional, even bizarre antagonisms which bore little resemblance to the conventional civil processes we know today.

As tempers flared and rhetoric waxed hot in the Whig-Democrat controversy over bank reform and other issues, at least two Whig leaders, one of them William Tradewell, sought to settle Read himself by challenging him to a duel. Read, temperate by nature, declined both. But, in what might have been a hasty aside, Read remarked that if he had to fight anyone, it would have to be the Whig's "bulldog" himself, Augustus Alston. At the frantic urging of friends, Alston decided to challenge Read and, to the surprise of many, Read accepted.

From that day on, Read was considered a doomed man, not only because, aside from earlier war days, he was only a casual, inexpert user of firearms, but because Alston was a practiced pistol expert. On the day of the duel, December 12, 1839, a confident Alston instructed his wife and sisters to prepare a big "victory" banquet for himself and friends on his return. The terms of the encounter—"duel to the death"—were agreed upon before the two met at an isolated rural location that chill, misty morning.

Whether from some intuitive hunch after careful assessment of his opponent's character (his quick temper for one thing), or simply due to some personal favor for it, Read, as challengee, chose the Yager rifle for weapons. It was the most deadly of weapons at short range—and it had an unusually sensitive hair-trigger. As their seconds—and a few picked bystanders—looked on, the two men walked the ten paces and wheeled. But Alston, whether from eagerness or uncertain balance, discharged his weapon before he could raise it and aim. He suddenly clutched the rifle to his breast as Read coolly aimed his rifle and fired. The ball shattered through Alston's rifle trigger and the challenger fell dead.

Even though, within its deadly terms, the duel was considered "fair," Alston's grieving bitter sisters called it "murder" since Alston fired before he could properly aim. They thereupon took the bullet removed from their brother, recast it, and sent it to brother Willis, in Texas, demanding that he return and avenge his brother's death with the same bullet. Learning of the sisters' plans, citizens came to Read and urged him to stay armed, which he did.

It was a festive evening, January 6, 1840, as General Read, who had since been elected legislative Speaker, was hosting friends at the traditional Speaker's Ball at the old City Hotel. As the banquet proceeded in merriment, a tall figure wearing a long cloak and hat pulled down, suddenly entered the scene and strode toward Read. Several onlookers gasped, exclaiming, "It's Willis Alston!" as the latter then tossed his hat off, threw back his cape, and charged at Read with a drawn bowie knife. Read by now had drawn his gun and fired at Willis, slightly grazing his hand. The two then struggled until others pulled them apart. Read suffered only minor cuts; Willis was not further injured.

After this incident, Willis dropped out of sight for a while, but he remained in the remote vicinity—planning. Over a year passed. then one day Willis contacted a friend, Michael Ledwith, and arranged to stay at the latter's house in town. He knew that Read strolled past this house often, and so he waited—with a double-barrel shotgun.

It was a fair day, that April 27, 1841, as Read strolled past the Ledwith house with a friend. The first barrel-load caught Read in the back, seriously wounding him. He wheeled about, just as Alston walked up very close to him and fired the second barrel at his head. Read died instantly.

His friend meanwhile summoned authorities and Alston was arrested and jailed. But he later escaped by means, according to one historian, of a group of friends "and about $30,000 in bribes." He then fled back to Texas.

Alston was settled in the town of Brazoria, Texas, for about three months when a Dr. Stewart, also a Brazoria area resident, learned of Alston's presence there. The doctor, a former Tallahasseean who had known Read and had learned of his murder, became incensed that Read's killer should be living in that community. Alston learned of the doctor's remarks about him and wrote them down on a sheet of paper. One day the two met on horseback and Willis stopped the doctor and handed him the sheet of paper, asking him to declare whether or not he had made the remarks. As the doctor took the piece of paper, he dismounted from the side opposite Alston, drew his gun, stepped around the horse and shot Alston in the stomach. Though badly wounded, Willis grabbed his shotgun and fired at the doctor, killing him at once.

Once again, Willis was arrested and jailed. As he recovered from his wound, he remained in high spirits, often playing a fiddle given him by a friend. One night a visiting servant, who had wrapped a rope around his body cleverly enough to elude detection, passed the rope on to Willis as part of an escape plan.

But on this same night, grieving friends of the doctor had other plans, however ill-starred. They stormed the jail, overpowered the marshal, and dragged Alston outside in a blanket. They then fired a volley of bullets into the last of the Alston brothers.

After such senseless blood-sheddings, was there a sudden moral revulsion? Did the "good citizens" of Florida suddenly realize they were condoning an unusually aberrant form of homicide? Sad to say, legislative attempts to outlaw dueling were repeatedly defeated. And when, years later, a toothless anti-dueling bill finally passed, it contained so many clauses condemning a person for declining a duel, that its intent for all practical purposes was tacitly nullified.

The arrogant (but curiously servile) homage to fantasies of royal and courtly splendor still lingered strongly among the plantation set. At the death of Willis Alston, an area newspaper, *The Florida Mirror,* could quite seriously proclaim of the Alstons: "A lion-like passion at the slightest insult— generous of life and gold alike—fitter in their imperious habits and princely ways for the days of chivalry and realm of barons than for our prosaic days and our commonplace land."

This was, unwittingly, perhaps more a diagnosis than a eulogy. The royal pretensions and the "princely ways," like the Code Duello itself, seemed symptomatic of some darker and deeper social malady. And whatever its nature, it seemed almost destined to be cleansed by fire within a generation. And it was.

57.

The "Binder Boys" Burst the Great Boom Bubble

A shipwreck and a killer storm sealed the fate of the last land bust while shopkeepers tried to become millionaires overnight.

Any perceptive history buff of Florida's often erratic—sometimes manic—real estate market is no doubt wincing as he watches the teetering of the Gold Coast's condominium "overbuild" today, especially in Miami.

His mind's eye cannot help recalling grainy images of another era when seedy little figures dressed in shabby white knickerbockers swarmed over the same turf like voracious locusts—the "binder boys." Of course, the new "binder boy" may be more fashionably tailored, his modus operandi less abrasive and more sophisticated, but his genus remains the same—a fast-buck speculator whose machinations once triggered the greatest bust in Florida's history.

The seeds of the great Florida land boom of the 1920s—that classic study in mass delusion—were probably planted earlier in the World War I era when Prest-o-lite millionaire Carl Fisher dredged up his golden sandbar, Miami Beach. Amid much circuslike hoopla and celebrity-gathering for lot sales, Fisher turned the first national spotlight on the Gold Coast.

But other seeds gestated, too. The postwar years found people's pockets bursting with war profits. They were eager to travel, go places, and Henry Ford's cheap and sturdy "Model T" made mass mobility a first-time reality. The more affluent, also, began a mass switch from southern Europe's winter playgrounds to Florida's closer and more salubrious sunshine. New roads like the Dixie Highway, from Canada to Miami, made travel easier. So did S. D. Warfield's new Seaboard Coast Line railroad, cutting into Henry Flagler's once undisputed Florida East Coast railroad territory.

Thus, real estate expansion, which up to 1921 was lively but unfrenzied, began to take on feverish intensity as more visitors poured into the Gold Coast, especially Miami, the epidemic's center. An inevitable housing shortage sharply spurred new building, land prices began to soar and speculators found quick and huge profits to be turned from once arid scrub or pine land. National magazines began to ballyhoo the quick fortunes to be made by just ordinary "little people" in Florida real estate. A New York boilermaker turned his $1,000 savings into $190,000 in cash and acreage within months; a South Carolina stenographer paid $350 for a Miami lot and sold it weeks later for $65,000; one shabby derelict boasted of parlaying two bottles of bootlegged gin into $60,000; the City of Miami itself faced a crisis when policemen, firemen, and other city employees quit their jobs to get in on the "gold rush."

As the speculative hordes poured in, prices soared even higher. A front-foot on Flagler street zoomed to $50,000, while overgrown woodland eight miles inland sold for $25,000 an acre. Lots were sold like hot dogs, straight off the blueprints, site unseen, often up to 100 times their true value. Food became scarce and housing scarcer. People slept in cars, on benches, in parks or on beaches. Miami became a sweating madhouse with (at one count) 5,917 real estate brokers on the bustling scene.

But the small fry were peanut shuckers compared to the grandiose dreamers. George Merrick employed celebrities like William Jennings Bryan to sell $150 million in lots in his exclusive southwest Miami subdivision, Coral Gables. Northward, flamboyant Palm Beach architect Addison Mizner sold $14 million in lots on opening day for his fabulous Venetian-styled city, Boca Raton. Magnate Joseph Young spent $40 million turning a batch of tomato farms into his Hollywood-by-the-Sea. N.B.T. Roney and Ohio's ex-governor James Cox paid $3 million for undeveloped Seminole Beach. Within six hours it was gobbled up for $8 million. (Most of these men were virtually wiped out when the bust came.) By the end of 1925, $7 billion worth of Florida real estate had changed hands.

By now, both the state and its chamber of commerce, along with Governor John Martin, were promoting Florida nationwide as strike-it-rich land. To entice wealthy migrants, the legislature even hastily revised the constitution to cancel income and inheritance taxes. But reactions were setting in, too. Northern and Mid-Western bankers became so disturbed by the exodus of people—plus huge cash deposit withdrawals—that many of them ran full-page newspaper ads, such as: "You're going to Florida to do what? To sell lots to the other fellow who is going to Florida to sell lots to you. That's about all you can do in Florida—unless you want to work." And when the northern Scripps-Howard newspapers somberly predicted a looming land-bust, the state's press responded with vitriol, one of them running a front-page banner shrieking: "Shut Your Damn Mouth!" while another threatened to sue the chain for malicious slander.

But of all the dubious speculators, the unscrupulous "binder boys" came to symbolize the basically manic character of this fantasy paper kingdom—and the cause of its collapse. With no intention of actually buying a property, they would pay a small sum down for a binder option on it, and resell the binder many times before the first large payment was due, an often long interval for county clerks who were already overwhelmed with title searches and deed recordings. A lot's price would spiral many times on one binder while each link-buyer in this dizzy daisy chain reaped a windfall profit. Millions changed hands in such a manner—at least on paper—and few if any heeded the dire warnings of soberer heads like Miami banker E. C. Romfh, who acutely perceived what such hysteria must lead to.

Even as this papier-mâché Tower of Babel began to sway ominously, Miami was a scene of chaos. Two large vessels that overturned, or grounded, one after the other in Miami's harbor channel, choked off desperately needed food and building supplies for months, while scores of ships could neither enter nor leave port. On land, essential rail repairs kept 900 freight cars stuck in Miami yards, with 1,200 more jammed back-to-back northward, prompting the emergency freight embargo. Meanwhile, in New York, a bad bear market reduced scores of would-be boom investors and a national probe of Gold Coast real estate frauds further cooled investment ardor. Finally, in late summer 1926, the great tower crashed mightily, drowning hundreds of investors, large and small, overnight in a sea of paper. Then, on September 15, 1926, as if to dramatically punctuate the debacle, a killer hurricane roared up the Gold Coast, smashing like matchsticks the often gimcrack new buildings, killing 150 people, and leaving thousands of homeless. Florida's greatest aberrancy had ended—abruptly, tragically, and totally.

Bustling Miami today certainly shows no signs of repeating so colossal an episode of madness. But symptoms are surfacing as one observes the new "binder boys" who in recent years have been cashing in on the Gold Coast's condomania—distorting condo sales, undercutting prices, and creating false market pictures that have already had devastating side-effects for scores of financiers and builders. One can only wonder how many busts it will take before the state's business and political leaders finally identify a disease that may soon prove endemic enough to resist immunization by any nostrum.

58.
Tampa Terror and the Cigar Strike of 1910

The cigarworkers' strike of 1910 exposed race prejudice in a manner long to be remembered.

The City of Tampa today is one of the most progressive and enlightened communities in the South, with a liberal outward bending that bodes much promise for its future.

But once, 65 years ago, the city wrote a shameful chapter of lynching, lawlessness, and terror that shook the community and left deep scars for more than a generation. The event was the great general cigarworkers' strike of 1910.

In those years, Tampa virtually lived off its only industry—cigars. An allied structure of bankers, merchants, professions, trades, and press waxed fat from the clear Havana stogies that poured by millions out over the world each year. It accounted for 65 percent of city revenues and 75 percent of its payrolls. It moved Tampa from a sleepy get-by village of 2,000 in the mid-1880s to 37,782 souls in 1910. The city had lavished free land, buildings, and subsidies on Vincente Martinez Ybor and other manufacturers and had enjoyed up to 1910 a literal industrial "utopia."

The cigarworkers—mainly Cuban and Spanish but with some Italians—with an aesthetic sense of their craft, considered themselves as much artists as workmen and, indeed, they produced the finest of the original pure clear Havanas. Unions were coming into their own in those days and the cigarworkers were then organizing under the International Cigarmaker's Union of America (AFL). All building tradesmen in the city then were union and the ICUA was a legitimate chartered national union. In fact, a former cigarmaker, Samuel Gompers, was then president of the entire American Federation of Labor. By June 1910, the cigarmakers had organized 37 of the main Tampa factories and formally petitioned the Cigar Manufacturers Association for recognition. Since there was no dispute over wages, hours, or working conditions—only union recognition—they foresaw no problems, a routine formality only. But the CMA refused recognition. The ICUA's young and able leader and head of its Joint Advisory Board, José de la Campa, tried various appeals to avert a strike but when factory owners locked out 50 percent of the workers that month, the union struck, and over 8,000 men and nearly 2,000 women went out.

The city's separately-owned newspapers—the *Tribune* headed by Colonel W. F. Stovall and D. Lambright, and the *Times,* owned by D. B. McKay (who was also mayor)—at first assumed the traditional posture of impartiality, a "hands-off" fairness. This seemed laudable since each had industry-related financial interests. But this posture soon proved to be only that, a posture, and the press was to assume one of the most ignominious roles in journalistic history. (Aside from the traditional names, the Tampa press of today has no ties or relations whatever with the press of 1910.)

On July 21, de la Campa appealed to the city's Board of Trade to assist in arbitration but its secretary, W. R. Powell, somewhat vaguely and ambiguously, replied that information received from "most reliable sources" prevented that body from involvement in the dispute. A few days later, the owners closed all factories.

Curiously, during July and August, the press had been running repeated stories on the need for more police in the city. The union's Joint Advisory Board leaders and the workers had maintained a peaceful and orderly regime in the strike and were somewhat disturbed by these police calls. Aside from one minor scuffle, there had been no "incidents" as such.

Out in the surrounding rural areas dwelled numerous individuals whose ways of life, and livelihoods, were dubious at best, lawless at worst. Some doubtless were amused at the irony of "city folk" calling them in to assist as "special police." But the appeal to them as "Americans" (i.e., Anglo-Saxons), plus the extra silver dollars and maybe even the chance to have some "fun" seemed irresistible. They soon began to increase in number on Ybor and West Tampa streets, scuffling with workers occasionally and lending an air of intimidation generally. Finally, after a strong show of unity by the city's unions and others with the cigarworkers in a huge downtown Labor Day parade, McKay publicly announced the hiring of some 300 of these "special police." The press at this time had already begun to inject an ugly note of prejudice into its news columns by identifying only Anglo-Saxons as "Americans" and all others by race or nationality. The impartial mask was slipping; it would soon fall totally.

On September 14, around lunchtime, as was their custom, a crowd of workers was gathered in front of the Bustille Bros. & Diaz factory in West Tampa just as J. F. Easterling, the firm's bookkeeper, was about to enter the building. Suddenly, from the edge of the group, a shot rang out and Easterling fell wounded. In the ensuing excited confusion, the unknown assailant had quietly slipped away. Easterling would linger for days in the hospital before dying, his assassin never known.

The press at once began screaming in chorus at the "blood-lust possessed . . . nationalities" who had "the temerity to assault an American" and darkly hinted the complicity of cigarworkers. The union itself denounced the shooting and disclaimed any connection to it. The press had already spurred the organizing of a "citizens' committee"—bankers, merchants, lawyers, etc.—and began inflammatory appeals to them to "do something."

A week later, two men, Angelo Albano, 25, and Castronse Figarretta, 45, were arrested as suspects. They had allegedly been seen in the crowd at Bustillo, though not with any weapon. Then as deputies drove the pair by horse-drawn hack to the town jail that same night, they were stopped at gunpoint on Howard Avenue by three carloads of from 25 to 30 men who seized the prisoners, took them to a tree at the corner of Howard and the present Kennedy Boulevard and lynched them. Albano was shot once in the stomach. Authorities located the death site soon after but, inexplicably, left the bodies hanging until morning; a note pinned to one victim's trousers warned others to "take note or go the same way." Crowds quickly gathered next morning, including Figarretta's wife and daughters who fell prostrate at the scene. Photographers suddenly appeared but, after protests by the Italian consulate, Governor Albert Gilchrist suppressed selling the grisly photos. Figarretta had been associated with the grocery business and Albano sold insurance prior to their deaths. Neither was connected to the union. It had been a full moonlit night but deputies could not identify the men, although Constable James Keagin said they were all "Americans" with "painted faces." Nor could they identify any of the three cars, even though few people owned cars in 1910.

Perhaps as shocking, however, was a *Tribune* editorial calling the lynching "a lesson" with "determined men" superceding "the weakness and inadequacies" of the jury system. "Every person in that group deserved hanging," it shrieked. The union by now genuinely feared some covert "terror" campaign, especially when de la Campa, G. P. Bradford, and board attorney Robert McNamee began receiving anonymous lynch threats. McKay's "street squads"—"street goons" in the union's view—were openly attacking strikers in isolated places.

In this period, McKay wrote in his *Times:* "It is impossible to understand the attitude of the American Union workingmen of the city who had been misled into sympathizing and supporting" the cigarworkers. The words, with their subtle appeal to prejudice, were soon answered. In a resolution by the carpenters, in which all unions joined, continued moral and financial support was pledged the cigarman. The resolution further read: "It has come to our notice the Mayor . . . has without warrant of law imported from various rural districts a larger number of men for police duty, whose strongest recommendation is the reputation for lawlessness of the districts from whence they came . . . [and whose] presence . . . is better calculated to provoke disorder than to preserve the peace." They admonished McKay to stop "the troublemakers and agitators who are . . . directing the destinies" of the factory owners.

McKay conceded only that a few were "unfit for service" and had been let go; the remainder were "unbiased" men. The press' bias was another matter. The "gentlemen" of the union's board had now become "undesirable," destroying the city's economy. Frantic editorials called for "erradicating . . . this element." The workers were "poor, misguided ones . . . stricken mute under the sway of fanatical leaders . . . trying to shake them to the tune of 30 cents a week dues." The workers secretly wanted to return to work, they claimed (even though a private ballot referendum held in October showed only 15 votes to return). When Easterling died September 29, the *Tribune* claimed that factory owners were "fleeing the city for their lives." In fact, the number who had left the city were busily setting up branch factories in cities from Key West and Miami to Jacksonville; the rest were safely at home. The only single incident here reported was a factory owner's partner who, mistaking an innocent pedestrian in some bushes as an "assassin," whipped out a pistol. In his excitement, he shot himself, but the bullet passed harmlessly through his coat-sleeve.

The press, meanwhile, listed some 800 "prominent citizens" for its "committee" and flatly declared that they were "the only law." The remaining 37,000 citizens were not mentioned, although many, including business and professional people, were openly sympathetic to the workers, contributing food, clothing, and other aid to their families. The press was now almost demanding that merchants refuse workers credit and that landlords start eviction proceedings. It even called for the arrest of workers as vagrants since they had "no visible means of support."

The factory owners, supposedly "fleeing for their lives," were now emboldened to reopen their factories and begin importing by boat "replacements" from Havana and Key West, 25 to 50 at a time, while some 200 "committee" members, armed and riding in cars, patrolled the streets to "protect" the replacements. In truth it was the workers themselves who began to fear for their lives and livelihoods.

Then, on October 17, after giving speeches at the Labor Temple on Eighth Avenue urging workers to ignore "terrorist tactics" and stick out the strike, de la Campa, J. F. Barthlum, and Britt Russell were arrested by deputies under a vague charge of "conspiring to incite" the men. Over protests by attorney McNamee, they were held for days without bond. Tried by a somewhat selected jury, they were convicted shortly after and sentenced by Judge Horace Gordon to a year each, as the press gloated, "on the chain-gang." Then, shortly after this arrest, an armed mob of the "committee," headed by Colonel Hugh C. Macfarlane, stormed into the Labor Temple, driving workers out of it, smashing chairs, tables, and other furniture, and seizing all the union's records and papers. The mob's reasons: to find "evidence" linking union leaders to the Easterling shooting! It took a grand jury weeks to show there was no such evidence, and the union would later sue the city for $20,000 damages. The *Tribune* meanwhile piously declared that if the acts were illegal, it was "a mere technicality" since the mob had been "armed with the law of right."

Meanwhile, the harsh glare of a national spotlight began to smart the eyes of the local vigilantes. In a major speech, carried in papers over the nation, AFL president Gompers blasted the city's "leaders." Citing the sanctioning of "grave outrages"—lynching, strikebreakers, mob actions— the eminent labor leader declared Tampa "a lawless and disreputable community." While publicly lashing at "unfair" charges from "outsiders," a subdued press and committee cringed at the unexpected publicity and quickly invited Governor Gilchrist down to "investigate." After several days, once meeting with the workers and the remainder with "the other side," Gilchrist pronounced that "no undue violence" had occurred in Tampa. He then promptly left town. An elated press splashed headlines over this cursory probe's "findings." The union felt crushed.

The strike lingered on into the new year but the dispirited workers now saw clearly the hopeless odds against them. Their meager funds long since exhausted, some evicted from homes, their food credit lost, their leaders jailed, "street goons" still stalking about with a "lawless" committee hovering in the background with "replacements" (however unskilled) totalling nearly 1,000—the workers agreed, on January 26, to return to work.

They drew a few agreements from the manufacturers—no reprisals against workers, no undercutting of price and wage scales (the cartabon), and strict observance of child labor laws. But on their only real strike goal— union recognition—they had failed. This would come in later years.

But the proud cigarmaker knew what terrible and powerful forces it had taken to defeat him and, in this, he might take some grim satisfaction. Beyond that, he only knew that he would never forget that dark time when his city was once "a lawless and disreputable community" indeed.

59.
The Infamous "Gulags" of Florida's Past

Sentences to prison were sentences to slave labor and probably death. The system lasted more than half a century.

We are staggered and appalled today at accounts of Gulag Archipelagoes in the Soviet Union (Stalin's horrendous counterpart to the infamous Siberia of czarist days).

But once upon a time in Florida, there was maintained a penal system that for sheer brutality would have rivaled anything devised by a Stalin or a czar.

In fact, for more than half a century—the latter 19th and into the 20th— it was a system that began and continued in "almost unrelieved barbarity," according to one of its own official participants. Historians often allude to this dark chapter with vague generalities about certain "abuses" and "injustices," and it is not surprising that there are no popular histories written of Florida prisons. For it was indeed what it was called in 1885 by author George Washington Cable, "a disgrace to civilization."

Even before the Civil War, the notorious "convict lease system" was practiced unofficially in Florida. But in 1877 it was actually made official penal law. Motivated largely by greed, venality, corruption and prejudice, this act served virtually to institutionalize an evil that, in spite of the efforts of outraged citizens through the decades, would not be abolished until 1923.

And there would be little record of it specifically had not one man who had served as a captain in some of these prison "camps" decided to bring it to public attention in an unusual and graphic little book, *The American Siberia,* published in the late 1890s. The author, J. C. Powell, in a narration curiously mixed between confessional and apologia, does not have to embellish his day-by-day revelation of the terrible inhumanity visited upon countless thousands of wretched souls, most of whom would find release from this sustained barbarity only in death.

In the years after the Civil War, Florida was economically destitute, its government in constant turmoil from warring political factions; corruption was almost endemic. At this time, the huge arsenal at Chattahoochee was converted into an insane asylum and state prison, and Colonel M. Martin was named by Governor Harrison Reed to be its warden. The state then turned over all of its convicts to Martin and paid him over $30,000 in bonuses to take charge. Martin soon made a fortune by working the prisoners in his wine vineyards and on other farms. The colonel was also speaker of the state legislative assembly and was able to secure lucrative appropriations to feed and clothe his charges, although these funds rarely saw their intended purpose. Instead, Martin operated what Powell labelled "a horror den."

Scantily clothed and fed, the prisoners were worked exhaustively, seven days weekly, from dawn to dusk. For the slightest infractions, they endured tortures of medieval origins, not only leather strap beatings and air-tight sweat-boxes, but the Spanish inquisition's "water treatment," whereby a bound prisoner had water forcibly poured into him until his stomach distended and, in slow agony, the life was literally squeezed from him. Another common punishment was hanging by thumbs with leather cords, the toes just clear of the ground. As the prisoner writhed and shrieked, every muscle in his body was seized with painful cramps. Survivors of this ordeal were easily recognized by their grotesquely elongated thumbs, knobbily deformed at the tips.

Guards always kept fixed bayonets on their muskets by which to repeatedly prod a prisoner who might lag in a forced run or fall from exhaustion at labor.

As word of these atrocities spread, a scandal appeared imminent. But Governor Marcellus Stearns stifled it by transferring, by lease, half the prisoners to some northern railroad lessees who were building the St. Johns & Eustis Railroad. This proved little more than swapping one hell for another. In this tropic marsh and palmetto jungle, no provisions had been made for either food or shelter. Crude makeshift shelters forced convicts to sleep in mud and slime. The meager rations quickly ran out and, during brief releases from the hard labor, the men were forced to scour the woods for roots and palmetto cabbage, their only sustenance. Soon the camp was ravaged by every disease that starvation and exposure could induce—fever, skin maladies, scurvy, pneumonia, dysentery, and others. When scores of prisoners died, Powell relates, the work had to be halted.

After George Drew became governor (1877-81), the Chattahoochee prison was discontinued and convict leasing became law. The door was now open to a system of abuse and degradation of human life unparalleled in state history. Private interests flocked to get their share of this relatively "free" labor. Prisoners were put to forced labor in cotton fields, brickyards, railroads, lumber mills, and other profitable ventures. Few if any restrictions were placed on lessees as to the hours they worked their charges or how they punished them. A common, and notorious, enterprise was turpentining. Powell, who had supervised some of these camps, said of this labor: "The work is severe to a degree almost impossible to exaggerate, and it is very difficult to control sufficient quality of free labor to properly cultivate any great number of trees."

While there were many poor white convicts, the greater number of prisoners were black. When the Democratic Bourbons regained power once more in Reconstruction days, they lashed back at blacks more cruelly than in slave days. To ensure a steady flow of free labor, local judges would convict as vagrants, and send to these chain-gang camps, blacks whose only crime was voting, looking for work, refusing certain work conditions, or trying to homestead or own land. A sentence to many of these work camps— especially in turpentine—could often mean simply a death sentence. The men were usually worked—literally—to the last "pound of flesh." Some were deemed fortunate if they received even as much as the sparse regulation ration of bacon fatback, cornbread, and field peas. They were beaten with leather whips often just on personal whim by low-paid, semi-literate guards who sometimes were ex-convicts themselves. Their waist-chains, attached to their leg stride-chains, were never removed. An unruly prisoner would have the additional attachment of a 50-pound iron ball, permanently. If a prisoner survived this physical and psychic ordeal, the vermin-infested filth of his crude log quarters would almost ensure him of disease. Powell said many camps became virtual hospitals, with dysentery the most common, and fatal, disease. Records of prisoners were rarely kept, but if Powell's estimate of the number of prisoners who died from whippings, shootings, starvation or disease (then dumped into the customary shallow dirt graves) is accurate, then a vast stretch of North Florida today is just one very long unmarked cemetery.

Needless to say, men would often risk their lives to escape this tropic Siberia. Scores were successful; hundreds were not. They had to elude first the tenaciously unerring fox-hounds, used in all camps. This could only be done by reaching the cane brakes of the Suwanee River, or St. Marks, or the swampy areas northward. But even trained backwoodsmen could get lost in the dense forests, lagoons, swamps, palmetto flats, and labyrinthine jungle that was then Florida. It was not unusual for a hunter to stumble over a seeming bundle of filthy rags in a lonely wood, only to lay bare the bones of some desperate, lost escapee.

But if an escapee could reach any settler in the area, he was almost "home free," because the reaction of common people in North Florida— white or black—to the convict lease system was one of furious if impotent rage. Whether black or white, an escapee could almost be assured of getting his shackles "hacked" and a swap of "stripes" for a shirt and trousers. Powell reports that in Taylor and Lafayette counties, for example, law officials refused even to serve warrants, for fear of their lives, so strong was the revulsion to this sytem.

The convict lease system also spawned another infamous outgrowth—peonage. Debt-ridden sharecroppers could be forced to "work out" a debt to a plantation owner, or an employer could pay a prisoner's fine and assume almost unlimited "work custody" over him. Unscrupulous contractors, especially at the county level, often forced prisoners into debt and retained them as workers long after their sentences were completed.

A great number of the fortunes of North Florida "pioneer" citizens were obtained from the use of these systems—men like Green Chaires, a wealthy Tallahassee planter; Major H. A. Wyse, who supplied turpentine gum to Dutton, Ruff & Jones; or E. B. Bailey, of Monticello, who, in shifting some prisoners to the phosphate mines, added what Powell described as a "new dimension of horrors to the system."

Through the years, various governors, some few legislators, editors, educators, religious, and civic leaders sought, without success, abolishment of this infamous practice. Too often, many lawmakers were themselves engaged in this unsavory business. Or, like Governor W. S. Jennings, in 1900, they simply sought more profit for the state by raising the contractors' pay per year per convict from $26.50 to $150. When finally the legislator passed a bill abolishing the system in 1911, it was vetoed by Governor Albert Gilchrist.

It took a tragedy and a little spotlighting from a faraway state—North Dakota—to finally catalyze public action. In late 1921, a North Dakota farm boy, Martin Tabert, 22, was arrested in Tallahassee for hopping a freight train. He was convicted of vagrancy and turned over to a lumber company that had a lease contract with Leon County. While at a camp at Clara in Dixie County, the youth died in February 1922, after being flogged to death by a whipping boss. The boy's parents were told he had died of "fever and complications." But a probe instigated at the demand of the Dakota legislature revealed the real cause and a furor of national publicity entered the case. Some officials involved lost their jobs and the whipping boss was tried for murder (and later acquitted). And yet the tragedy galvanized a milestone achievement. In 1923, Governor Cary Hardee signed separate bills forbidding the whipping of prisoners and abolishing forever the infamous leasing system.

The path from "an American Siberia" to the relatively modern and humane penal system of today seemed long and tortuous. But history can often serve man benevolently, simply by showing him where he has been and how easily he got there and why he must be ever vigilant that he never travel that path again.

60.
Armed Only with Integrity, Governor Carlton Faced Violence

Doyle Carlton was governor during the early Depression days when criminal elements descended on Florida.

The early 1930s were tough years to be Florida's governor. There was boom and bust, natural disaster, and the Great Depression. But Florida's 25th governor, Doyle Elam Carlton (1929-1933), also had to contend with powerful criminal gambling elements, who literally bought a chunk of the legislature out from under him and then threatened him. (At one point, President Herbert Hoover sent in federal lawmen to guard Carlton.) This was the time during which the notorious "Hialeah bill," which legalized parimutuel betting for the first time, passed over the governor's veto.

Carlton, 44, was a man whose simple virtues and integrity might have made him one of the state's most productive governors. But sadly, he was caught up in the vortex of national forces that few then could comprehend, much less anticipate. Thus one might easily understand the governor's lament of how "at times, one feels oppressed with the overwhelming sense of responsibility."

Born in Wauchula to a pioneer family, Carlton graduated first from Stetson University and then took degrees from Chicago and Columbia universities before marrying Nell Ray and opening a Tampa law practice in 1912. He successfully sought a state senate seat (1917-1919) and worked on behalf of child labor laws, women's suffrage, free textbooks, and worker's compensation.

In 1928 Carlton entered a five-man Florida gubernatorial race that was already aflame with bigotry, arising mainly over the Democratic presidential candidate, New Yorker Al Smith, a Catholic and a "wet" on prohibition. Carlton's strongest opponent, former governor Sidney J. Catts (1917-1921), used a toxic blend of religious and sectional demagoguery to incite such a strong anti-Catholic vote that Florida voted Republican (Hoover) for the first time in 50 years.

But Carlton trounced runner-up Catts decisively in both the first and second-choice voting (the one-two choice system that eliminated second primaries) and won in November with 61 percent.

He took office just as Florida began to feel the full impact of its boom-to-bust economy—widespread unemployment, bankruptcies, and bank failings. Thus, when the great 1929 stock market crash hit, 150 Florida towns were already in financial default, and the state government was in an unconstitutional condition of debt. Worse yet, state spending in 1928 under former Governor John Martin had exceeded receipts by almost $2.5 million.

Declaring taxation and financing to be the state's major problems, Carlton set out to slash the state budge by a quarter-million dollars and abolish "useless offices" at state and local levels and consolidate others. He kept road building on a pay-as-you-go plan, proposed stricter banking laws, relieved county taxpayers by sharply reducing millages and fought the "menace" of local bonding districts.

But Carlton clashed repeatedly with the legislature, holding it in numerous extra sessions as new tax revenues were sought to replenish depleted state coffers. Opposing most moves for new taxes, Carlton compromised on a penny gas-tax addition.

But his severe test came with the lure of a new "easy revenue" method: a parimutuel bill to legalize betting at horse and dog tracks. Powerful groups backed by millionaire Joseph Widener had recently organized the Hialeah Race Track in Dade County and were exerting all-out pressure for the bill. They were joined by equally wealthy Northern underworld figures sponsoring their own tracks. There was talk of payoffs in cash and bootlegged liquor, talk which prompted torrid senate floor fights and cries of "bribery." The bribes and booze must have been enough, for the bill passed. Carlton vowed to veto it, declaring that "the moral issue far outweighed all others."

Carlton later recalled a bribe offer "by a man who told me that my signature (on the bill) was worth $100,000. I told him, 'if it's worth that much, then I believe I'll keep it.' " He then received physical threats, and President Hoover personally offered federal agents down to guard the executive.

The bill was vetoed, but legislators overrode it by the slimmest of margins.

Carlton was unable to bring the economic recovery to the state that he so tirelessly strove for. But he worked hard to elect the man who would greatly aid such recovery in the years ahead through massive federal projects and reforms: Franklin D. Roosevelt. From the time he left office, the former governor came to symbolize "a strong moral force in public affairs," to such an extent that he would serve in various presidential advisory capacities until his death at 87 in October 1972.

61.
The Flagler Divorce Law Furor

Laws protected Mrs. Flagler from divorce because she was insane, but her famous husband railroaded a change that caused a furious debate.

Henry M. Flagler was castigated at the time, but historians hold him in a kinder light. His contributions overshadow the divorce.

When the wife of Henry Morrison Flagler sat down to breakfast one morning and casually announced that she was engaged to be married to the "Czar of all the Russias," the Czar of all Florida developers almost choked on his Florida grapefruit.

This story is perhaps apocryphal, but not in the essential element that would provoke one of the state's most controversial legal storms—the "Flagler Divorce Bill"—at the turn of the century. And when, within weeks after his divorce, Florida's own "Daddy Warbucks," as historian John Ney fondly—and injudiciously—labeled Flagler, turned around and married his not-quite "Little Orphan Annie," the storm swelled into a statewide chorus of denunciatory censure from press, pulpit, and parlor. Almost overnight, Florida's "greatest benefactor" had suddenly become Florida's "greatest villain."

Even today, this black mark lingers against the man who, otherwise, in true Warbucks style gave away countless sums of money to financially strapped individuals and groups, brought jobs and opportunities to tens of thousands of settlers and, more importantly, opened the entire east coast of a frontier state to the most phenomenal development in its history.

And yet in more sober historical retrospect, the facts indicate that the rail mogul may have been the victim of an historical "bad rap"—unjustly maligned in a tragic situation that would humanly compel no alternative to

246

the one he chose. The "facts" surrounding the divorce were, in fact, sequentially simple.

Flagler was no stranger to marital misfortune. His first wife, Mary Harkness, had a severe bronchial illness that kept her a semi-invalid until her death in 1881. A devoted Flagler never left her side, even as he was building the giant Standard Oil monopoly with partner John D. Rockefeller, Sr. His friendship with the nurse who attended his wife's last days ended in his marriage to her at age 53. Thirty-five-year-old Alice Shourds, a practical nurse and former aspiring but unsuccessful actress, was described at the time as having blue eyes, red hair, and the proverbial temper to match. Now one of the world's richest men, Flagler had already begun his "love affair" with Florida and during that second marriage would push his railroad south from Jacksonville, building lavish resort colonies as he went along—at St. Augustine, Ormond Beach, and the most permanent of them, at Palm Beach.

Alice lacked certain social and educational advantages but compensated with a zealous ambition for social standing among the gilded Florida resort crowd—the Vanderbilts, Astors, Goulds, Whitneys, and Wanamakers. She plunged furiously into their social whirl of balls and parties, but even as she did so, her erratic and volatile temperament seemed to wax stronger. She would sometimes disrupt social functions with petty tantrums, gossip maliciously with others, and affect the most exaggerated forms of "social" speech, according to historian Sidney Martin. Strongly enamored of her, Flagler was gently tolerant of her "moods" and would brook no criticism of her. Her behavior, while often unseemly, appeared to be normal.

But in the early 1890s, she became unusually preoccupied with a Ouija board and often spent hours alone in her room playing with it. She would at times shun her husband's attentions and it was in this period that she began confiding to disconcerted friends her plans to marry "the Czar of all the Russias." Her Ouija board, she solemnly related, had already told her of the Czar's love for her. Finally she related this and other bizarre confidences to a family friend, Dr. George Shelton, while he visited the Flagler New York residence in 1895. The doctor became alarmed, especially when she noted that this would all take place after Flagler's death. Informed of the physician's observations, the shaken Flagler agreed to let several prominent specialists in mental disorders examine his wife. (One of them first had to pose as a detective to clear a house "full of Russian spies" against which she had barricaded herself in her room.) Their diagnosis was unanimous and the distraught husband agreed to her confinement.

A year later, she had improved enough to be permitted to stay at the Flagler resort home at Mamaroneck, New York, where a joyful Flagler—prematurely—reported her "cured." She wasn't. And, when she managed to come by a Ouija board from a neighbor, she began a rapid relapse and a medical attendant later pronounced her "mental equilibrium . . . completely destroyed." She was confined once more to her sanitarium cottage where Flagler spared no expense for her comfort and treatment, but she never responded. On August 4, 1899, the New York Supreme Court, on medical petition, ruled her incurably insane with "chronic delusional insanity."

During this period, Flagler had gradually emerged from a bout of depression and had renewed an acquaintance with a young lady, Mary Lily Kenan. He had first met Mary, then 24, in 1891 at a party given by his wife. An accomplished vocalist and pianist, Mary on various occasions had sung many of his favorite songs and now, on renewed meeting, he found himself drawn to her. Mary was an orphan who lived with relatives in Wilmington, North Carolina. The Kenans were an old Wilmington family and Mary, while not exactly a beauty, had considerable charm and grace. Flagler began escorting her to social functions and outings and their friendship soon became warmer and more intimate. But gossip, which was the favorite pastime of Palm Beach, finally goaded Mary to insist that they marry. A frustrated Flagler wanted to remarry but neither New York, his lawful residence, nor Florida permitted divorce on grounds of insanity. Finally the desperate railroader changed his residence to Florida, had some political friends quietly introduce a divorce bill which was passed in record time and signed on April 25, 1901.

An immediate uproar ensued throughout the state. The press—with the lone exception of the Ocala *Banner* that defended him—flayed him with indignant editorials, labeled the new law "Flagler's Divorce Bill" and darkly hinted that the bill cost him $20,000 "properly distributed" to lawmakers. In street and pulpit he was scurrilously denounced as "villainous" and "immoral," with innuendoes suggesting even more lurid conduct. But this storm of criticism reached a crest when, shortly after obtaining his divorce, on August 24, 1901, the 71-year-old mogul married 34-year-old Mary in North Carolina. The name "Flagler" by now had become a household word in the state—and rarely a very nice word. (The bill would be repealed four years later.) Ignoring the reaction, the couple honeymooned in far-off Mamaroneck and later returned to Palm Beach where Flagler presented his young bride with a "cottage," the fabulous $2.5 million marble palace, "Whitehall."

Although they endured considerable social abuse in the early years, Mary proved to be a devoted wife and an accomplished hostess. She entertained often and lavishly at "Whitehall" and gradually the social detraction subsided. Their marriage was at least a contented one until Flagler's death on May 20, 1913. The bereaved Mary began ailing and survived her husband by only four years.

Meanwhile, in a peaceful sanitarium cottage in upstate New York, serenely oblivious to the legal earthquake of which she had become the catalyst, totally unaware even of the existence of her former spouse, Alice Shourds continued to paint her cheeks with red yarn dye, blacken her eyebrows with burnt cork, give herself facials with coffee cream, and excitedly discuss with a host of imaginary friends her approaching marriage to "the Czar of all the Russias." She lived in good health otherwise to the age of 82 and died of a brain hemorrhage on July 10, 1930.

62.
Near Riot at the Jacksonville Prizefight

When Jacksonville offered to host a much-touted prizefight, it opened the door for a brawl on a much larger scale.

It was a duel for the world's heavyweight boxing championship and all eyes of the international sports world were fixed on the little town of Jacksonville, Florida, that January day in 1894.

But before it was over, the state was plunged into controversy, a near riot developed, troops were called out, and it seemed that Governor Henry L. Mitchell himself was ready to step into the ring to stop what he called "a disgraceful and brutal" spectacle.

The little seaport town itself certainly had mixed feelings when it found itself host to the title fight between America's James J. "Gentleman Jim" Corbett—recent defeater of "the great John L. Sullivan"—and England's renowned champ, Charles Mitchell (no kin to the governor certainly). And soon the city was divided into two camps. Those who joined Mayor (later U.S. Senator) Duncan Fletcher and others in declaring that "prizefighting tends to lawlessness" and arouses "the brutal instincts of humanity" lined up against the Duval Athletic Club, which sponsored the event, along with a mixed gaggle of sporting bloods, gamblers, touts, promoters, and those who eagerly anticipated a brisk and lucrative business from the crowd.

The affair began quietly enough. Upon learning that a world's title fight was being arranged by the respective managers of Corbett and Mitchell, a group of local boosters organized the Athletic Club in October 1893 for the sole purpose of offering Jacksonville as the fight site. The club made an offer, the principals accepted, and the purse was set at $20,000, winner take all. But no sooner had arrangements been concluded and a public announcement of the event made when Governor Mitchell ordered the contest cancelled, threatening the use of force, if necessary, to prevent it. Other public and official protests followed. The mayor denounced the fight, and the local clergy held a mass citywide meeting to stop it. First the state and then the national press joined the controversy, some approving the contest but most, including Florida, opposing it and echoing the views of the New York *World* which condemned prizefighting as "immoral and bloody." The Legislature would later enact a bill making "prizefighting, pugilistic exhibitions and kindred offenses" crimes. At the time, the governor intended to construe an anti-dueling law as covering prizefights. Meanwhile, angry groups favoring the fight gathered in the city streets, shouting epithets at anti-fight factions and making threatening signs of defiance toward official interference.

But the Athletic Club was determined to hold the bout on schedule on January 25, 1894, at 2:30 P.M., at the old fairgrounds in Fairfield, within the city limits. They attempted to elude the law by calling it not a fight, but a "boxing match with five-ounce gloves." Corbett had already arrived and gone into training at Mayport. Mitchell arrived two weeks later, but, to "test the law," authorities arrested him. The fighter posted $1,500 bond and then set up his training camp at St. Augustine.

Duval County Sheriff Napoleon B. Broward (the future governor) favored drastic measures to halt the fight, including either jailing the two pugilists or seizing the fighting arena to prevent either combatants or ticketholders from entering. The governor backed away from these measures somewhat with the slightly circuitous reasoning that until the fight actually took place, no crime had yet been committed.

In the meantime, tempers of both anti- and pro-fight forces in the city were heating up with shouts, threats, and occasional scuffles. Emotions grew even hotter as the big day approached; in fact, tensions were building so ominously that city authorities declared martial law. On January 17, the Gates City Rifle Company, of Sanford, was ordered to march to Jacksonville and the Second Battalion of the state troops was alerted. Two days before the fight, the state militia arrived. As they paraded through the crowded streets, they were greeted by fight enthusiasts with hissing, booing, and even sand- and rock-throwing. A "High Noon" atmosphere seemed to be smoldering.

Elsewhere the city was hosting the largest crowds ever assembled there for any event. Sportsmen, gamblers, tourists, curiosity seekers, with a liberal lacing of assorted pickpockets, petty thieves, and dubious ladies, jammed the major hotels and lodging houses to capacity, many coming from as far away as New York and Chicago. Still others were forced to sleep in parks and vacant fields.

Finally, facing the adamant governor, a potentially explosive crowd, and, not least, a financial disaster, the club "played its trump card," as historian T. F. Davis put it. It employed one of the state's most prominent lawyers, Colonel A. W. Cockrell, to seek an injunction against state interference with the "proposed scientific glove contest." Hearings lasted up until the eve of the fight, and Circuit Judge Rhydon M. Call decided in favor of the club.

On fight morning, a torrential rain had churned the streets with mud, but the crowds were slogging their way to the arena as early as eleven o'clock. Tickets, at prices from $10 to $25 each, had long since been sold out. Greenbacks flashed openly as betting became hot and heavy, Corbett being a 10-to-4 favorite, while other boisterous fans entertained themselves with hip flasks and baskets of beer. A sensation was created when one woman, dressed in men's clothes (no woman then would have dared to attend a prizefight), entered and took a seat. But not a few of the prominent locals present easily recognized her as Clara Desplaines, owner of a famous brothel in Kansas City.

Finally, the two contenders entered the ring. The crowd was momentarily subdued up until the gong rang for the first round; the spectators then erupted into cheering and catcalls.

The fight itself was almost an anticlimax, in view of the ballyhoo and controversy that had preceded it. The first round was judged about even. In the second, Corbett floored Mitchell just before the bell rang. The third round saw "a groggy" Mitchell go down twice for a nine count. Then Corbett rushed in quickly, swinging a powerful right to Mitchell's nose. The latter fell hard, this time out cold, and Corbett retained his title.

As soon as Mitchell was revived, authorities arrested both men on misdemeanor assault charges. Each posted $5,000 bond and then returned north. The following February, Corbett was tried first and was acquitted. This verdict prompted the state to drop the case against Mitchell. The stormy controversy seemed to have been quickly forgotten.

And yet, in retrospect, the whole affair seemed almost to resemble some surreal comic opera. Or, as former Governor LeRoy Collins wrote years later: "What a ruckus over a prizefight! Why, today, we are subjected to more violence than that in a single, thirty-second television commercial about acid indigestion." He had a point.

63.
Bad Faith and Avarice Felled a Banking Empire

The high-flying Union Bank of Tallahassee made borrowing very easy. But its freewheeling lending practices failed the test of time, and bondholders on two continents lost their money.

Have they taken all the fun out of banking?

If so, then perhaps the caution of our modern pillars in pinstripes may only be overreaction to the excesses of the bankers who came before them. And this would certainly be true on considering the granddaddy of all Florida banks, the Union Bank of Tallahassee, the state's first. Talk about a frolic in the green; it's had no peer since.

The Union Bank, from its start, seemed dedicated to the proposition that banking could be not only fun and exciting, but also extremely profitable. Employing some rather novel banking methods, it infused throughout antebellum central Florida an exhilarating spree of prosperity. Indeed, it seemed that everyone in the state would soon be joyously rolling in clover. Unfortunately, they weren't exactly sure of whose clover they were rolling in, and this slight oversight would eventually shatter the whole concept of fun-loving finance. But, while the spree lasted, there was some high and merry stomping under the magnolias.

Organized by John G. Gamble of Tallahassee and promoted by Governor William DuVal as "a planters' bank," the Territorial Legislative Council chartered it on February 12, 1833, on an 11-7 vote. This charter had some novel features. For example, the stockholders of the bank were the chief borrowers of its capital, the capital itself having been borrowed originally through the issuance of what came to be called "faith bonds." No one was exactly sure what a faith bond was except that it pledged the faith of the territory—that is, its citizens. Therefore, four expert legal opinions were sought as to the bonds' validity. All four, including that of renowned statesman Daniel Webster, said it was quite all right. The charter also combined the functions of both banking and moneylending for long terms of credit on mortgages of real estate and chattels.

Some features prompted some spoilsport grumblings, such as that of James Wescott, territorial secretary, who warned that such a charter "will be found pregnant with the most mischievous and disastrous results." But such grousing was quickly drowned out by the euphoria that greeted the new bank.

Some irregularities cropped up, too. The stock-subscription books—opened to "land-owner citizens" only—were supposed to be opened throughout Florida, but were opened in three places only—Tallahassee, Marianna, and Pensacola. Middle Florida thus controlled most of the subscriptions, and the stock seemed centered in small groups. John Gamble, the bank's first and only president, owned 584 shares ($100 per share), and his brother, Robert Gamble, had 754 shares. Other Leon Countians together held 13,727 shares. In addition, the books stayed open long beyond the 60-day time limit, from April 10, 1833 to January 22, 1835. The 40-year charter allowed the bank a first-year capitalization of $1 million; after this time, up to $2 million more. This capital was raised on the faith bonds, 1,000 at $1,000 each, sold by the bank at par, redeemable within 24 to 30 years. The bonds were sold in New York, Philadelphia, and London, and the bank opened in January 1835.

The bank's instant popularity was understandable. Stock subscribers secured their holdings not with cash but with 20-year mortgages on land, homes, or slaves. A $3,000 stockholder could then draw two thirds of this in currency, or $2,000. Moreover, most settlers had bought their land for $1.25 to $2 an acre. The loan appraisers valued it at $5 an acre, so the bank was lending 50% to 100% over the planter's entire investment.

And many of these good citizens were not above playing a little numbers game called "working the appraiser." A planter would show them the slaves on the plantation, whisk him to his house for lavish wining and dining, then take him to the next plantation—where the same slaves had been quickly transferred, only now answering to different names. It was nearly always good for a "bonus" of a few thousand.

"Landamighty, the Union Bank is the best thing afloat; a man can just go to sleep and wake up rich," enthused a matron of the day, explaining how one could mortgage land and slaves, get a loan, buy more land and slaves, raise one or two good cotton crops, get another loan buy more land and slaves, and so on.

True enough. A fever of land speculation only enhanced the prosperity that seemed to be intoxicating nearly all of northern mid-Florida. The living was extravagant. And it intensified with the feverish expectation of more to come.

There were some dampening notes at the end of 1835—a severe frost wiped out many crops, and the Second Seminole War had commenced with fury, inflicting heavy losses in slaves, livestock, and even homes. But the euphoric borrowing and buying generally continued unabated.

Then came the financial Panic of 1837. The bank paused in its spree long enough to take stock and found that its extensive loans, large overdrafts, heavy overhead expenses, large fees and commissions to attorneys and special agents, and defaults had all severely depleted liquid assets. On May 10, 1837, it suspended all specie payments. Despite this suspension, it went ahead with plans to sell its remaining $2 million in faith bonds. But it drew sharp public resentment by giving older stockholders preference on purchase of the 20,000 shares of new stock. The older holders got 17,000 of these, while many would-be subscribers were turned away.

Older buyers also had their now-inflated original security reappraised. Land was valued now up to $15 or more per acre. A stockholder could borrow more than he did the first time on the same security.

Meanwhile, President Gamble hurried off to Europe in early 1838 to peddle his bonds; 200 were sold in New York, another 100 in Amsterdam, and the largest number, 966, in London. The remaining 704 bonds he left with an agent in London. (These would remain unsold, even at a heavy discount from par.)

The Union Bank of Tallahassee had a brief life as a high-flying institution.

Soon it was clear that the bank's heady days were about over. The ravages of the Indian war began to squelch the land boom, and the excesses of many planters rendered them unable to meet their staggering loan obligations. In addition, the Legislative Council's banking committee, alarmed at the massive indebtedness facing Florida's citizenry from the $2 million bond issue, began a probe of the bank's operation. The committee's report was drenched in caustic irony: "The idea of a bank founded on borrowed capital had been ill understood, now it was perfectly comprehensible. To become suddenly rich, to become offhand the proprietor of the land, slaves, houses and equipages simply by pledging property on a loan, with 20 years credit, which property could be bought with money thus obtained, was to enjoy in reality the vision of fiction. The charter of the bank was an El Dorado..."

Despite the bond sale, the bank's financial decline steadily worsened. Many planters faced ruin, corruption charges flew, reputations fell, old friends became enemies, duels were fought, neighbors shunned neighbors. By 1842, public sentiment had become so inflammatory that the council unanimously repudiated the faith bonds, denying that the territory had any authority to issue them. The following year the council suspended all operations of the Union Bank; it would never reopen. For some 20 years, the bondholders would try through three nations to get their money back; they never did.

Historian Ellen Call Long, in *Florida Breezes,* recalls a conversation of that day between a Tallahassee lady and her guest, an exchange that might also serve as a sadly quaint epitaph of sorts:

The lady: "We were once . . . a very frugal, unpretentious people, neighborly and helpful, until recently."

Guest: "What has made that change?"

Lady: "Little pieces of tissue paper, engraved with the usual vignettes and promises."

BIBLIOGRAPHY

Numbers below refer to chapter numbers.

1. Grismer, Karl H. *The Story of St. Petersburg.* St. Petersburg, P. K. Smith & Company, 1948.

   Official Opening Program and Pictorial History, Gandy Bridge, November, 1924. Special Collections, Hillsborough County Main Library, Tampa.

2. Ingram, James M. "John Perry Wall:" A Man for All Seasons." *Journal of the Florida Medical Association.* 53(1966): 709–17.

   McKay, D. B. *Pioneer Florida* v. II. Tampa, The Southern Publishing Co., 1959.

3. Holt, Rackham. *Mary McLeod Bethune: A Biography.* New York, Doubleday and Company, 1964.

   Embree, Edwin R. *13 Against the Odds.* New York, Viking Press, 1944.

4. Blackman, E. V. *Miami and Dade County, Florida; Its Settlement, Progress, and Achievement.* Washington, D.C., Victor Rainholt, 1921.

   Muir, Helen. *Miami, U.S.A.* Coconut Grove, Hurricane House Publishers, Inc., 1953.

5. Cox, Merlin A. *David Sholtz: The New Deal Governor (1932–36), of Florida."* *Florida Historical Quarterly* 43(1964):142–52.

   Tebeau, Charlton. *A History of Florida.* Coral Gables, University of Miami Press, 1971.

6. Hurston, Zora Neale. *Dust Tracks on a Road.* Philadelphia, Lippincott, 1942.

   Hemenway, Robert E. *Zora Neale Hurston: A Literary Biography.* Urbana, University of Illinois Press, 1977.

7. Howe, George D. "The Father of Modern Refrigeration (John Gorrie)." *Florida Historical Quarterly* 1(1909):19–23.

   Jahoda, Gloria. *The Other Florida.* New York, Charles Scribner's Sons, 1967.

8. Grismer, Karl. *The Story of Sarasota.* Sarasota, M. E. Russel, 1946.

   McDuffee, Lillie B. *The Lures of Manatee.* Nashville, Press of Marshall and Bruce Company, 1933.

9. Zilg, Gerard Colby. *DuPont, Behind the Nylon Curtain.* New Jersey, Prentice-Hall, Inc., 1974.

   James, Marquis. *Alfred I. DuPont, The Family Rebel.* New York, The Bobbs-Merrill Company, 1941.

10. Hanna, A. J. *The Music Master of Solano Grove (Frederick Delius).* New York, American Society of the French Legion of Honor, 1943.

    Jahoda, Gloria. *The Road to Samarkand: Frederick Delius and His Music.* New York, Charles Scriber's Sons, 1969.

11. Muir, Helen. *Miami, U.S.A.* Coconut Grove, Hurricane House Publishers, Inc., 1953.

    Parks, Arva Moore. *The Forgotten Frontier.* Miami, Banyan Books, Inc., 1977.

12. Thornbrough, Emma Lou. *T. Thomas Fortune: Militant Journalist.* Chicago, University of Chicago Press, 1972.

13. Lanier, Sidney. *Florida: Its Scenery, Climate, and History.* Philadelphia, J. B. Lippincott, 1875.

    Jackson, Lena E. "Sidney Lanier in Florida." *Florida Historical Quarterly.* 15 (1936)118–24.

14. Griswold, Oliver. *The Florida Keys and the Coral Reef.* Miami, The Graywood Press, 1965.

    Walker, Hester Perrine. "Massacre at Indian Key . . . " *Florida Historical Quarterly.* 5(1926):18–42.

15. Bigelow, Gordon E. *Frontier Eden: The Literary Career of Marjorie Kinnan Rawlings.* Gainesville, University of Florida Presses, 1966.

    Bellman, Samuel Irving. *Marjorie Kinnan Rawlings.* New York, Twayne Publishers, 1974.

16. Kuehl, Warren F. *Hamilton Holt: Journalist-Internationalist-Educator.* Gainesville, University of Florida Presses, 1960.

17. Frantzie, George. *Strangers at Ithaca.* St. Petersburg, Great Outdoors Publishing Company., n.d.

    Pent, R. F. *The History of Tarpon Springs.* St. Petersburg, Great Outdoors Publishing Company, 1964.

18. Grismer, Karl H. *The Story of St. Petersburg.* St. Petersburg, P. K. Smith, 1948.

    Bacon, Eve. *Oakland, The Early Years.* Chuluota, Florida, The Mickler House, Publishers, 1974.

20. Frisbee, Louise. *Peace River Pioneers.* E. A. Seemann Publishing Company, Miami, Florida, 1974.

    McKay, D. B. *Pioneer Florida, Vol. II.* Tampa, The Southern Publishing Company, 1959.

21. Hanna, A. J. and Kathryn A. *Lake Okeechobee.* New York, The Bobbs-Merrill Company, 1948.

22. Redford, Polly. *Billion-Dollar Sandbar.* New York, E. P. Dutton & Company, Inc., 1970.

    Kobler, John. *Capone: The Life and World of Al Capone.* New York, G. P. Putnam's Sons, 1971.

23. Sewell, John. *Memoirs and History of Miami, Florida.* Miami, Franklin Press, 1933.

    Shappee, Nathan D. "Zangara's Attempted Assassination of Franklin D. Roosevelt (1933)." *Florida Historical Quarterly.* 37(1958):101-10.

24. McKay, D. B. *Pioneer Florida Vol. II,* Tampa, The Southern Publishing Company, 1959.

    Tebeau, Charlton W. *The Story of the Chokoloskee Bay Country.* Coral Gables, University of Miami Press, 1955.

25. Hanna, A. J. *A Prince in Their Midst.* Norman, Oklahoma, University of Oklahoma Press, 1946.

    Long, Ellen Call. *Florida Breezes.* Gainesville, University of Florida Presses, 1962.

26. Jahoda, Gloria. *Florida, A Bicentennial History.* New York, W. W. Norton & Company, Inc., 1976.

    Shofner, Jerrell H. *History of Jefferson County.* Tallahassee, Sentry Press, 1976.
27. Prior, Leon O. *Lewis Payne, Pawn of John Wilkes Booth."* Florida Historical Quarterly* 43(1964):1-20.

    Weichmann, Louis J. *A True History of the Assassination of Abraham Lincoln . . . "* New York, Alfred A. Knopf, 1975.
28. Amory, Cleveland. *The Last Resorts.* New York, Harper & Row, 1952.

    Roberts, Kenneth L. *Florida.* Harper & Brothers, New York, 1926.
29. Woodman, Jim. *Key Biscayne: Romance of Cape Florida.* Miami, Hurricane House Press, 1961.
30. Phillips. Leon. *That Eaton Woman, In Defense of Peggy O'Neale Eaton.* Massachusetts, Barre Publishing; New York, Crown Publishers, Inc., 1974.

    Eaton, Margaret O'Neale. *The Autobiography of Peggy Eaton.* New York, Charles Scribner's Sons. 1932.
31. Mahon, John K. *History of the Second Seminole War, 1835-1842.* Gainesville, University of Florida Presses, 1967.

    Hartley, William and Ellen. *Osceola, the Unconquered Indian.* New York, Hawthorne Books, 1973.
32. Cochran, Jacqueline. *The Stars at Noon.* Boston, Little, Brown and Company, 1954.

    Jahoda, Gloria. *The Other Florida.* New York, Charles Scribner's Sons, 1967.
33. Hartley, William and Ellen. *A Woman Set Apart.* Dodd, Mead, 1963.
34. Walker, Jonathan. *Trial and Imprisonment of Jonathan Walker.* Gainesville, University of Florida Presses, 1974.
35. McKay, D. B. *Pioneer Florida Vol. II.* Tampa, The Southern Publishing Company, 1959. (From an unsigned article in the *Philadelphia Times* in 1882, a verbatim report by an Army officer present at the occasion).
36. Darrow, Anna. "Old Doc Anna." *Journal of the Florida Medical Association,* 55(1968):749-56.

    Will, Lawrence. *Cracker History of Okeechobee.* St. Petersburg, Great Outdoors Publishing Company, 1964.
37. Montague, Richard. *Oceans, Poles and Airmen.* New York, Random House, 1971.

    Dunn, Hampton. *Yesterday's Lakeland.* Tampa, Bay Center Corporation, 1976.
38. Gannon, Michael V. *The Cross in the Sand.* Gainesville, University of Florida Presses, 1965.

    Oré, Luis Jeronimo de, Bishop. *The Martyrs of Florida.* New York, Joseph F. Wagner, Inc., 1936.
39. Johnson, Kenneth R. "Florida Women Get the Vote." *Florida Historical Quarterly.* 48(1970):299-312.

    Taylor, Elizabeth, A. "The Woman Suffrage Movement in Florida." *Florida Historical Quarterly.* 36(1957):42-60.

40. Strickland, Alice. *The Valiant Pioneers*. Volusia County Historical Commission, 1963. University of Miami Press, 1963.

Hebel, Ianthe Bond. *Centennial History of Volusia County, Florida*. Daytona Beach, College Publishing Company, 1995.

41. Pierce, Charles. *Pioneer Life in Southeast Florida*. Miami, University of Miami Press, 1970.

42. Hanna, A. J. and Kathyrn A. *Florida's Golden Sands*. The Bobbs-Merrill Company, Inc., New York, 1950.

Morison, Samuel Eliot. *History of U.S. Naval Operations in WW II, Vol. 1*. Boston, Little, Brown, 1947–62.

43. Cabell, James Branch and A. J. Hanna. *The St. Johns, A Parade of Diversities*. New York, Farrar & Rinehart, 1943.

44. Bartram, William. *Travels*. New Haven, Yale University Press, 1958.

Van Doren, Mark, Editor. *The Travels of William Bartram*. New York, Dover Publications, 1928.

45. Carson, Ruby Leach. "Florida, Promoter of Cuban Liberty." *Florida Historical Quarterly*. 19(1941):270–92.

Harner, Charles E. *A Pictorial History of Ybor City*. Tampa, Trend Publications, Inc., 1975.

46. Covington, James. W. "Cuban Bloodhounds and the Seminoles." *Florida Historical Quarterly* 33(1954):111–19.

Giddings, Joshua R. *The Exiles of Florida*. Gainesville, University of Florida Presses, 1964.

47. Motte, Jacob Rhett. *Journey Into Wilderness*. Edited by James F. Sunderman. Gainesville, University of Florida Press, 1953.

48. Parker, Daisy. "John Milton, Governor of Florida: A Loyal Confederate." *Florida Historical Quarterly*. 20(1942):346–61.

Douglas, Marjory Stoneman. *Florida: The Long Frontier*. New York, Harper & Row Publishers, 1967.

49. Bok, Edward W. "Bok Tower—America's Taj Mahjal." *Scribner's Magazine*, New York, February, 1929.

Bok, Edward W. *The Americanization of Edward Bok*. New York, C. Scribner's Sons, 1922.

50. Mehling, Harold. *The Most of Everything: The Story of Miami Beach*. St. Petersburg, Great Outdoors Publishing Company, 1964.

Redford, Polly. *Billion-Dollar Sandbar: A Biography of Miami Beach*. New York, E. P. Dutton and Company, 1970.

51. Pettengill, George W., Jr. *The Story of the Florida Railroads*. Boston, Railway and Locomotive Society, Inc., 1952.

Prince, Richard E. *The Atlantic Coast Line Railroad*. Salt Lake City, Utah, Wheelwright Lithographing Company, 1966.

52. Lazarus, William C. *Wings in the Sun: The Annals of Aviation in Florida, 1895–1950*. Orlando, Ty Cobb's Florida Press, 1951.

53. Woodford, Milton M. "A Connecticut Yankee Fights at Olustee: Letters From the Front." Edited by Vaughn D. Bornet. *Florida Historical Quarterly.* 27(1949):237–59, 385–403.

Tebeau, Charlton. *A History of Florida.* Coral Gables, University of Miami Press, 1971.

54. Will, Lawrence E. *Okeechobee Hurricane and the Hoover Dike.* St. Petersburg, Great Outdoors Publishing Company, 1961.

55. Kennedy, Stetson. *Palmetto Country.* New York, Duell, Sloan & Pearce, 1942.

Jahoda, Gloria. *The Other Florida.* Charles Scribner's Sons, New York, 1967.

56. Collins, LeRoy. *Forerunners Courageous.* Tallahassee, Colcade Publishers, Inc., 1971.

Long, Ellen Call. *Florida Breezes.* Gainesville, University of Florida Presses, 1962.

57. Ballinger, Kenneth. *Miami Millions.* Miami, The Franklin Press, 1936.

Muir, Helen. *Miami, U.S.A.* Coconut Grove, Hurricane House Publishers, Inc.

58. Long, Durward. "Making of Modern Tampa: . . . " *Florida Historical Quarterly.* 49(1971):333–45.

The Tampa Tribune and *The Tampa Times.* Microfilm issues of 1910. Hillsborough County Public Library, Tampa.

59. Powell, J. C. *The American Siberia.* Chicago, W. B. Conkey Company, 1893.

Eckert, Edward H. "Contract Labor in Florida During Reconstruction." *Florida Historical Quarterly.* 47(1968):34–50.

60. Tebeau, Charlton. *A History of Florida.* Coral Gables, University of Miami Press, 1971.

61. Martin, Sidney Walter. *Florida's Flagler.* Athens, Georgia, University of Georgia Press, 1949.

62. Davis, T. Frederick. *History of Jacksonville, Florida.* St. Augustine, The Record Company, 1925.

Collins, LeRoy. *Forerunners Courageous.* Tallahassee, Colcade Publishers, Inc., 1971.

63. Abbey, Kathryn T. "The Union Bank of Tallahassee: An Experiment in Territorial Finance." *Florida Historical Quarterly.* 15(1937): 207–31.

Tebeau, Charlton. *A History of Florida.* Coral Gables, University of Miami Press, 1971.

INDEX

Agee, Alice Mae (Mrs. David
Sholtz) 22
Airplane Law 210-12
Albano, Angelo 237
Allison, Carl & James 205
Alston, Augustus 227-30
Alston, Gideon 228-30
Alston, Willis 228-310
Ambrose, James ("Uncle
Jimmy") 208-9
Anderson, Elbert 42-5
Armour, James A. 170
Ashley Gang 85-9, 149
Askew, Gov. Reubin 108
Austin, W. W. 167
Avery, Fred 205

Bailey, E. B. 243
Baker, Bob 87
Baker, Fred 88
Baldwin, Florence
(Countess Nugent) 48
Ball, Ed 39-40, 107
Ball, Jessie (Mrs. Alfred R. duPont) 39
Barr, Mary (Mrs. Kirk Monroe) 48
Barron, Dempsey 107
Bartram, William 183-6
Barthlum, J. F. 237
Beachy, Lincoln 211
Beasley, Edmund D. ("Alligator")
& Anna 46
Bedell, Deaconess Harriet M. 136-40
Beight, George 59
Bellamy Brothers 103
Belle Glade 219-21
Bethune, Mary McLeod 13-16, 51
Bethune-Cookman College 15, 28
"Binder Boys" 233-4
Bok, William 201-3
Bok's Singing Tower &
Sanctuary 201-3
Bolding, Jeffrey 37
Boom & Bust 7, 20, 23, 38-41, 78, 80,
91, 105, 106, 138, 204-6, 232-4,
245, 253-5

Bowden, H. L. 167
Bowleg, Chief Bill 36
Braden, Joseph & Hector 34
Bradford, G. P. 237
Branch, Gov. John 142, 228
Brees, Anton 203
Brickell 17-18
Brooks, George 161
Broward, Gov. Napoleon 224, 251
Brown, David 172
Brown, Maria 48
Bryan, William Jennings 161
Burdine, Roddy 92
Busset, H. L. 161
Butler, W. M. 171

Caldwell, Stafford 21
Call, Judge Rhydon M. 251
Call, Gen. Richard Keith 103-4, 122-3,
195, 198
Campa, Josae De La 235-8
Campbell, John T. 100
Cancer de Barbastro, Fra. Luis 155-8
Capone, Albert Francis ("Sonny") 93
Capone, Alphonse ("Scarface Al")
90-93
Carlton, Gov. Doyle Elam 23,
92, 244-5
Carney, Dick 48
Carney, Maggie 18
Cattle Industry 81-4
Catts, Gov. Sidney J. 162, 244
Chaires, Green 243
Chamberlain, Mrs. Ella C. 159-61
Chapman, Dr. Alvan Wentworth 32
Chekika, Caloosa Chief 59-61
Cheney, John K. 69
Chevrolet, Louis 167
Clark, Frank 161
Cigar Industry 235-9
Civil War & Reconstruction 37, 51-2,
54, 109-11, 141-3, 197-200, 213-6
Clarke, Sen. Scott D. 106

Cochran, Jacqueline ("Jackie") 131-5
Cockrell, Col. A. W. 250
Coconut Grove 19, 46-9
Cohen, Isador 19
Collier, Barron 41, 136, 139
Collins, John 205
Collins, LeRoy 103, 252
Collins, William ("Pogey Bill") 149
Comstock, Mrs. Frank 20
Cooley, Mrs. Rozelle 160
Cooley, William 118
Coral Gables 7, 238
Corbett, J. F. 100
Corbett, James J. ("Gentleman Jim")
    250-252
Cornell, Edward 151
Corse, Mrs. Montgomery 43
Corcoris, John 69-71
Cosden, Joshua 113
Cowkeeper, Seminole Chief 186
Cowpunchers 81-4
Crawford-Smith, Alexina
    ("Zenia,"Mrs. Hamilton Holt) 68
Crime & Criminals 85-9, 90-93, 94-7,
    98-101, 108-11, 179, 182, 206, 244-5
Cross, Mrs. W. H. 95
Cufney Tiger, Chief 138
Curtiss, G. H. 167

Dade, Francis L. 118, 128
Darrow, Dr. Anna Albertina
    ("Doc Anner") 149-51
Dauer, Manning J. 108
Davis, D. P. ("Doc") 7
Davis, T. F. 260
Davis, William W. 199
Day, Mary (Mrs. Sidney Lanier) 55-7
Daytona Beach Races 165-9
Dean, G. W. 100
deCamp, Marie Antoinette
    (Mrs. E. C. Romfh) 78
Demens, Peter W. (Piotr Alexewitch
    Dementier) 72-4
Demogeot, Victor 167
Desoto Tiger, Chief 86
d'Hedouville, Count Jean 48

Delius, Frederick 42-5
Desplaines, Clara 252
Dimicks, E. N. ("Cap") 172-3
Disston, Hamilton 73
Dorelis, Countess Dolly Hylan
    Heminway Fleischmann O'Brian 114
Douglas, Charles 42-3
Douglas, Marjory Stoneman 138
Drew, Gov. George 240
Dueling 10, 227-31
Dunlap, Tully 79
duPont, Alfred Irenee 38
Durrance, Charles M. 21
Duval, Gov. William P. 103, 124, 253
Dyal, C. D. 38-40

Earhart, Amelia 133
Easterling, J. F. 236
Eaton, John H. 121-5
Eaton, Margaret (Peggy O'Neale) 121-5
Eatonville 26
Elder, Ruth 152-4
Elliott, Eugene 8
Eppes, Francis 228
Eppes, Susan Bradford 111
Eubanks, Pressie (Mrs. John Wall) 10
Ewan, J. W. ("Duke of Dade") 17-8

Ferman, Fred 100
Finegan, Gen. Joseph 213-15
Figaretto, Castronse 237
Firestone, Harvey 92
Fisher, Carl Graham 92, 204-6, 232
Fitzpatrick, Col. Richard 192
Flagler, Henry 17-9, 165-7, 173, 246-9
Fleming, Gov. Francis P. 12
Fletcher, Duncan 161, 250
Ford, Henry 167
Fortune, Timothy Thomas 50-53
Frank Charlie 138
Freezes 18-19
Frow, Joseph & John 47
Fuller, H. Walter 6

Gadsden, Col. James 103
Gamble, James N. 15

Gamble, John G. 103, 253-4
Gamble, Maj. Robert 34
Gandy Bridge Co. 6
Gandy, George Sheppard ("Dad") 5-8
Giblin, Vincent 92
Giddings, Rep. Joshua 192-3
Gilchrist, Gov. Albert 237, 239, 243
Gill, Mrs. Joe 95-6
Glass, James 59
Gomez, Arthur 21
Gompers, Samuel 235, 239
Gordon, Fritz 92
Goredon, Judge Horace 238
Gorrie, Dr. John 30-33
Gray, Catherine Daingerfield Willis
    (Princess Murat) 103-4
Grieg, Edvard 44-5
Grismer, Karl H. 8, 74

Haig, Mary (Mrs. J. R. Motte) 196
Haldeman, George 151-3
Hamblin, Rep. A. C. 161
Harmon, H. F. 171
Hannagan, Steve 206
Hardee, Gov. Cary A. 8, 21, 23, 243
Hardie, Dan 96-7
Harkness, Mary (Mrs. Henry Flagler)
    247
Harney, Lt. Col. William S. 58-9, 61,
    192, 196
Harris, Col. Frank 10
Hart, Thomas S. 21
Hathaway, J. F. 165
Hemingway, Ernest 64
Henderson, Parker, Jr. 91
Hendrickson, Wilbur ("Wild Bill") 86
Henry 118-20
Hialeah Race Track 78, 244-5
Hines, E. A. & Thomas 48, 49
Holate Fixico, Chief 145-8
Hollins, Dixie 39
Holt, Hamilton 66-8
Hopkins, Edward 198
Housman, Capt. Jacob 58-9, 61
Howe, Charles 60
Howey, W. J. 24

Howse, Caroline (Mrs. John Milton)
    197
Hurricanes 35-6, 129, 204, 219-22,
    234
Hurston, Zora Neale 25-9

Ingraham, James W. 19, 149
Ingram, Dr. Joseph M. 11

Jackson, Pres. Andrew 122-3
Jackson, Dr. James & Mary 19
Jackson, Page 8
Jahoda, Gloria 107
Jenkins' Ear War 179-82
Jenkins, Robert 179-82
Jennings, Gov. W. S. 243
Jesup, Gen. Thomas S. 126, 128-9, 192
Johnson, Charlie 208-9
Johnson, Malcolm 228
Johnston, Alva 113
Justice in Florida 223-6, 237-9

Kavasilos, Demosthenes 70
Kenan, Mary Lily (Mrs. Henry Flagler)
    248
Kennedy, Stetson 225
King, Buck 82
King, Judge Ziba 81
Kirkman, Mary (Mrs. Richard K. Call)
    122, 124
Kiser, Mrs. Earl 92
Kissimmee 210-12
Knight, Marion B. 107
Knight, Peter O. 22
Ku Klux Klan 51, 225

Lake Worth 170-4
Lambright, D. 236
Lanehart, Will 171
Lang, August 170
Lanier, Sidney 54-7
Lockhart, Frank 168
Lodge, Albert 208
Long, Ellen Call 198, 256
Lowe, Kid 86
Lowery, Woodbury 158

Lum, Henry B. 47, 48
Lummus, J. E. 19
Lummus, John N., Jr. 91
Lynn, Ray 88

McArdle, T. H. 151
McClellan, S. S. 208-9
McCormack, Arthur 79
McDay, D. B. 57
McDonald, Arthur 167
MacFarlane, Flora 48
McFarlane, Col. Hugh C. 239
McKay, D. B. 236-8
McKay, Matilda 11
McNamee, Robert 237-8
Maharaja of Baroda 114
Mahon, John 196
Marriott, Fred 167
Marti, Jose 188
Martin, Gov. John W. 21, 23-4, 233, 246
Martin, Col. M. 240-41
Martin, Sidney 247
Massacre at Cape Florida Lighthouse 117-20
Medary, Milton B. 202
Menendez, Manuel 188
Merrick, George 7, 114, 233
Merritt, J. R. 88
Miami 17-20, 219, 232-4
Maimi Beach 204-6
Middleton, Clarence 87-8
Miller, Albert 88
Miller, Mary Doughton (Mrs. Tully Dunlap) 79
Milton, Gov. John 197-200
Mitchell, Charles 250-52
Mitchell, Gov. Henry L. 250
Mizelle, Napoleon Bonaparte ("Bone") 81-4
Mizner, Addison 7, 238
Mobley, Hanford 87-8, 149
Monroe, Kirk & Mary 48
Monroe, Commodore Ralph M. 19-20, 46-7, 49
Moore, Charlie 171

Moore Haven 219
Morgan, W. J. 165-7
Mott, Capt. John 60
Motte, Jacob Rhett 194-6
Muis, Helen 18
Munos, Juan 157
Murat, Prince Achille 102-5
Murphy, T. M. 210
Myhre, Milford 203

Nugent, Count James L. 48

Oglethorpe, Gen. James 179-81
Oldfield, Barney 167, 205
Olds, Ransom E. 165
Olmstead, Frederick Law 202
Olustee, Battle of 213-6
Orange Belt Railroad 72-4
Osceola, Chief 126-30, 191-2, 196

Palm Beach 7, 112-4, 170, 172-4, 219, 221
Peacock, Charles & Isabella 46, 47, 48
Peacock, John Thomas ("Jolly Jack") 42
Penal System 240-3
Pensacola 254
Pent, John & Edward 47
Peonage 243
Perrine, Dr. Henry 58-61
Perry Arthur 40
Perry, John Sr. 112
Pierce, Charles W. 170-71, 174
Pierce, Hannibal Dillingham 170-71
Plant, Henry Bradley 207
Plant System Railroad 207-9
Poinsett, Joel R. 58-9
Politics 21-4, 33, 106-8, 121-5, 159-62, 179-80, 197-200, 225, 233-4, 243, 244-5, 248, 250-51, 253
Porter, Dr. Horace 46
Powell, J. C. 240-42
Powell, Lewis Thornton (AKA Lewis Payne) 108-11
Powell, W. R. 236
Princess of Ghika 114

Purman, W. J. 52

Rawlings, Marjorie Kinnan 63-5
Read, Leigh 227-30
Reed, Gov. Harrison 240
Reid, Territorial Gov. Robert 192
Rice, John 68
Rice, Leland 150
Roberts, Kenneth 113
Roesch, Judge & Mrs. Robert H. 83
Rollins College 66-8
Roosevelt, Franklin D. 16, 21, 94-7
Romfh, Edward Coleman 19, 38,
    77-80, 234
Romfh, Mildred 79
Rosan, M. 32-3
Russ, Joe 51
Russell, Britt 238

St. Augustine 247
Santini, Adolphus 99
Sarasota Settlement 34-7, 36
Sargent, Charles Sprague 47
Seaboard Airline Railroad 207-9
Seminole Wars 34, 36, 58, 118-20,
    124, 144-8, 191-4, 254
Seminole Indians 36, 136-40, 144-8,
    149-51, 186
Sewell, John & E. J. 19
Seymour, Gen. Truman A. 213-16
Sholtz, Gov. David 21-4, 97
Shourds, Alice (Mrs. Henry Flagler)
    247-9
Simmons, Dr. Eleanor Galt 48
Smallwood, Charles S. ("Ted")
    99-101
Smiley, Carrie C. (Mrs. T. Thomas
    Fortune) 52
Smith, Capt. Elliott 60
Snell, Hamlin 34
Solano Grove (Delius place) 42-4
Sponge Industry 69-71
Stearns, Gov. Marcellus 240
Stotesbury, Mrs. E. T. 113
Stovall, Col. W. F. 236
Stowe, Charles E. 49

Stranahan, Mrs. Frank 161
Sturdy, James 60
Sturtevant, Ephraim 17
Submarine Warfare 175-8

Tabert, Martin 243
Tallahassee 227-31, 253-6
Talof Hadjo 145-8
Tampa 187-90, 235-9
Tarpon Springs 69-71
Tebeau, Charlton 6
Thompson, John W. B. 118-20
Thompson, Uly O. 97
Thompson, Wiley 127-9
Timberlake, John 122-3
Toland, Sam 99
Towle, Capt. W. H. 99
Townley, Thomas 19
Tracy, Joe 89
Tradewell, William 228
Trammel, Sen. Park 161
Traub, Charles 168
Turpentine Industry 223-6
Tuttle, Julia DeForest Sturtevant
    ("Mother of Miami") 17-20

Union Bank of Tallahassee 253-5
Upthegrove, Laura ("Queen of the
    Everglades") 85-6, 88-9, 149

Vanderbilt, William K. 165, 167
Vans Agnew, P. A. 210-211

Walker, Gov. David 56
Walker, Jonathan 141-3
Wall, Dr. John Perry 9-12, 31
Wall, Thomas F. 43, 45
Warren, Gov. Fuller 107
Watson, Edgar J. 98-101
Watson, J. W. 19-20
Watson, J. Tom 21
Whitehall (Flagler place) 248
Weedon, Dr. Frederick 129
Wescott, James 253
Whitaker, Nancy Catherine Stewart 36

Whitaker, William H. ("Father of Sarasota") 34-7
Whitehair, Francis 22
Williams, James 61
Williams, John C. 73
Women's Suffrage 159-62
Woodford, Pvt. Milton M. 213-6
Worth, Col. W. J. 145-7
Wrecks & Wreckers 171-3
Wyatt, Col. William 34

Wyatt, Mary Jane (Mrs. Wm. H. Whitaker) 36-7
Wyse, Maj. H. A. 243

Ybor, Vincente Martinez 235
Ybor City 188
Yellow fever 9-12, 31
Young, Joseph 233

Zangara, Giuseppe 94-7